Using C
with *curses, lex* and *yacc*

Using C
with *curses*, *lex* and *yacc*

Building a Window Shell for
UNIX System V

Axel T. Schreiner

Carl Hanser Verlag

Prentice Hall

First published in German 1989 under the title
*C-Praxis mit curses, lex und yacc: Eine Window Shell
für UNIX System V* by
Carl Hanser Verlag, Munich and Vienna

First published in English 1990 by
Prentice Hall International (UK) Ltd
66 Wood Lane End, Hemel Hempstead
Hertfordshire HP2 4RG
A division of
Simon & Schuster International Group

**Printed in Great Britain at
the University Press, Cambridge**

Library of Congress Cataloging-in-Publication Data

Schreiner, Axel T.
    Using C with curses, LEX and YACC : building a window shell for
UNIX system V / Axel-Tobias Schreiner.
      p. cm.
    ISBN (invalid) 0−13−932864−5 : $44.95
    1. UNIX system V (Computer operating system) 2. C (Computer
program language) I. Title.
QA76.76.O63S39 1990
005.4′3—dc20   90-7044
                                                   CIP

British Library Cataloguing in Publication Data

Schreiner, Axel-Tobias
  Using C with Curses, Lex and Yacc : building a window
  shell for Unix System V.
  1. Computer systems. Software packages
  I. Title II. C-Praxis mit Curses, Lex und Yacc,
  (*English*)
  005.3

  ISBN 0−13−932864−5

---

3 4 5   94 93 92

Contents

Preface

By now C is almost one of the older programming languages. There is the current informal standard based on the description by Brian Kernighan and Dennis Ritchie, and there is the official ANSI standard. C compilers are available for almost all existent computers and operating systems. There are C dialects and extensions for parallel execution and object-oriented programming, and there are a multitude of books and courses on C.

This book is not simply another C book. As a matter of fact, the basic skills of C programming and of using UNIX system calls and tools are assumed as prerequisites. If one needs to brush up on using UNIX, a good introduction would be the book by Brian Kernighan and Robert Pike (1984).

Instead we discuss the environment for developing with C and use those UNIX tools which make C programmers much more productive. C programs can employ a large number of powerful library functions which significantly simplify text handling, dynamically storing information, accessing files, or portable programming of dialogs with arbitrary terminals. Additionally, there are programs like the compiler generators *lex* and *yacc*, which take little effort to implement, e.g., command languages so that they can be easily maintained. *awk* is a string programming language which can be mastered quickly, and which is perfectly suited to generate C code from tables specified in a very problem-oriented fashion.

Using C is like any craft which is best learned under apprenticeship in a shop. Using C productively and securely in the environment of all the standard tools available with UNIX is best illustrated by a significant, larger example where the entire toolset is employed. Such an example clearly illustrates how C and the tools are used step by step to derive solutions which can be easily extended and re-used in other projects.

This book presents the development of an interactive program which contains a command language with a calculator with C operators, dynamic strings, and C library functions. The program maintains screen windows with the *curses* function library and it solves the typical problems in this context. It demonstrates access to many files and other processes including a line-oriented dialog. Our example is a window shell, i.e., a program where separate calculations can be performed in various areas of the screen and where shell commands can be executed. We discuss how to embed commands in screen management and we develop a window manager which is used to define and manipulate the screen areas.

curses are a famous − if not infamous − collection of C functions which were extracted from the *vi* editor by Ken Arnold at Berkeley and made into a library in their own right. The *termcap* database describes all possible and impossible properties of practically every terminal in existence. *curses* use this database to provide for full screen applications under UNIX which can be run unchanged on a multitude of different terminals. As regards portable C programs, *curses* are as important for screen-oriented programming as *stdio* is to file access.

Today, therefore, *curses* are widely available, if not liked, by UNIX programmers. Unfortunately, the input functions of the original implementations were quite buggy and the documentation remained so sketchy that it was quite difficult to develop challenging applications.

System V has improved the situation somewhat: Mark Horton at Bell Laboratories replaced *termcap* by the *terminfo* database – this one is precompiled and can thus be accessed much more quickly. *curses* have been revised and extended for *terminfo* and the input functions have been improved. At least when this book was written the library appeared to contain fewer severe errors than before.

The window shell demonstrates possibilities and limitations of the *curses* library at the same time. This aspect of the discussion takes precedence over the usefulness of the program itself. This book is more concerned with using *awk*, *lex*, *yacc*, and *curses* than with developing yet another, optimally comfortable shell. The parts of the window shell are more important than the window shell itself: e.g., the view manager, a desk calculator reminiscent of C with a macro facility, functions to view files and pipes, functions to embed a dialog with other programs and for excursions to programs taking over the entire screen.

The book especially tries to demonstrate the evolution of larger programs. Major parts of the window shell are developed individually and then integrated with the view manager. Hopefully, this will demonstrate how new implementation techniques can be designed and made to work within a more complex framework.

Chapter 1 is a user guide for the desk calculator *calc*, for the *curses* simulator *cdc*, and for the window shell *wish* which are all developed in this book. Section 1.1 is a short overview, the remaining sections present many details which can be skipped during a first reading.

In the second chapter we look at the step by step development of *calc* using the compiler generators *lex* and *yacc*. It is very important that *calc* can be easily extended to serve as backbone for command languages and that *calc* has a very compact, line-oriented interface by which it may be easily connected to arbitrary interactive environments. Section 2.8 summarizes the interface which is used in the following chapters.

Chapter 3 presents *curses*. First, we look at three very small programs: *nv* shows text files on the terminal screen and could be used to look at output from *nroff* and *col*. If a terminal supports it, boldface output can be shown using reverse video. *sane* is a program to return a messed up terminal to some reasonable state. Finally, *doodle* is a rudimentary drawing program where the cursor is moved on the screen and where text can be deposited at the cursor. *nv* demonstrates the most important *curses* output functions, *sane* shows how to access the *terminfo* database directly, and *doodle* is mainly concerned with input and decoding of function keys and with the various terminal modes.

In the second half of Chapter 3 the desk calculator is connected to the terminal screen using *curses*. Next we see how *curses* can be used to divide a terminal screen into windows so that *calc* only uses part of the screen. Here we look at various techniques for scrolling to simulate a terminal within a window. In Section 3.7 we develop the desk calculator into *cdc*, a program where almost all *curses* functions can be exercised interactively directly on the screen.

curses have bugs. They are a complicated package of functions, and their subtleties are hardly sketched in the documentation. Nevertheless, *curses* are portable to many UNIX systems and terminals (and even to MS-DOS) and it pays to master them. The trick is to understand them well enough so that bugs (or 'features') may be spotted, isolated, and circumvented if necessary. This is why techniques like scrolling are explained in detail and why *cdc* was built and presented as a testing ground for learning by experiment.

curses support a rudimentary window concept. Flashy applications, however, require much more support than *curses* have to offer. If possible, window management should be separated from the applications running within the windows. Therefore, Chapter 4 presents a general 'view manager' module to show how *curses* can be used to implement an environment, where applications can easily be coded to run in many windows on a single terminal screen. Using the cursor, windows can be moved, re-sized, erased, etc.

The remaining chapters deal mostly with systems programming problems arising from communicating with several processes (apparently) at the same time. Chapter 5 describes a number of viewing techniques, for files, a help database, the log of a previously run process, and a pipe from a process running concurrently. The chapter also shows a general technique to run a variety of different applications simultaneously under control of the view manager.

Chapter 6 introduces *pads*, a new feature of *curses*. Pads are windows which can be larger than the terminal screen, and which can be accessed with most *curses* functions. We look at the beginnings of a screen editor to see how completely *curses* can simulate an intelligent terminal on an arbitrary one.

Finally, Chapter 7 shows how a two way communication with a concurrent process can be confined to a view and presents a line-oriented input routine with timeouts. We also look at some complications arising from the fact that an interactive program is no longer connected to a terminal for standard input and output.

The Appendix contains short descriptions of the programs and functions developed throughout this book. There are one-line definitions of all the library functions and system calls supported by *calc*, *cdc*, and *wish*, and of all the *curses* functions. Chapter 1 and the Appendix serve as a description of the source programs in this book, which may be obtained from the publisher. *wish* itself consists of almost 5000 lines of source code; the development steps consist of about 30 working programs which can be extracted from the sources. This should permit rather detailed studies.

wish started out as a farewell party for my 'Software' course at the university of Ulm in fall 1987. I made an early version of *cdc* to discover the fine print behind *curses* and to simplify demonstrations in class. A design study appeared in my *Sprechstunde* column in *unix/mail* 1/88, and many readers requested the sources. Their reaction prompted me to write this book.

wish owes a lot to thoughtful criticism by Dr Ernst Janich and former students at Ulm. My wife Carol read the entire book and corrected my German English ways. The people at Hanser and Prentice Hall were once again patient enough to wait until we got it just right. To all of them go my sincere thanks.

Ramsau, Easter 1990   Axel T. Schreiner

## CHAPTER ONE

The Window Shell
wish

1.1 Overview

wish is a UNIX program, where the terminal screen is divided into several working areas, termed
views.† Each view can be individually selected. It is then foremost on the screen perhaps cover-
ing other views. When *wish* is first called, view 0 is selected:

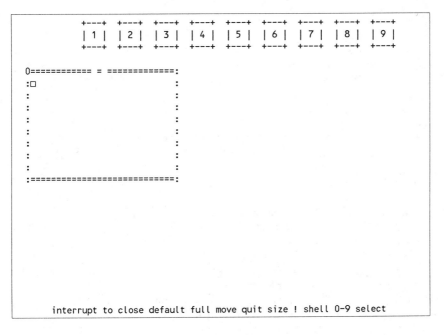

The cursor is at the top left of the selected view. In the picture above it is represented by □.
Depending on the capabilities of the terminal, parts of the bottom row are optically emphasized,
e.g., by reverse video (dark characters on light background).

† It would be preferable to call a working area a *window*. However, this word has a specific meaning in the context of
curses.

At first a line-oriented command language applies within the selected view. The language is based on a desk calculator for integer arithmetic with the C operators, dynamic strings, and with a large number of constants and functions from the C library. We will look at the details in Section 1.2. Section 2.7 will show how easily more functions can be added.

The desk calculator accepts some statements to deal with views. **fw** (*full window*) makes the current view as large as possible, **dw** (*default window*) returns to the original position and size. **cw** (*change window*) selects another view which is specified as an integer expression or character constant.

```
+---+ +---+            +---+ +---+ +---+ +---+
| 2 | | 3 |            | 5 | | 6 | | 7 | | 8 |
+---+ +---+            +---+ +---+ +---+ +---+
9================================ = ========================================:
:         EXINIT=so /usr/axel/.exrc                                         :
:         1============ = ============:                                     :
:         :wert = 10                  :                                     :
:         :          10               :                                     :
:         :cw 4          4============ = =============:                     :
:         :             :++ wert                      :                     :
:         :             :       11                    :                     :
:         :             :getlogin(), getuid()         :                     :
:         :             :       "axel"                :                     :
:         :             :       10                    :                     :
:         :=============:□                             :                     :
:         TERMINFO=/usr:                               :                     :
:         TZ=MEZ-1     :                               :                     :
:         USE=/usr/axel:==============================:                     :
:         VISUAL=/bin/vi                                                     :
:         _=wish                                                            :
:cw 1                                                                       :
:                                                                           :
:===========================================================================:
        interrupt to close default full move quit size ! shell 0-9 select
```

The screen will look as above after the following input:

```
cw 9                 # select view 9
fw                   # (within view 9) full screen
export               # show environment
cw 1                 # select view 1
wert = 10            # (within view 1) new variable
cw 4                 # select view 4
++ wert              # (within view 4) increment variable
getlogin(), getuid() # library functions
```

As you can see, *wish* knows names and values of exported shell variables – and they can be changed, too. *wish* itself, however, uses a single symbol table for all views.

A view is deselected using **cw**, but it remains on the terminal screen. An input of length 0, i.e., *control*-D at the beginning of an input line, terminates work within a view. The view is then removed from the screen and a representative *icon* appears at the top of the screen. If we reselect the view later, *wish* will display it with its original content. If we terminate work in all views, *wish* itself terminates. All ten icons cannot, therefore, appear on the screen together.

A view first serves as a desk calculator; as a reminder we see an assignment symbol at the top center of the view's frame. The other features of *wish* can be selected by a number of special character symbols:

= *statements*	desk calculator
< *file name*	view a file
? *term*	explain a term
! *command*	view output from a command
& *command*	execute command, view log
$ *command*	dialog with a command
: *file name*	edit a file

The special character symbols were of course selected to be similar to the usual UNIX conventions. The pipeline symbol | may be used in place of ! and % may be used in place of $. The pipeline symbol | and the background command symbol & may even follow their *command* argument. !! is an abbreviation for the last input line in each view.

A special character symbol prevents an input line from being interpreted as a sequence of desk calculator statements. If the input line consists only of the symbol, it changes how the following input lines in this view are interpreted: the symbol appears at the top center of the view's frame and is implicitly prefixed to each input line. The various features of *wish* are described in detail in the following sections.

```
+---+  +---+        +---+  +---+        +---+  +---+
| 1 |  | 2 |        | 4 |  | 5 |        | 7 |  | 8 |
+---+  +---+        +---+  +---+        +---+  +---+
0--------- < view.h ---------+  6============ = ============:
|#ifndef VIEW_H            |  :cw 9                        :
|                          |  :exit(0)□                    :
|#ifdef  GLOBAL            |  :                            :
|#define INIT(x) = x       |  :                            :
|#else                     |  :                            :
|#define GLOBAL   extern   |  :                            :
|#define INIT(x)           |  :                            :
|#endif                    |  :                            :
+-------- \n \b cdfmqs! 0-9 -+  :============================:


3--------- $ sh -i -------123  9---------- | who -----------+
|$ date                    |  |axel     tty02       Aug |
|Wed Aug 31 15:28:42 MEZ 1988| |axel     tty03       Aug |
|                          |  |axel     tty01       Aug |
|                          |  |  |                       |
|$                         |  |  |                       |
|                          |  |  |                       |
|                          |  |  |                       |
|                          |  |  |                       |
|                          |  |  |                       |
+--------------------------+  +----------- \n cdfmqs! 0-9 -+
      interrupt to close default full move quit size ! shell 0-9 select
```

Here we first selected the views 0, 3, 6, and 9, and used the *move* option of the view manager to arrange them in the positions shown; the view manager is discussed in Section 1.4. View 0 is used to look at the file *view.h* and view 9 contains the output from *who*; we will look at file display in Section 1.5. View 3 talks to a Bourne Shell. Dialog input and output are shown entirely within the view, but we cannot fully simulate a terminal there; Section 1.7 looks at dialogs. Using the view manager, we selected view 6 and the cursor is at the end of an input line there. **exit( )** is a built-in library function and a quick and orderly way to terminate *wish*.

The output area of a view has two states which are distinguished by the appearance of the frame. View 6 in the example is in desk calculator state, the other views are in output state. The top of the frame shows the input that has put the view into output state. When we have finished looking at an output, the view manager restores the desk calculator state of the view and displays the previous input lines.

1.2 Desk Calculator

The desk calculator supports interactive integer arithmetic and dynamic string operations. Expression syntax is loosely based on C. A large number of values, library functions, and system calls are built into the calculator. These tables can easily be expanded; therefore, this description may not quite apply to the latest release available on your system.

The calculator can be generated as a stand-alone program. The implementation is discussed in Chapter 2. The present section describes only how the desk calculator part of the *wish* command language can be used. A few other statements for interaction with *wish* are also understood by the desk calculator, but they will be discussed in later sections of Chapter 1.

Lexical Conventions

The calculator is line oriented. If an error is found, the rest of the current line is ignored and a new line is requested.

White space and comments are ignored, except that white space may be necessary to delimit input symbols. *Comments* begin with # and extend to the end of an input line. However, # within a character or string constant does not start a comment.

Identifiers denote integer and string variables, macros, and built-in values and functions. An identifier starts with a letter and consists of letters and digits. The underscore _ is considered to be a letter. All characters of an identifier are significant.

There is a large number of *reserved words* which cannot be used as identifiers. Statement keywords and the names of built-in values and functions are reserved. This part of the implementation is table driven, and names can easily be added or deleted.

An input line can contain several *statements*. They may be separated or terminated by commas or semicolons.

Constants

The calculator supports character, integer, and string constants just like C. Base 10 is used to output integer values, strings are displayed without escaping control characters.

Character constants are enclosed in single quotes and may be specified using \ escape sequences (hexadecimal notation is not supported). They must be fully contained on an input line or within a macro definition. Character constants have integer values.

Integer constants are digit strings. They are normally interpreted in base 10 and must fit into the **int** range of the host system. The base prefixes **0** for base 8 and **0x** or **0X** for base 16 can be used. Upper- and lower-case letters **a** through **f** serve as additional digits.

String constants are character sequences enclosed in double quotes. They must be fully contained on an input line or within a macro definition. The usual \ escapes may be used, but they may cause problems on some terminals. Strings may be empty.

Macro Preprocessor

Scanning strictly from left to right, input lines are preprocessed. If an identifier has been defined as a macro name, it is replaced. If the macro name is immediately followed by a left parenthesis on the input line, an argument list is replaced together with the macro name. The argument list consists of arguments separated by commas and extends to the closing right parenthesis; the entire macro call must be contained on one input line.

An argument may contain balanced parentheses and commas within parentheses. It may also contain arbitrary character or string constants. If an argument contains another macro call, the call is expanded as the replacement text is scanned.

The replacement text from the macro definition refers to the arguments positionally with the symbols **$1**, **$2**, etc. Only nine arguments and the macro name **$0** can be referenced.† Extra arguments are ignored, references to missing arguments are replaced by no text. If $ is not followed by a digit, it quotes the next character, i.e., **$$** represents a single $. A trailing $ in the replacement text is silently ignored.

A macro definition consists of an entire input line. Such a line is not preprocessed and contains the following information:

```
def name replacement
```

def is reserved and must be followed by at least one blank. **name** is the macro name to be defined; it cannot be a reserved word. **replacement** is optional; if specified, it must be separated from **name** by at least one blank.

Macro definitions may be listed by specifying **def** without a **name** as a statement. Macros may be undefined using an entire input line, which is not preprocessed, containing the following information:

```
undef name
```

undef is reserved and must be followed by at least one blank. **name** is the macro name to be undefined; it must be a defined macro name. Once undefined, **name** is a new identifier.

---

† Since the replacement text is processed again for macro calls, using **$0** is probably a bad idea.

Variables

Variables can store integer or string values. They receive and change their type by assignment. If an assignment operation such as + = or an increment operator such as + + is applied to a new identifier, the identifier is initialized with zero or an empty string.

The statement **set** shows all currently defined variables. String values are surrounded by double quotes. The statement

```
unset name ...
```

undefines all variables specified as arguments.

Environment

The calculator has access to environment variables. Initially, all environment variables become string variables in the calculator, unless their names are reserved words. The statement **export** displays all currently defined environment variables. **export** can be specified with one or more variable names to add them to the environment; if a variable name is new it is initialized as an empty string. An **unset** statement can be used to remove an environment variable.

The environment is passed from the calculator to other programs. Integer variable values are represented as sequences of decimal digits, just as **export** shows them.

The functions **getenv**(3) and **putenv**(3) are built in and apply to the environment kept in the symbol table.

Integer Arithmetic

An integer expression is a statement. The resulting value is displayed. The calculator supports the following C operators for integer arithmetic:

= *op*=	assignment, operator assignment
|	bit-wise or
^	bit-wise exclusive or
&	bit-wise and
<< >>	shift, left and right
+ -	addition, subtraction
* / %	multiplication, division, remainder
! ~ -	logical and bit complement, minus
++ --	increment and decrement
( )	grouping
[]	string subscript

The table is shown in increasing order of precedence. Operator assignments exist for all binary operators. There is a large number of built-in integer values and functions with integer results.

String Operations

A string expression is a statement. The resulting string is displayed. All string values are managed dynamically; however, running out of heap space is fatal.

There are two string operations: assignment and concatenation. Concatenation has higher precedence and is specified by juxtaposing two string values with or without **+** in between. Assignment is specified using **=**. The operator **+ =** denotes concatenation, i.e.,

```
a += b; c = c d; strcat(e, f)
```

express similar operations. Assignment is grouped from the right, concatenation is grouped from the left.

A subscript operation may be applied to a string value. If the value is the result of a string expression, it must be enclosed in parentheses. The result of subscripting is a single character, i.e., an integer value. For example

```
c = (a = "abc")[2]
```

assigns a string value to the variable **a** and an integer value to **c**.

There is a built-in string value **version** identifying the calculator. Most of the string functions from the C library are also built in.

Built-in Values

The statement **const** displays the built-in values. They may be used just like variables, but they cannot be exported, erased, turned into macros, or assigned to.

The following values are built in. They are taken from the header files of the host system.

File control:

```
F_DUPFD
F_GETFD     F_SETFD
F_GETFL     F_SETFL
```

open(2) arguments:

```
O_RDONLY    O_WRONLY    O_RDWR
O_APPEND    O_CREAT
O_NDELAY    O_TRUNC
```

File types and modes:

```
S_IFIFO     S_IFCHR     S_IFDIR     S_IFBLK     S_IFREG
S_ISUID     S_ISGID
S_IRUSR     S_IWUSR     S_IXUSR
```

Signals:

SIGHUP	SIGINT	SIGQUIT	SIGILL	SIGTRAP
SIGFPE	SIGKILL	SIGSYS	SIGPIPE	SIGALRM
SIGTERM	SIGUSR1	SIGUSR2		

Key names from *curses* (3):

KEY_A1	KEY_A3	KEY_B2	KEY_BACKSPACE	KEY_BREAK
KEY_C1	KEY_C3	KEY_CATAB	KEY_CLEAR	KEY_CTAB
KEY_DC	KEY_DL	KEY_DOWN	KEY_EIC	KEY_ENTER
KEY_EOL	KEY_EOS	KEY_F0	KEY_HOME	KEY_IC
KEY_IL	KEY_LEFT	KEY_LL	KEY_NPAGE	KEY_PPAGE
KEY_PRINT	KEY_RESET	KEY_RIGHT	KEY_SF	KEY_SR
KEY_SRESET	KEY_STAB	KEY_UP		

All of these values are integers. There is a single character value: **version** is a string identifying the calculator.

Built-in Functions

If a built-in function name is specified as a statement, i.e., without an argument list, the calculator displays the names of all built-in functions which accept similar argument lists. For example:

```
strcpy
        strcat() built-in
        strcpy() built-in
```

The following functions are built in. They cannot be exported, erased, or turned into variables or macros. They perform as advertised in the System V Interface Definition (1986).

System calls:

_exit	access	chdir	chmod	chown
exit	getegid	geteuid	getgid	getpgrp
getpid	getppid	getuid	kill	link
mknod	mount	nice	pause	setgid
setpgrp	setuid	sync	umask	umount
unlink				

Library functions:

_tolower	_toupper			
abort	abs	atoi		
getenv	getlogin			
isalnum	isalpha	isascii	isatty	iscntrl
isdigit	isgraph	islower	isprint	ispunct

isspace	isupper	isxdigit	itoa	
KEY_F	keymap			
putenv				
rand				
sleep	srand	strcat	strchr	strcmp
strcpy	strcspn	strlen	strpbrk	strrchr
strspn				
toascii	tolower	toupper	ttyname	

exit( ) terminates *wish* gracefully, **_exit( )** leaves the terminal screen messed up. **getenv( )** and **putenv( )** interface with the calculator as described above. **itoa( )** converts an integer value into a string. **KEY_F( )** returns the key value for a numbered function key. **keymap( )** changes key mapping as explained in Section 4.7.

1.3 Interactive *curses*

cdc is a special version of the desk calculator supporting interactive access to (almost) all *curses* functions. Input is normally read from the terminal, *curses* functions apply to the terminal screen. Input can also be read from one or more argument files. A single minus sign as a command argument denotes the terminal. *cdc* has the following options:

-c *n*	allocate *n* lines to statement echo
-o *log*	copy statements and replies to *log*
-v	echo statements read from input file

By default, one third of the terminal screen, and at least three lines, are dedicated to statement echo. By default, statements read from an input file are not echoed unless they cause an error.

The *curses* simulation is entirely faithful if statements are read from a file and not echoed. If statements are read from the terminal, or echoed from a file, there can be some interference between statement echo and statement output on the terminal screen. If *cdc* is used for serious testing, statements can first be executed from the terminal to produce a log file. The log file can then be submitted as a command argument for *cdc* to verify operation without any input interference.

General Aspects

cdc supports the desk calculator language exactly as described in Section 1.2. There are many more built-in values and functions, and hence many more reserved words.

Output from the statements is truncated at the right margin, scrolled, and paginated. If the question **more?** is answered with **q**, only the end of the output from one input line is shown. The question **more?** also appears, if an argument file produces an error. In this case, **q** will terminate *cdc*.

cdc supports a shell escape. If an input line starts with an exclamation mark, the rest of the line is passed to the shell for processing. Upon return, *cdc* will pause for a key to be pressed. The same shell escape is also supported as the library function **system( )**. The function accepts a string expression as an argument and returns the exit code as an integer value.

If input is read from the terminal, *cdc* supports a history feature. A line consisting only of **!!** will recall the previous non-blank line. This line is echoed in place of **!!**.

Windows

cdc supports *curses* windows. Variables can store integer, string, or window pointer values. No attempt is made, however, to guard against stray window pointers, or to reclaim memory once windows become inaccessible. *cdc* performs exactly as *curses* does.

There are two constant window pointer values: **curscr** and **stdscr**. Other values can be created using **newwin( )**, **newpad( )**, or **subwin( )**.

Window pointer values may be assigned, passed as function arguments, or used with the structure selection operator **− >** to get the integer values of most components.

Built-in Values

In addition to the built-in values described in Section 1.2, the following values are also available:

Attributes and masks:

```
A_BLINK         A_BOLD          A_DIM           A_REVERSE       A_UNDERLINE
A_STANDOUT
A_CHARTEXT      A_ATTRIBUTES
```

Terminal dimensions:

```
COLS            LINES
```

Default window pointer values:

```
curscr          stdscr
```

Other constants:

```
ERR             FALSE           OK              TRUE
```

The values are taken from the host system header files. The selection of names corresponds to System V release 2.

Access to Window Components

The structure selection operator **− >** is available for read-only access to component values. The operator always returns integer values. Row and column information is also available through built-in functions as described in Section 3.4.

Component names:

_attrs	_begx	_begy	_bmarg	_clear
_curx	_cury	_flags	_leave	_maxx
_maxy	_nodelay	_scroll	_tmarg	_use_idl
_use_meta	_use_keypad			

Component functions:

begx	begy
curx	cury
maxx	maxy

Built-in *curses* Functions

The following macros and functions from the *curses* library are directly available as built-in functions. They perform as described in Chapter 3. A capsule summary and references to examples are contained in the appendix.

addch	addstr	attroff	attron	attrset
baudrate	beep	box	clear	clearok
clrtobot	clrtoeol	delch	deleteln	delwin
erase	erasechar	flash	flushinp	has_ic
has_il	idlok	inch	insch	insertln
keypad	killchar	leaveok	longname	move
mvaddch	mvaddstr	mvdelch	mvinch	mvinsch
mvwaddch	mvwaddstr	mvwdelch	mvwin	mvwinch
mvwinsch	newpad	newwin	overlay	overwrite
scroll	scrollok	setscrreg	standend	standout
subwin	touchwin	unctrl	waddch	waddstr
wattroff	wattron	wattrset	wclear	wclrtobot
wclrtoeol	wdelch	wdeleteln	werase	winch
winsch	winsertln	wmove	wsetscrreg	wstandend
wstandout				

The next group of functions and macros from the *curses* library is also available as built-in functions. If input is read from a file, the library functions are called directly. If input is read from the terminal, the user's terminal state is restored as far as possible before the library function is called.

cbreak	doupdate	echo	endwin	getbegyx
getch	getmaxyx	getstr	getyx	initscr
intrflush	mvgetch	mvgetstr	mvwgetch	mvwgetstr
nl	nocbreak	nodelay	noecho	nonl
noraw	pnoutrefresh	prefresh	raw	refresh
typeahead	wgetch	wgetstr	wnoutrefresh	wrefresh

The **getstr** functions create dynamic string values for their argument variables. The **getyx** functions change their argument variables into integers. **initscr( )** is called implicitly by *cdc* and should not be called again. **endwin( )** will terminate *cdc* just as **exit( )** does.

Other Built-in Functions

A few more built-in functions are provided for convenience. Details are explained in Section 3.7.

```
copywin(wa, wb, ya, xa, y0b, x0b, y1b, x1b, ov)
fill(ch)
sane()
state()
wfill(w, ch)
wframe(w, nr, nc, y, x)
wframe2(w, nr, nc, y, x)
wstate(w)

    WINDOW * wa, * wb, * w;
```

copywin( ) copies a rectangle from **wa** to **wb**. If **ov** is set, only non-blanks are copied. **fill( )** and **wfill( )** fill **stdscr** or a window with a single character. **sane( )** restores default settings to the terminal, e.g., **echo( )**, **nocbreak( )**, etc. **state( )** and **wstate( )** display information about **stdscr** or a window. The display is erased once the screen is refreshed.

wframe( ) and **wframe2( )** draw a single or a double frame with given dimensions or extending to the border with the origin at a point in a window. These functions are explained in Section 3.5.

1.4 View Management

wish manages several working areas, called views. A *view* is either opened or closed. A closed view is displayed as an *icon*, i.e., a small box near the edge of the terminal screen with the view number or name shown inside. An open view is displayed as a double or single frame somewhere on the terminal screen with the view number or name displayed in the top left corner and perhaps state information displayed on the frame. Icons can never be obscured; views can cover each other.

wish supports command arguments to control the number of views, initial size, etc. The options **−b**, **−l**, **−r**, and **−t** determine the position of the icons at the bottom, left, right, or top edge of the screen respectively. The option **−n** controls the number of views. The options **−i** and **−f** determine the sizes of an icon and a default frame. Options are described more precisely below.

Initially, the first view is open and all other views are closed. Depending on the number of views, the first view is called zero or A. It is displayed as a double frame to indicate that it is accepting commands such as desk calculator statements.

Certain commands will change the view into a single frame to indicate that the view is carrying out some other operation. The double frame and the old interior will reappear once the operation is completed. Possible operations will be described in the remaining sections of this chapter.

There are three commands to control views. **fw** (*full window*) changes the view to use the full terminal screen, excluding the icon area and the prompt. **dw** (*default window*) changes the view to the size and position when first opened. **cw** (*change window*) takes an integer expression argument denoting another view to be opened. The view may be specified as a small number or as a character constant.

An end of file in place of an input line will close the current view and change to the most recently used view. *wish* will be terminated if no more views are open.

At the bottom of the terminal screen *wish* displays a message describing view management options available through an interrupt. When an interrupt is caused, e.g., by pressing the *break* key, the cursor moves to the icon position of the current view and *wish* reads a single character. **c** closes the current view and changes to the most recently used view. **d** changes to the default frame for the current view. **f** changes to the full terminal screen. **m** places the cursor at the top left corner of the current view and permits moving the view. **s** places the cursor at the bottom right corner and permits changing the size of the view. **!** suspends *wish* and executes a shell. *wish* is resumed and the screen is replotted when the shell exits. The path to the shell is taken from the environment variable **SHELL**. *control*-D or **q** terminate *wish*. A digit or an upper-case letter will open and select a new current view.

Moving or resizing a view is accomplished by moving the cursor to the desired new top left or bottom right corner and pressing *return*. The cursor can be moved with arrow keys or with **hjkl** as in the *vi* editor. **h**, *erase*, or backspace move to the left, **l** or space move to the right, *tab* moves to the next tab position, **k** moves up, **j** moves down. The keys at the diagonal of the keypad move diagonally, *kill* and the center key of the keypad move back to the start of the operation, the *home* key moves to the top left position, and the *lower left* key moves to the lower left position possible for the cursor. Another interrupt aborts the operation.

When a view is moved, its contents remain unchanged. If the view is made smaller, the last part of the text above the cursor is preserved. If the view is made bigger, the old text is arranged in the top left part of the new view. Since text is cut at the right margin, a new larger view is incomplete.

The View Management Module: *vm.c*

View management is provided by a separate module within *wish* which might be useful to other applications. The module manages the following data structure:

```
typedef struct view View;
        struct view {
                WINDOW * v_icon;          /* icon */
                WINDOW * v_frame;         /* frame */
                WINDOW ** v_sub;          /* interiors */
                WINDOW * v_view;          /* current: icon or sub[v_now] */
                char * v_user;            /* user's extension */
                int v_pid;                /* secondary process */
                unsigned v_top;           /* counts top calls */
                short v_seq;              /* used to sort by top calls */
                char v_now;               /* current interior */
        };
```

.v_icon, **.v_frame**, and **.v_sub**[*i*] are allocated windows, where *i* ranges from zero to a limit set by the user. **.v_sub**[0] is a subwindow of **.v_frame**. The user may set a legitimate index into **.v_now** and call **vopen()** to display a new interior. **.v_user** is a pointer to an extension area which can be allocated during initialization, but which is otherwise not under control of the view manager.

Public components of the view data structure should only be accessed with the following access macros from the header file *view.h*:

vframe(vp)	frame window (read only)
view(vp)	current interior window (read only)
vnow(vp)	index selecting view()
vpid(vp)	process id

vp is a pointer to the view data structure.

Initialization

The view manager is initialized by a call to **vmain()**. The first argument must be a dispatcher function to be called within each open view. Further argument groups are optional and can appear in any order. The last argument must be zero. The following argument groups can be specified:

selector	additional values	effect
V_ARG	(int) argc, (char **) argv, (char *) opt	command argument list and getopt(3) descriptor
V_BOT		icons appear at bottom
V_FRAME	(int) FLINE, (int) FCOL	default frame dimensions
V_ICON	(int) ILINE, (int) ICOL	icon dimensions
V_INFO	(int (*)()) vinfo	called by vopen()
V_LEFT		icons appear at left
V_LUSER	(int) sizeof (* v_user)	extension area size
V_NSUB	(int) NSUB	number of interiors
V_NVIEW	(int) NVIEW	number of views
V_RIGHT		icons appear at right
V_SIG	(int) vsig	signal to get to manager
V_TOP		icons appear at top
0		terminates argument list

Suitable defaults are provided. Icons appear at the top; they are three lines high and five columns wide. There are ten views, each with one interior; the default frame is ten lines high and thirty columns wide. **vmain()** will terminate with a fatal error message if impossible requests are made.

If an argument list is passed with **V_ARG**, a number of options can be changed through command arguments. Since arguments to **vmain()** are processed in order, command arguments can be rendered ineffective by subsequently passing other values to **vmain()**. The command arguments are parsed by **getopt**(3) under control of the option string passed with **V_ARG**, and unexpected arguments are silently ignored. The following command arguments can be recognized:

`-a`	do not use alternate character set
`-b`	icons appear at bottom
`-f` *rows,cols*	default frame dimension
`-i` *rows,cols*	icon dimension
`-l`	icons appear at left
`-r`	icons appear at right
`-t`	icons appear at top
`-n` *num*	number of views
`-q`	enter manager with *quit* signal

The following options select the maximum number of views on a typical terminal. It should be noted that a view may require 4 KB or more memory even with a single interior.

```
$ wish -l -i1,3 -f5,30 -n20
```

Main Loop

If a command argument list is passed to **vmain( )** and a command argument is not followed by correct parameters, **vmain( )** will immediately return -1. Otherwise, the first view is opened and the dispatcher function is called with a pointer to the current view data structure.

Whenever a view is opened, **vopen( )** is called with a pointer to the view data structure. **vopen( )** brings that view to the front of the terminal screen. If an information function was specified with **V_INFO**, it will be called by **vopen( )** with the view data structure pointer as argument.

Once **vopen( )** has been completed, **view(vp)** points to the current interior window. This window may be changed by assigning a suitable index to **vnow(vp)** and calling **vopen( )** with a pointer to the view data structure to make the new interior current. Clearly, the index must be within the range of interiors specified as **V_NSUB**.

The dispatcher function is expected to draw on **vframe(vp)** from the information function, if any, and on **view(vp)** from the dispatcher function.

If the dispatcher function returns to **vmain( )**, the current view is closed, i.e., it is returned to icon state. If there are more open views, the most recently topped view is topped again, and the dispatcher function is called again. The cycle continues until there are no more open views. At this point, screen processing is terminated and **vmain( )** returns zero.

Signals

vmain( ) connects each of the signals **SIGHUP, SIGINT, SIGQUIT**, and **SIGTERM** to an internal function **quit( )** unless the signal is ignored when **vmain( )** is called. **quit( )** terminates screen processing, resets the signal to its state upon entry to **vmain( )**, and issues the signal again. Further signals in the range **SIGHUP** to **SIGTERM** can be added to this mechanism by passing them to **vcatch( )**.

If a signal is passed to **vmain( )** with **V_SIG**, it is set up as an entry point to the view manager. The signal is reset to its original state before **vmain( )** returns. This access is intended for the signals **SIGINT** or **SIGQUIT**. If a signal is set up, a prompt is displayed indicating the features of the view manager.

View Management Functions: *vm( )*

The appearance of views is controlled by the function **vm( )** which takes a character and a code as arguments. **vm( )** can be called directly, or it can be entered through the signal set up as **V_SIG**. In the latter case, the character is read from the terminal and the code is set to zero. The following management options are supported:

argument	effect
c	close current view, select previous
d	default frame for current view
f	full screen frame for current view
m	move current view
s	change size of current view
!	execute **SHELL**
q *code*	
control-D *code*	terminate the process
\0 *letter*	
\0 *number*	select view, open if necessary

vm( ) will always return to the top of the main loop in **vmain( )**, i.e., the dispatcher function will be called again in the current or new view. It is the responsibility of the dispatcher function to control the terminal state, i.e., **echo( )** and **cbreak( )**.

Process Management

Each view may control a separate process. The view manager, however, is a single process, and the system call **wait**(2) may have surprising results with respect to a single view.

Therefore, the view manager supports a process id component **vpid(vp)** as part of the view data structure. If a view calls **fork**(2) it should post the process id in **vpid(vp)**. If the view wants to wait for the process to terminate, it should wait until **vpid(vp)** is zero. As long as that is not the case, process termination should be checked by using **vwait( )** in place of **wait**(2). The function **vwait( )** works just like **wait**(2), but it posts process termination among all views.

Function Summary

The following table summarizes the functions supported by the view management module *vm.c*:

```
crt_off()                              end screen processing
crt_on(s) char * s;                    resume screen processing
exit(code)                             quit
fatal(fmt, ...)                        message and quit
vcatch(sig)                            intercept signal
vm(ch, code)                           manipulate view, return to main loop
int vmain(f, ..., 0) int (* f)();      main loop
vopen(vp) View * vp;                   change interior, make view current
int vwait(sp) int * sp;                wait for and record process completion
```

Unless **s** is a null pointer, **crt_on( )** will output **s** as a prompt and wait for input before resuming screen processing. The screen is redrawn at the next refresh operation.

The Key Mapping Module: *getkey.c*

The view manager uses cursor input to move and resize views. Terminals do not necessarily support a convenient set of function keys. Therefore, the key mapping module *getkey.c* supports a dynamic mapping between input key presses and key values used by the application.

```
int keymap(from, to)
int loadmap(fnm) char * fnm;
int mvwgetkey(wp, y, x) WINDOW * wp;
```

keymap( ) arranges for the value **to** to be returned for the key press **from**. The old assignment is returned. The return value zero indicates no previous assignment. If **to** is zero, **from** is mapped to itself. The return value -1 indicates an error: **to** must be an ASCII character or one of the *curses* key names.

loadmap( ) reads a list of mappings from a file. The file name can be passed as argument. If the argument is a null pointer, the file is read from a standard directory based on the environment variable **TERM**. If the map was loaded successfully, **loadmap( )** will return zero. The format of the map file is described in Section 4.7. Here is an example for the extended keyboard of an IBM PC with XENIX:

```
#       XENIX console keymap

ascii                   # up to 128 key names or numbers can follow here
        0  ^A ppage ^C ^D sf npage ^G
        ^H ^I ^J    ^K ^L ^M ^N    ^O
        ^P ^Q ^R    ^S ^T ^U ^V    ^W
        ^X sr ^Z    ^[ ^\ ^] ^^    ^_

        040             # white space cannot be used
        '!'             # character constants can
```

```
keypad                        # renaming can follow here

    f(10)   f(0)    # fix getch() decoder bug
    f(1)    ic      # KEY_F1 will be mapped to KEY_IC
    f(2)    dc
    f(3)    dl
    f(4)    home
    f(5)    clear
    f(6)    eos
    f(7)    eol
    f(8)    ll


    home    a1      # keypad keys are mapped to diagonal
    ppage   a3
    ll      c1
    npage   c3
```

Various bugs in the *curses* input mechanism can also be circumvented here.

mvwgetkey( ) is the input function which is subject to key mapping. The cursor is moved to row **y** and column **x** in the window **wp** and the window is refreshed. **keypad**( ) decoding is turned on, i.e., **echo**( ) and **nocbreak**( ) are implicitly suspended. One key press is read, mapped, and returned. **keypad**( ) decoding is turned off again. Zero can only be returned, if key code zero is not mapped.

1.5 Viewing Text

A view can be used to look at a text file, to query a help database, to watch output produced by a concurrently executing command, or to run a command to completion and look at its log. Special input lines request these operations. They are not part of the desk calculator language described in Section 1.2. Therefore, they are not subject to macro substitution.

> `< ` *file name*   view a file
> `? ` *term*   explain a term
> `! ` *command*   view output from a command
> `& ` *command*   execute command, view log

The pipe operator | can be used in place of !. The pipe operator | and the background operator & can also be specified following a command.

A view can be set up to interpret its input lines as display commands in any of the four categories by default. If a selection symbol is specified without an argument, it sets the default. The symbol is displayed on the top of the view frame as a reminder. Calculator commands can still be executed with = as a prefix. The symbol = alone will reset the view into calculator mode.

Long output lines are truncated at the right edge of the view. They cannot be restored when a view is enlarged. Since output is paginated, it may be a good idea to make a view fairly wide before display operations are started.

While a display command is active, the frame surrounding a view is changed into a single frame. The cursor is positioned at the beginning of the last text line. This may not be the bottom of the view at end of file or when the view is enlarged. The display command appears on the top line of the view frame and possible inputs are shown on the bottom line. The following inputs are available:

newline	advance one screen
backspace	back up (if possible)
q	quit, return to input mode
c	close current view, select previous
d	default frame for current view
f	full screen frame for current view
m	move current view
s	change size of current view
!	execute **SHELL**
letter *digit*	select view, open if necessary

+ and − can also be used to move forward and backward. The current *erase* character is equivalent to *backspace*, and *control*-D has the same effect as **q**. All of these inputs are subject to key mapping. Any input not otherwise assigned will cause a move forward.

Files

wish can display text files. Control characters other than white space are escaped with ^. Codes outside ASCII do not break *wish*, but their appearance depends on the terminal.

Lines are displayed as strings, i.e., text following a null byte is not shown. Long lines are truncated at the right edge of a view. Very long lines are split into several input lines. *wish* will not break if it displays a binary file, but the output is useless.

A text file is shown as a sequence of non-overlapping screens. *newline* or equivalent advances to the next screen. An unassigned input character advances by one line. *backspace* or equivalent backs up to the beginning of the file.

Help

wish can query the usage database described in the last chapter of Schreiner (1987). The database can be generated from the sources of on-line manual pages normally available on a UNIX system. Appropriate software tools and a sample database with information about *wish* are part of the software for this book available from the publisher.

By default, the database is a file *wish.use* in a standard directory. The directory can be set with the environment variable **USE**. A new database name is specified on an input line preceded by two question marks. Two question marks without an argument request the default database.

A query positions the view in the database to the first entry where the key starts with the *term* specified in the query. If the query is a single minus sign, the view is positioned to the beginning of the database. One database entry is shown in a view. Since the entries are expected to be short, a single view should be sufficient for the display. *newline* or any unassigned input character advances to the next entry. *backspace* or equivalent backs up to the previous entry.

Output from a Command

If a command is issued with the selector **!** or **|**, the command is executed concurrently with *wish*. Standard input for the command is the null device; standard output and diagnostic output are piped to *wish* and displayed in the view. The command should not interfere with the terminal used by *wish*, i.e., it should not try to access */dev/tty*.

wish uses the *interrupt* signal to enter view management. This signal is set up to be ignored by the concurrent command. If a view is closed or deselected, UNIX will block the concurrent command once the connecting pipe is full. If output of the command is no longer viewed, i.e., if *wish* is terminated or if the user issues **q** to the view displaying output from the command, the command receives a **SIGPIPE** signal. By default, it will then quit.

Command output is viewed just like a text file. *newline* or equivalent will advance by screens, unassigned input characters will advance by lines. However, a pipe cannot be backed up. *backspace* or equivalent will be ignored.

Log of a Command

If a command is issued with the selector **&**, the command is executed to completion before the output can be viewed. Standard input for the command is the null device; standard output and diagnostic output are collected in a temporary file. During this period, the frame surrounding the view is changed to a single frame and the reminder **waiting** appears in the prompt area on the bottom of the frame. Signals are handled as described for a concurrent command. Once the command has completed, its output can be viewed just like a file, i.e., **\b** will return to the beginning of the output.

1.6 Editor

A view can be used to edit a small text file. Editing is initiated with a command using the prefix **:** and a file name. During editing, the file name is shown on the top edge of the view.

If the file exists, it is loaded into memory. If the file does not exist, an empty file is created initially, but it will be removed if editing is aborted. Line length is limited to the width of the terminal screen, and long lines are silently truncated during input from the file. The number of lines is not limited, but if no more memory is available, editing is aborted. Tab characters are converted to white space. Trailing white space is not written into a file.

Editing is terminated with *control*-D and aborted with *control*-X. If editing is aborted, the original file remains unchanged. If editing is terminated properly, the file is overwritten.

During editing, the view acts as a window into the edited text. The terminal cursor denotes a position in the text, and the view will follow this text cursor through the text. For example, if the terminal cursor is at the bottom of the view, and if a key is pressed to move the cursor downward, the view will be positioned lower in the text so that the text position denoted by the cursor is near the center of the view. Similarly, the view will follow horizontally if the text is wider than the view.

This editor is mode-less, i.e., if a key press represents a visible character, the character is deposited at the cursor in the text. Cursor movement is based on the function keys of an intelligent terminal. All keys are subject to key mapping as described in Section 1.4. The following keys are recognized:

control-D	terminate editing, overwrite file
control-X	
kill key	abort editing, file unchanged
backspace	move one column left
erase key	move one column left
KEY_BACKSPACE	move one column left
KEY_LEFT	move one column left
KEY_RIGHT	move one column right
KEY_DOWN	move one row down
KEY_UP	move one row up
KEY_A1	move left and up
KEY_A3	move right and up
KEY_C1	move left and down
KEY_C3	move right and down
KEY_B3	move to center of left edge of view
KEY_LL	move to bottom left of view
KEY_HOME	move to top left of view
KEY_SF	move view one line down in text, keep cursor at text position
KEY_SR	move view one line up in text, keep cursor at text position
KEY_NPAGE	move view one page down in text, cursor to top left of view
KEY_PPAGE	move view one page up in text, cursor to bottom left of view
KEY_DL	delete line at cursor, cursor to next line
KEY_IL	insert blank line before line under cursor, cursor on new line
KEY_DC	delete character at cursor, cursor to next character
KEY_IC	insert blank character before character at cursor, cursor on new character
KEY_CLEAR	if at beginning of text, erase entire text; otherwise move to beginning
KEY_EOS	if at beginning of a line, erase rest of text; otherwise move to beginning of line
KEY_EOL	erase from cursor to end of line

newline	erase from cursor to end of line, move to next line
return	
tab	add blanks to next tab stop
other	if visible, insert character into text, move cursor past it

If the cursor would be moved out of the actual text, it is moved toward the beginning of the text. Lines in the view that do not correspond to text lines are marked with ˉ. The first line can be empty, but it cannot be deleted.

1.7 Dialog with a Command

A view can be used to conduct a dialog with a concurrent process. The concurrent process should expect to read complete input lines. Its standard and diagnostic output are collected in a pipe and displayed in the view. The number of the concurrent process is displayed on the top right part of the view frame, the command initiating the dialog is shown in the center.

The dialog is initiated by a *wish* command line with the prefix $ or %. The concurrent process is the result of executing the command line with the Bourne Shell.

The dialog can also be initiated by a command line consisting only of **sh**. In this case, the concurrent process is the result of executing the shell selected by the environment variable **SHELL**. If there is no such variable, the Bourne Shell is used. The process receives **sh** and −**i** as command name and argument.

The concurrent process inherits its signal state from *wish*. **SIGPIPE** and **SIGALRM** are set to default state, and the view management signal is ignored.

Line Interface

wish reads input characters from the keyboard and echoes them into the view. Normal line editing conventions may be used, i.e., *newline*, *return*, and *control*-D terminate an input line. The *erase* and *kill* characters may be used to edit within a line, and *control*-D at the beginning of a line indicates end of file.

Input and output can be intermixed. While *wish* only passes complete lines to the concurrent process, it periodically suspends waiting for input from the keyboard to display accumulated output from the process in the view. This arrangement is a fairly faithful simulation of line-oriented terminal input for the concurrent process. Typeahead is supported and will be stored in the pipe to the concurrent process.

Process Termination

control-D at the beginning of a line specifies end of input from the keyboard. In this case, a **SIGPIPE** signal is sent to the concurrent process and the view is returned to command state. Alternatively, *wish* senses if the concurrent process terminates, and will automatically return the view to command state.

Interruptible Input: *winput( )*

Intermixing input and output within a view is by far the most interesting aspect of process communication. This is accomplished with a function **winput( )** that is carefully designed to support line input, which may be interrupted and resumed at a later time.

```
int winput(wp, buf, col, bpp, lim, timeout)
        WINDOW * wp;
        char buf[], ** bpp; unsigned char col[];
        unsigned timeout;
```

winput( ) reads characters from the keyboard, displays the echo in the window indicated by **wp**, and stores the edited input line in **buf**[ ]. If a line is completed, **winput( )** returns the number of characters stored. If *control*-D is entered at the beginning of a line, **winput( )** returns **EOF**. Only visible characters are stored, and normal line editing conventions apply. However, **winput( )** cannot backspace over the top of **wp**.

    lim indicates the size of the vectors **buf**[ ] and **col**[ ]. The result is always terminated with a null byte, therefore, **lim** must be at least two. If *return* or *newline* terminate an input line, **\n** is stored at the end of the result in **buf**[ ].

    If **timeout** is zero, **winput( )** will continue until **lim**−1 characters have been stored, or until a line is terminated with *control*-D, *newline*, or *return*. The result cannot be zero.

    If **timeout** is not zero, **winput( )** will return zero as long as a line is not complete. The function will return either if a character is read or after **timeout** seconds have expired. Line completion and end of input are reported as before.

    col[ ] is required for line editing. **winput( )** stores the relative column position of each character there to simplify backing up over tab characters.

    bpp is required to make input resumable after timeouts. **winput( )** is serially reusable even when two input lines are collected in parallel. ***bpp** must point to the next location in **buf**[ ] where a character may be stored. The pointer should be initialized when a new input line is started, but it should then be reserved for **winput( )**.

    winput( ) reads input with **getchar**(3) and assumes **noecho( )** and **cbreak( )** to be set. **keypad( )** should be **FALSE** and **scrollok( )** would normally be **TRUE**. Input starts at the current position in **wp**.

## CHAPTER TWO

A Desk Calculator
scan, *scanl* **and** *calc*

2.1 Design

wish manages output on a terminal screen and distributes keyboard input to various activities, but it is not a menu-oriented or function-key-driven program. The backbone of *wish* is a simple command language, and it is very important that this language may be easily changed and extended. A desk calculator for integer arithmetic is in itself a useful program; if we design it as closely related to C as possible, we minimize the learning effort for our users. If we provide a link between the desk calculator's symbol table and the shell's environment variables, we have a natural way to transfer information to other programs. We must provide for some string manipulation in the calculator, however, and we need an escape mechanism to issue commands, etc. C has a preprocessor, and we should implement something similar.

As we have shown in a previous book (Schreiner and Friedman, 1985), a quick way to make a language is to describe its lexical aspects using *lex*(1) and its syntactic aspects using *yacc*(1). Section 2.2 deals with lexical analysis using *lex* for a strictly line-oriented application and provides an interface that can easily be connected to a screen interface later. Section 2.3 describes syntax analysis for C-like integer arithmetic and shows how we can handle strings. Section 2.4 discusses symbol table management based on binary search tree functions from the C library. In Section 2.5 we connect the environment and our symbol table. Section 2.6 introduces a simple preprocessor that interfaces nicely with our line-oriented lexical analysis. Section 2.7 demonstrates how easily we can add built-in functions to our desk calculator, and provides general mechanisms to extend the calculator language. Section 2.8 summarizes how the calculator can be used in other projects.

2.2 Lexical Analysis: *scan.l*

Lexical analysis is concerned with assembling input characters into symbols for syntax analysis. An easy description of the problem is a list of patterns for the various symbols – identifiers, numbers, character constants, C operators, comments, etc. – which we need to assemble. Lesk and Schmidt's *lex* is a UNIX tool to convert such a pattern list into a C program to do the pattern recognition. Patterns are regular expressions similar to those used in *ed*, *awk*, or in the various *grep* programs. C statements are attached to each pattern and will be executed when input text matching the pattern has been found. An array **yytext[ ]** then contains **yyleng** characters – the assembled input symbol. The C statements may assign a value describing specific aspects of the symbol to **yylval** and they should **return** an integer value describing the symbol class. For example, the following part of our lexical analysis source *scan.l* deals with assignment operator symbols:

```
shift    "<<"|">>"
space    [ \n\t]
white    [ \t]


%%


"+"{white}*"="          { Return(token(PASGOP)); }

([-*/%|^&]|{shift}){white}*"=" {
#ifndef DEBUG
                        yylval.y_int = yytext[0];
#endif
                        Return(token(ASGOP));
                }

{shift}                 {
#ifndef DEBUG
                        yylval.y_int = yytext[0];
#endif
                        Return(token(SHIFT));
                }


.                       Return(token(yytext[0]));
```

shift is a name for the pattern to recognize shift operators < < and > >, and **white** denotes the pattern to recognize white space on a line: a space, or a tab character. **space** additionally includes newlines.

Following *%%*, the pattern/action table so far contains four entries: for + = we will return the token **PASGOP** (*plus assignment operator*), where + and = may be separated by white space; for any of the other combined assignment operators − =, * =, etc. we assign its first character **yytext[0]** to **yylval.y_int**, where we assume **yylval** to be a **union** containing such an alternative, and we return the token **ASGOP**; for the two shift operators we assign the first character to **yytext[0]** and return **SHIFT**; finally, for an arbitrary character not matching the previous patterns we return the character itself.

We need two more patterns to recognize white space and comments and then we are nearly off and running:

```
{space}+                |
"#".*$                  ;
```

Newlines are only included here: white space in general is not significant, but a token such as + = is not allowed to extend over more than one input line.

Our action for both patterns is the same: one or more white space characters and a sequence of arbitrary characters beginning with # and extending to the end of a line are both to be ignored. | as an action asks *lex* to connect to the action following the next pattern; an empty C statement ; is a simple action to ignore some input.

Testing a *lex* Program

Clearly, at this point we do not know what our syntax analysis later might want to receive in **yylval** (and actually we don't even write that part of the code). We might also not yet find it necessary to distinguish **PASGOP** from **ASGOP**. However, we should have a way to test our lexical analysis thus far. Consider the following code, which is placed prior to %% in *scan.l*:

```
%{
#ifdef  DEBUG

        char * yylval;

        main()
        {
                while (yylex())
                        printf("%-.10s is \"%s\"\n", yylval, yytext);
                return 0;
        }

#       define  token(x)        "x"
#       define  Return(x)       return yylval = x, 1

#else

#       include "syn.i"
#       define  token(x)        x
#       define  Return(x)       return x

#endif
%}
```

lex copies text within %{ and %} directly to the generated C program. From the pattern/action table *lex* constructs a function **yylex()** which performs pattern recognition and executes our actions; an action may **return** an integer value: the result value of **yylex()**. *lex* arranges to return zero upon end of input, and we should arrange to return non-zero values for our symbols.

We will define **DEBUG** to compile a test version *scan* of our lexical analysis. A dialog with *scan* looks as follows:

```
$ scan
+= = << << = x1 # a line of input for testing
PASGOP is "+="
yytext[0] is "="
```

```
SHIFT is "<<"
ASGOP is "<< ="
yytext[0] is "x"
yytext[0] is "1"
```

main( ) calls **yylex( )** and displays the result: the token that syntax analysis will later receive and the text currently stored in **yytext[ ]**. **yylex( )** is supposed to return an integer value, which cannot necessarily be used to hide a character pointer. Therefore, in the test version we define **yylval** as a character pointer and use it to pass the token as text. The definition for **token( )** takes a token name and converts it to text.† **Return( )** passes the text to **yylval** and returns a non-zero value from **yylex( )**. Later, an include file *syn.i* should provide numerical values for token names such as **PASGOP**, and the definitions for **token( )** and **Return( )** become much simpler.

Starting the *Makefile*

wish will consist of many source files and compilation is best managed using Feldman's *make*(1). Now is the time to start a *Makefile* to describe how our various sources should be compiled. So far we call *lex* to construct a C source *scan.c* from the lexical analysis source *scan.l*, and we use the C compiler *cc*(1) to produce the task *scan*:

```
all:
CWD     = Wish
SHELL   = /bin/sh
T       = scan


pr:     Makefile
pr:     scan.l


all:    $T
rm:                ; rm -f *.[io] scan.c
rmall:  rm         ; rm -f $T


# scanner test programs

scan:   scan.c  ; $(CC) $(CFLAGS) -o $@ -DDEBUG $? -ll
                  rm -f scan.o
scan.c: scan.l  ; $(LEX) -t scan.l > scan.c
scan.o: scan.c syn.i
```

---

† The definition may have to be changed to use #x as replacement text, if the C preprocessor conforms to the new ANSI standard.

```
# general subroutines

pr:      # CWD $?                              # source printer
         @set -xv; \
         for i in `ls $?`; \
         do      pr -l72 -e -h $(CWD)/$$i $$i; \
         done | lp
         >$@


.PRECIOUS:      pr
```

make reads *Makefile*, a table describing the relationship between source files, targets such as object files, task images or other files, and the commands to produce targets from sources. Depending on the time stamps of the files, *make* tries to minimize the recompilation effort. A line such as

```
scan.c: scan.l   ; $(LEX) -t scan.l > scan.c
```

is typical: the target *scan.c* results from the source *scan.l* by executing the command following the semicolon. $(LEX) is a predefined macro in *make*: the name of the *lex* processor, normally just **lex** itself. Macros can be defined or redefined in the *Makefile*; they provide text replacement, and some macro names interact in subtle ways with *make* itself. A line such as

```
SHELL    = /bin/sh
```

is typical: **/bin/sh** is the replacement text for the macro name **SHELL** which would be called as $(SHELL). This name happens to decide which shell *make* will use to process the command lines in *Makefile* − we shall see later that choosing the right shell may make a significant difference.

For projects such as *wish* we build a certain number of options into our *Makefile* which can be extended during development. If *make* is called without arguments, it will build the first target in *Makefile*. We introduce the target **all** at the beginning and let it depend on all tasks that we wish to build. Since a file *all* is never built, *make* without arguments will always check to build all tasks.

The task list could be specified directly as sources for **all**, but if we define a macro **T** with the task names, we can overwrite this macro when calling *make* and thus limit how much *make* will build:

```
make T=
```

would do nothing. Targets can appear several times in a *Makefile*, but only once with a command part. Macros, however, are replaced as they are read. This is why we place an empty target **all** at the beginning of *Makefile* and later repeat it with the macro $T.

Our makefiles usually contain targets such as **rm** to remove temporary files, **rmall** to remove everything that is not a source file, and **pr** to list changed source files on the printer. *scan.c* is a temporary file, created from the lexical analysis source *scan.l*. Here we cannot do away with the extension **.c** required by the C compiler. For other intermediate files we will always use the extension **.i** and we can, therefore, use a wildcard to remove them. **rmall** removes temporary files by depending on **rm**, and then removes the tasks $T. Option −**f** suppresses an error return from *rm*(1); this way an unsuccessful *rm* will not immediately abort *make*.

pr is a fairly standard subroutine for a *Makefile*. **pr** depends on all files that we wish to print. This list is the replacement text of the predefined macro $?. With **ls** $? we construct an alphabetized list of all files on which **pr** depends. If *pr* is itself a file, the list will contain only those source files newer than *pr*. With the **for** loop we pass each file name in alphabetical order to the command *pr*(1). If *pr* is an empty file, the shell will still follow the search path to find the command *pr*. In this fashion we can add standard arguments, e.g., 72 lines per page for German paper, expansion of tabs for a dumb printer, and a header including the source directory name **$(CWD)** for filing purposes. All of these options are in a single place in the *Makefile*, so we can always copy this part of our makefiles, because it does not contain project-specific text.† Clearly, the file *pr* is **PRECIOUS**, i.e., it should not be removed if *make* is interrupted, because it is the time stamp to trace what source files still need to be printed.

Time to put flesh onto the skeleton's bones: the task *scan* depends on the temporary source file *scan.c* which depends on the lexical analysis source *scan.l*. We should use built-in macros such as **$(LEX)** or **$(CC)** to conform to *make* conventions. **$(CFLAGS)** is also a built-in macro, often with empty replacement text. Since *make* reads the environment prior to its own macro definitions, we could define **CFLAGS** in our shell *.profile* to always provide a private include directory or an optimization flag in the absence of an explicit definition of **CFLAGS** in *Makefile*.

$@** is a built-in macro denoting the current target; **$? is built in and stands for all (newer) sources of the current target. Using **$@** makes it much easier to change target names. Using **$?** saves typing, but if objects depend on source files as well as include files, **$?** might contain include file names, and a programming system such as *cc* generally is not amused when include files are passed as arguments.

Our line for *scan* above all specifies that **DEBUG** must be defined to compile the test version, and that the *lex* library −**ll** must be linked in. Some compilers might leave an object *scan.o* behind (at least if there is more than one source or object to be put together); compiled with **DEBUG** this object would contain a **main( )** function and would thus not fit with the rest of the project. Therefore, we remove *scan.o* if *scan* is compiled.

Scanning C Symbols

The basic mechanism for lexical analysis is in place and we have a way to check it out. Now we can add more pattern/action pairs to recognize all the other symbols we need in our desk calculator language. Obviously, the scanner can be extended at any time − after all, we are using *lex* to facilitate unforeseen extensions to this part of our system.

The pattern **.** recognizes any single character but newline; the associated action returns the character. As we shall see, letting single character symbols represent themselves is a convenient way to deal with them in syntax analysis. We will, therefore, only have to concern ourselves with assembling multi-character symbols. In ambiguous situations, *lex* will select the pattern/action pair that fits the longest input string; all other pairs should, therefore, precede the single character wildcard.

---

† *make* appears to support an undocumented **include** statement that permits file inclusion while a makefile is read. The unadorned file name follows **include**, and the entire line is replaced by the file contents. No macro expansion takes place on the **include** line.

```
"--"                          |
"++"                          {
#ifndef DEBUG
                              yylval.y_int = yytext[0];
#endif
                              Return(token(INC));
                              }
```

Sequences of special characters denoting an operator are usually specified explicitly. If we need comparison operators, etc., we can add them here in a similar fashion.

Just like the shift operators, the increment and decrement operators have equivalent usage. To keep the grammar of our calculator smaller, we define only one token **INC** for both operators and later distinguish them by their first letter in **yylval.y_int**.

Numerical constants consist of digit sequences, possibly preceded by a qualifier denoting base 16:

```
hex       [0-9a-fA-F]
num       [0-9]
%%

0[xX]{hex}+                   |
{num}+                        { long strtol();
#ifndef DEBUG
                              yylval.y_int = strtol(yytext, (char **) 0, 0);
#endif
                              Return(token(Iconstant));
                              }
```

The patterns use two more named patterns, **hex** for the hexadecimal digits and **num** for decimal and octal digits, which must be defined in the first section of the *lex* source. The constant value will be passed to the syntax analysis as an integer in **yylval.y_int**. Fortunately, this call to **strtol**(3) automatically recognizes and converts all three possible bases.

There are three kinds of character constants enclosed in quotes: a single character, an escaped character, and a character described by its octal value.† Determining the constant value is easy if we write three patterns:

```
\'[^'\\\n]\'                  {
#ifndef DEBUG
                              yylval.y_int = yytext[1];
#endif
                              Return(token(Iconstant));
                              }
```

A single character may not be a quote, a \, or a newline. The constant value is the integer value of the character.

---

† The ANSI standard offers a fourth possibility: hexadecimal representation.

```
\'\\[^0-7\n]\'          { register char * cp; char * strchr();
                          static char esc[] = "bfnrt", ape[] = "\b\f\n\r\t";
#ifndef DEBUG
                          if (cp = strchr(esc, yylval.y_int = yytext[2]))
                              yylval.y_int = ape[cp - esc];
#endif
                          Return(token(Iconstant));
                        }
```

Octal digits do not represent themselves as escaped characters, and a newline may not be escaped. A certain list **esc[ ]** of escaped characters represents a list **ape[ ]** of special values and we can use linear search with **strchr**(3) for the translation. Any other escaped character, in particular a quote, represents its own integer value.

```
\'\\([0-7]{1,3})\'      { long strtol();
#ifndef DEBUG
                          yylval.y_int = strtol(yytext + 2, (char **) 0, 8);
#endif
                          Return(token(Iconstant));
                        }
```

One to three octal digits can again be converted using **strtol**() – this time with base 8 as an explicit argument. The phrase **{1,3}** specifies that the preceding regular expression may be used one to three times; however, **{ }** has lower precedence than concatenation and thus requires appropriate parentheses for grouping.

```
\"([^"\\\n]|\\.)*\"     { char * strsave();
#ifndef DEBUG
                          if (cstring(yytext, yytext+1) == -1)
                              REJECT;
                          yylval.y_str = strsave(yytext);
#endif
                          Return(token(Sconstant));
                        }
```

String constants are enclosed in double quotes and contain zero or more characters. But for double quote, \, and newline, any character may appear unadorned. Any character with the exception of newline may follow \. Unfortunately, we will later need the internal representation of the string with \-escapes evaluated. **cstring**(), part of the software package of Schreiner (1987), is a suitable conversion function:

```
int cstring(out, in) char out[], in[];
```

cstring() copies from **in[ ]** to **out[ ]**, evaluates the escape sequences, stops at a non-escaped null byte or at an unprotected double quote, terminates **out[ ]** with a null byte, and returns the number of bytes stored into **out[ ]** prior to the null byte.

   If **cstring**() discovers a newline (escaped or not), or an escaped null byte, it will return -1. While our *lex* pattern excludes this possibility, we still provide error recovery: **REJECT** as an action rejects the pattern currently matched by *lex* and forces the scanner to make another selection. In our case, the characters of the string might end up being returned as single characters; a double quote alone will not be legal in our desk calculator language and thus we make sure that we receive an error indication.

Null bytes can be represented in **in[ ]**. Therefore, **out[ ]** might contain null bytes. In our case we are only interested in the string up to the first null byte; **strsave( )** uses **malloc**(3) to return a copy of its argument saved in dynamic memory.

One more class of C symbols remains: reserved words and user-defined identifiers. We could specify reserved words as individual patterns, just like the operator **INC**, but this would dramatically increase the size of the program generated by *lex*. It is preferable, albeit slower in execution, to use a single pattern to recognize every word as an identifier, and later employ table lookup to distinguish reserved words, user-defined identifiers, and macros.

```
alpha      [a-zA-Z_]
alnum      [a-zA-Z_0-9]
%%

{alpha}{alnum}*          {
#ifdef  DEBUG
                        Return(token(Identifier));
#else
                        return lexi_screen(yytext);
#endif
                        }
```

We will look at the details of **lexi_screen( )** in Section 2.4 and extend this code to perform macro substitution in Section 2.6. Once again we use two named patterns **alpha** and **alnum**, defined in the initial part of the *lex* source, to document our concept of letters and to simplify maintenance or extension.

Reading *lex* Input from Buffers: *lexi_buf( )*

Our desk calculator will be line oriented and the command lines are read through a screen management mechanism. Thus far, however, lexical analysis reads standard input. We need to change the input mechanism of **yylex( )** so that it uses buffers which we can fill elsewhere. The new test program is called *scanl*; here is its *Makefile* entry:

```
scanl:  scan.c  ; $(CC) $(CFLAGS) -o $@ -DDEBUG_LINE $? -ll $(local)
                rm -f scan.o
```

Under control of the preprocessor symbol **DEBUG_LINE** we define a new **main( )** program at the beginning of *scan.l* as follows:

```
%{
#ifdef  DEBUG_LINE

        char * yylval;

        main()
        {       char buf[BUFSIZ];

                while (gets(buf))
                {       lexi_buf(buf);
                        while (yylex())
                                printf("%-.10s is \"%s\"\n", yylval, yytext);
                }
                return 0;

        }

#       undef   input
#       undef   unput
#       define  DEBUG

#else
#ifdef  DEBUG

... main() as before ...
```

This time we read an input line with **gets**(3) into a local buffer which we make available to lexical analysis with a new function **lexi_buf**( ). Once a buffer is available, calls to **yylex**( ) will return successive symbols from the buffer. *scanl* is supposed to produce the same output as *scan* and **DEBUG_LINE**, therefore, needs to define **DEBUG** for the pattern/action part of the program.

lex arranges for **yylex**( ) to use three functions for input and output: **input**( ) is expected to return the next input character or zero as indication of end of file; **output**( ) is called with each character that cannot be matched by any pattern (in our case this cannot happen); **unput**( ) is called if a character needs to be pushed back into the stream read by **input**( ). By default, **input**( ) reads standard input, **output**( ) writes to standard output, and **unput**( ) interacts with **input**( ) to provide multi-character pushback.

The three functions are defined by *lex* as macros and need to be undefined early on. We can terminate the pattern/action part of the *lex* source with %%; the rest of the source is copied to the generated C program and usually contains new versions of functions such as **input**( ). We let a **Stream** consist of a pointer .buf to the current input buffer and a pointer .bp to the next input character. **lexi_buf**( ) expects to receive a static buffer as argument and it initializes a **Stream**:

```
%%

#ifdef  DEBUG_LINE
#undef  DEBUG
#endif

#ifndef DEBUG

typedef struct stream Stream;
        struct stream { char * buf, * bp; Stream * prev; };

static Stream _in, * in = & _in;
lexi_buf(buf)
        register char * buf;
{       extern int yyprevious;
        char * strcat();

        in -> buf = in -> bp = strcat(buf, "\n");
        NLSTATE;
}
```

Selection is a bit tricky: we require the line interface if **DEBUG** is not defined, and especially, if **DEBUG_LINE** is defined. In the latter case, we have earlier defined **DEBUG** to get the right actions; now we need to undefine **DEBUG** to get the line interface.

At this point of our development, a single static **Stream** will do; we could call it **in** and refer to its components as **in.buf** and **in.bp**. The purpose of the structure is to hide the somewhat likely names **buf** and **bp**. Once we add a preprocessor in Section 2.6, we will discover that we need a stack of **Stream**s. At that point we add the component **.prev**, rename **in** to **_in**, add the **Stream** pointer **in** and refer to the current components **in − >buf** and **in − >bp**. To keep our presentation closer to the final software distribution, we have already introduced the macro version above.

```
int input()
{       register char ch;

        if (ch = * in -> bp)
                ++ in -> bp;
        return ch;
}
```

input( ) returns the next character in the current **Stream**; if this is not a null byte, the next character pointer must be advanced.

```
unput(ch)
        register int ch;
{
        if (ch)
                -- in -> bp;
        if (* in -> bp != ch)
                fatal("unput");
}
```

unput( ) moves the next character pointer backwards, unless it is confronted with pushing back end of file. If the character to be pushed back is not the one originally in the current **Stream**, things probably got confused and **unput( )** unhappily calls **fatal( )** to output an error message and terminate the task. **fatal( )** later needs to worry about screen management; for now, a simple combination of **puts**(3) and **exit**(2) will do. Such a function should be found in a private library specified as $(**local**) in our *Makefile* entry for *scanl* above.

lex patterns may use ^ and $ to match beginning and end of an input line. ^ depends on the automaton being in **NLSTATE**, and $ depends on the next input character being newline. Initially, **yylex( )** is in **NLSTATE**; if **lexi_buf( )** silently adds \n to each input buffer† and if the end of the buffer is always reached, we would always be in **NLSTATE** at the beginning of the buffer. Syntax errors, however, break this cycle, and it is best to use the (undocumented) macro **NLSTATE** to make sure; experimentation reveals that **yyprevious** must also be declared.

The line interface to a *lex* program developed in this section can be used for other applications. For example, **lexi_buf( )** could produce a listing as each input line is passed to it. If we read from a file, **lexi_buf( )** should increment **yylineno** to aid in generating error messages (the default version of **input( )** does this, too).

2.3 Syntax Analysis: *calc.y*

Syntax analysis is concerned with assembling input symbols into phrases and ultimately into a *sentence*. An easy description of the problem is a grammar describing how a sentence, i.e., an input buffer, may be composed. A *grammar* consists of a list of *rules*; each rule explains a *non-terminal symbol* using one or more *formulations*; each formulation defines a *phrase* and consists of a sequence of zero or more non-terminal symbols, each in turn explained by some rule, or *tokens*, each assembled from the actual input during lexical analysis. One non-terminal, usually the one explained by the first rule in the grammar, is termed the *start symbol* of the grammar; the purpose of syntax analysis is to find phrases so that the entire input token sequence is derived from the start symbol. Johnson's *yacc* is a UNIX tool to convert a suitable grammar into a C program to do the phrase recognition.

An *action* composed of C statements can be attached to each formulation and will be executed when input text matching the formulation has been found. Input is processed from left to right, and formulations are selected bottom up. The last formulation selected will be one for the start symbol. In an interactive system, the action usually implements what the phrase means, e.g., if a formulation describes addition, the associated action will perform it. In a compiler or other programmable system, the actions usually build an internal representation of the sentence, to be acted on in a later phase of the program.

---

† ...in high hopes that there is enough room!

During lexical analysis, a value may be attached to a token by assigning the value to **yylval** before the token is returned as function value of **yylex( )**. Actions have access to the attached values: within an action associated with a formulation, **$1** is the value associated with the first symbol in the formulation, **$2** refers to the value for the second symbol, etc. If the symbol is a token, its value was assigned to **yylval** during lexical analysis. If the symbol is a non-terminal, a phrase has been found earlier for it, and an action probably was executed. Each action can attach a value to the non-terminal explained by its phrase; the value is assigned in the action to **$$**, or the action may call a C function specified elsewhere, which can assign the value to **yylval** just as lexical analysis assigns to **yylval**. By default, **$1** will be passed to **$$**.

Describing a language, i.e., a set of permissible sentences, by a grammar written from scratch is a non-trivial problem. Fortunately, programming languages tend to follow simple, standard architectures and grammars suitable for recognition can usually be built by adapting well-known patterns. Theoretical aspects of grammars and recognizers such as those built by *yacc* are thoroughly discussed in Aho, Sethi and Ullman (1986). A gentle introduction to using *yacc* is presented in Chapter 8 of Kernighan and Pike (1984), a more comprehensive user's view appears in Schreiner and Friedman (1985). Here we will show how we put our interactive desk calculator together, but we will not expound on better ways to a fancier recognizer.

First Steps

Once again we start with a very small subset of the final grammar, construct a test program for it, and extend the result as we go along. First, consider syntax alone: we want to process an input **buffer** consisting of at least one **stmt**. Several **stmts** should be separated by comma or semicolon; if we permit **stmt** to be empty, we can have many delimiters in sequence, and delimiters may also be specified at the end of the input buffer. Thus far, we have the following grammar:

```
buffer   : stmts

stmts    : stmt
         | stmts ',' stmt
         | stmts ';' stmt

stmt     : /* null */
         | ie
         | se

ie       : Iconstant

se       : Sconstant
```

For technical reasons − memory consumption, for one − we should use left recursion rather than right recursion to describe an iteration. : separates the non-terminal name from its first formulation, and | separates two formulations in the same rule. A rule can be terminated by a semicolon, but we prefer just to leave a blank line. Comments are as in C, white space is ignored (except for delimiting words), and single character symbols are tokens describing themselves as return values from **yylex( )**.

Not every **stmt** will be empty. For starters, we explain an integer expression **ie** as an **Iconstant** and a string expression **se** as a **Sconstant**. Both names have already been anticipated in our lexical analysis.

Since **Iconstant** and **Sconstant** are never explained, *yacc* could implicitly define them to be tokens. For technical reasons, however, tokens must be declared in the input to *yacc* prior to the grammar:

```
%union { int y_int; char * y_str; }

%token  <y_int> Iconstant
%token  <y_str> Sconstant

%token  <y_int> ASGOP INC PASGOP SHIFT
%%

... grammar as above ...
```

During lexical analysis we attach values to tokens. **Iconstant** is accompanied by an integer value, **Sconstant** by a dynamically saved character string. Each value is assigned to **yylval** which, therefore, must have a **union** type. The **%union** statement in the initial part of the *yacc* source declares the value type. If we plan to use a value deposited during lexical analysis, we must not only introduce the corresponding name with **%token**, but one of the alternatives in the **%union** must be mentioned after **%token** to explain to *yacc* how a reference to the value needs to be expanded.

Tokens themselves are represented as small integer values to be returned by **yylex( )** and to be understood by **yyparse( )**, the recognizer generated by *yacc*. It helps if both functions agree on the values: integer values in the range 1 to 255 in fact are character values specified as character constants within the grammar and returned by **yylex( )** directly; integer values beginning at 257 are assigned by *yacc* sequentially to each token name mentioned in the **%token** statements. *yacc* can be persuaded to deposit the results of **%union** as well as preprocessor definitions for the token names into a separate include file *y.tab.h* for the benefit of lexical analysis. **yyparse( )** is written into a file *y.tab.c*.

Making a Parser

We are ready to compile a minimal recognizer. Here are the additions to our *Makefile*:

```
local    = ../Lib/cstring.o ../Lib/fatal.o ../Lib/strsave.o
T        = scan scanl calc
YFLAGS   = -d
pr:      calc.y

rm:              ; rm -f *.[io] scan.c calc.c y*

# calculator test program

calc:   $(calc)        ; $(CC) $(CFLAGS) -o $@ -DDEBUG $(calc) -ll $(local)
                         rm -f calc.o

calc.c y.tab.h: calc.y ; $(YACC) $(YFLAGS) calc.y
                         mv y.tab.c calc.c

syn.i:  y.tab.h        ; -cmp -s $@ $? || cp $? $@
```

local must provide access to private functions such as **cstring**( ) etc., which are used in lexical analysis. Most likely, these will not be individual objects but will reside in a private library.

Our *yacc* source is in a file *calc.y* − another candidate for occasional printing under control of the target **pr**. While processing the source, *yacc* generates a number of temporary files which are left over if things go badly wrong. All these names start with y; therefore, we add the wildcard **y*** to our cleanup target **rm** and do not start our own file names with y. *yacc* deposits its output in a file *y.tab.c*. We prefer to rename this file to *calc.c*, since it is derived from the actual source file *calc.y*, and we add it to the removal list as well.

We are ready to describe how the new files are made. First we need to call *yacc* − within *make* known as $(YACC) − pass it our grammar in *calc.y*, and specify option −**d** so that token and type definitions are copied to *y.tab.h*. Within *make*, options for *yacc* are customarily passed using the built-in macro $(**YFLAGS**).

make will execute *yacc* as soon as we change *calc.y*, and *yacc* will overwrite the definitions in *y.tab.h*. Lexical analysis needs these definitions, but **yylex**( ) only needs to be recompiled if the definitions change. To save some compilation effort, we maintain the definitions for lexical analysis in a separate file *syn.i* which starts out as a copy of *y.tab.h*, but is only overwritten if *y.tab.h* is changed. **cmp** −**s** will silently fail, if its argument files differ or do not both exist. Only in this case will *cp*(1) be executed. − at the beginning of a command part in a *Makefile* keeps *make* from terminating as soon as the command fails. We connect *cmp* and *cp* using logical or: the Bourne Shell will execute a command following || only if the preceding command fails. Unfortunately, the C Shell does exactly the opposite. This is why we have explicitly defined **SHELL** to be the Bourne Shell in our *Makefile*.

If we execute *make* at this point, we receive a few complaints about missing functions: for lexical analysis we postulated **lexi_screen**( ) as connection to a symbol table; *yacc* additionally assumes a function **yyerror**( ) which is passed a character string argument as an error message. We are also missing a usable **main**( ) program. The *lex* library −**ll** happens to contain one, but it would call **yylex**( ) and not the function **yyparse**( ) which *yacc* generates. System V has a *yacc* library −**ly**. This library contains trivial functions **main**( ) and **yyerror**( ), and would have to be specified prior to −**ll**. Since we choose to read our own input buffers and pass them to lexical analysis through **lexi_buf**( ), we really must supply our own functions. We do so under control of **DEBUG** in the third part of the *yacc* source:

```
... grammar as before ...

%%

#ifdef DEBUG

#include <stdio.h>

int lexi_screen() { fatal("lexi_screen"); }

yyerror(s)
        register char * s;
{
        puts(s);
}

main()
{       char buf[BUFSIZ];

        while (gets(buf))
                lexi_buf(buf), yyparse();
        return 0;
}

#endif
```

Obtaining Output

Very little happens, if we execute this first version of our desk calculator. This is not surprising, since we did not specify any actions in the grammar. Recognition as such is a silent business:

```
$ calc
10, 20; "axel was here" ,,,
10 + 20
syntax error
"huh?"
^D
$
```

The system is more responsive, once we attach some calls to **printf**(3). We would normally be interested in the value of a string or integer expression:

```
        %type    <y_int> ie
        %type    <y_str> se
        %%

        stmt     : /* null */
                 | ie                  { reply("%d", $1); }
                 | se                  { reply("\"%s\"", $1), free($1); }


        ie       : Iconstant           /* $$ = $1; */


        se       : Sconstant           /* $$ = $1; */
```

Comments have been added as reminders that by default the value attached to the first symbol in a formulation will be passed as value attached to the non-terminal. Clearly, *yacc* needs to know about value types for non-terminals. This is usually specified with **%type** declarations in the beginning part of the *yacc* source.

Values attached to **Sconstant** originate in **yytext[ ]** and are stored in dynamically allocated memory during lexical analysis. Once we have finished with the value of a string expression we must free this space. Otherwise, dynamic memory will eventually be exhausted. Our code is not bullet-proof: as it stands, syntax errors more or less abort the recognition process and memory allocated to string values attached to active symbols is lost.

Output from our desk calculator will later have to be passed to our screen manager. This is why we introduce **reply( )**. Right now, **printf( )** would certainly suffice:

```
#define VARARG   , v1, v2, v3, v4, v5

reply(fmt VARARG)
        register char * fmt;
{
        putchar('\t'), printf(fmt VARARG), putchar('\n');
}


yyerror(s)
        register char * s;
{
        reply("?%s", s);
}
```

reply( ) might be called with a variable number of arguments. A more reasonable solution appears in Section 3.4. Right now, the definition of **VARARG** is a poor man's dirty alternative to *varargs.h*. Since error messages also need to go to the screen manager, we re-route the output from **yyerror( )** as well. Our desk calculator is now ready to talk back. Here is an example:

```
$ calc
10, 20; "axel was here" ,,,
        10
        20
        "axel was here"
```

```
10 + 20
        10
        ?syntax error
"new\nline"
        "new
line"
quit
lexi_screen
$
```

quit, of course, is assembled as an identifier, and our stub for **lexi_screen( )** terminates this version of *calc* with a call to **fatal( )**.

Teaching Arithmetic

The initial version of our desk calculator is working and we should extend it to do something useful. We can now add all aspects of C integer arithmetic that do not involve variables. We just write more formulations for the non-terminal symbol **ie** (*integer expression*). For example, an integer expression may consist of an integer constant **Iconstant** or of two integer expressions connected by the operator | to denote bit-wise *or*:

```
ie      : Iconstant           /* $$ = $1; */
        | ie '|' ie           { $$ = $1 | $3; }
```

The associated action attaches the bit-wise *or* of the two integer expression values **$1** and **$3** as result of the *or* operation.

Unfortunately, there is a technical complication. As it stands, the grammar does not specify associativity of the *or* operation. In what order should an expression such as

```
10 | 20 | 30 | 40
```

be evaluated? Where does our calculator implicitly assume parentheses for grouping? While it does not make any difference for *or*, the problem is certainly real for a non-commutative operation such as subtraction. In the initial part of the *yacc* source we can specify a table defining operator properties:

```
%left           '|'
%left           '^'
%left           '&'
%left   <y_int> SHIFT           /* << >> */
%left           '+' '-'
%left           '*' '/' '%'
%right          '!' '~'
%nonassoc.      '['
%%
```

Each **%left** statement defines a list of operator tokens which are left-associative, i.e., which group from left to right. **%right** similarly defines operators to group from right to left, and **%nonassoc** introduces operators that cannot be grouped implicitly.

The sequence of all **%left**, **%right**, and **%nonassoc** statements together has another pleasant property: it defines operator precedence. The first such statement introduces operators of lowest precedence, i.e., those which are evaluated last, and the last such statement introduces operators of highest precedence, i.e., those which are executed first. Operators defined within one statement have equal precedence and group as the statement indicates. The example of **SHIFT** shows that the statements can additionally specify the value type attached to the operators, if any.

```
ie      : Iconstant              /* $$ = $1; */
        | ie '|' ie              { $$ = $1 | $3; }
        | ie '^' ie              { $$ = $1 ^ $3; }
        | ie '&' ie              { $$ = $1 & $3; }
        | ie SHIFT ie            { switch($2) {
                                    case '<':   $$ = $1 << $3; break;
                                    case '>':   $$ = $1 >> $3; break;
                                 } }
        | ie '+' ie              { $$ = $1 + $3; }
        | ie '-' ie              { $$ = $1 - $3; }
        | ie '*' ie              { $$ = $1 * $3; }
        | ie '/' ie              { if ($3 == 0) response("?div by 0");
                                   $$ = $1 / $3;
                                 }
        | ie '%' ie              { if ($3 == 0) response("?mod 0");
                                   $$ = $1 % $3;
                                 }
        | '!' ie                 { $$ = ! $2; }
        | '~' ie                 { $$ = ~ $2; }
        | '-' ie %prec '!'       { $$ = - $2; }
        | se '[' ie ']'          { if ($3 < 0 || $3 > strlen($1))
                                        free($1), response("?index range");
                                   $$ = $1 [ $3 ], free($1);
                                 }
        | '(' ie ')'             { $$ = $2; }
```

With the operator table in place, the grammar can be extended very quickly. A few actions present minor complications: the two **SHIFT** operators must be distinguished by the attached value, i.e., the first character of the operator; dividing by zero or computing the remainder modulo zero should not be permitted; selecting a character from a string expression using a subscript is only legal if the index value is within range; the string value must be released whether a character has been selected or not. A new function **response( )** accepts arguments and passes them to **reply( )** for output, but it will not return:

```
#include <setjmp.h>

jmp_buf on_response;

response(fmt VARARG)
        register char * fmt;
{
        reply(fmt VARARG);
        longjmp(on_response, 1);
}


main()
{       char buf[BUFSIZ];

        setjmp(on_response);
        while (gets(buf))
                lexi_buf(buf), yyparse();
        return 0;
}
```

We use **setjmp**(3) in our main program and **longjmp**(3) to return from **response**( ) directly to the point where a new input buffer is read. **response**( ) can also be used to implement **yyerror**( ): in an interactive, line-oriented system the best error recovery strategy is probably just to abort the offending buffer with a brief message. As our string subscripting example shows, we must be careful to reclaim as much allocated memory as possible prior to aborting the recognition process. **setjmp**( ) and **longjmp**( ) take care to reset the automatic memory.

Minus signs exhibit another complication: the operator − has fairly low precedence if it takes two arguments and denotes subtraction, but is has high precedence if it takes one argument and denotes reversal of the sign. **%prec** is (nearly) a kludge in *yacc* to force a formulation to take its precedence from a different operator.

Dynamic String Concatenation

If we stick to C, we should support string concatenation through a **strcat**( ) function in the desk calculator. Section 2.7 deals with the implementation of built-in functions. However, it is convenient, and an interesting experiment, to add an operator for string concatenation. A tempting approach is to specify

```
se      : Sconstant            /* $$ = $1; */
        | se se                ( ... }
```

i.e., to indicate concatenation by juxtaposing strings. *yacc* complains that this grammar has a *shift/reduce conflict*, i.e., just as with *or* above, *yacc* is not sure which set of parentheses to assume silently:

```
"abc" "def" "ghi"       # input
( "abc" "def" ) "ghi"   # group from left
"abc" ( "def" "ghi" )   # group from right
```

We could accept *yacc*'s judgement. In case of such a shift/reduce conflict, *yacc* would group from the left, i.e., it would try to build the longest possible phrase. An experiment with the final version of the desk calculator shows, however, that we would later run into about 50 shift/reduce conflicts. Since there is an easy way to fix things here, let's not rely on *yacc* too much:

```
%type    <y_str> se, s
%%


se       : s                    /* $$ = $1; */
         | se s                 ( ... )


s        : Sconstant            /* $$ = $1; */
         | '(' se ')'           { $$ = $2; }
```

We need explicitly to group from the left in the grammar, i.e., we need to use left recursion. We have also introduced parentheses for explicit grouping in string expressions. This serves no useful purpose at the moment, but it avoids an unnecessary difference between string and integer expressions. Here is the action to dynamically concatenate string values:

```
         | se s
            ( (       char * malloc(), * strcat(), * strcpy();

                      if (! ($$ = malloc(strlen($1) + strlen($2) + 1)))
                              fatal("no room");
                      strcat(strcpy($$, $1), $2), free($1), free($2);

            } }
```

We need an extra set of braces to construct a C block which can enclose our function declarations. **strlen**(3) is used to measure the space requirements, **malloc**(3) obtains the space, a combination of **strcpy**(3) and **strcat**(3) constructs the new value, and **free**(3) releases the old space. If we cannot find enough memory, we terminate our calculator. It is tempting to call **response**( ), but it does not appear likely that our user could do much more at this point. Here is a sample session with this release of *calc*:

```
$ calc
10, 20; "axel was here"            # constants, delimiters
        10
        20
        "axel was here"
'\n' - 20, 10 / ('a' - 97), 'b'    # simple arithmetic
        -10
        ?div by 0

                                   # oops, 'b' is skipped
'\123' << 3, 01230                 # shifting
        664
        664
```

```
"abc" "def" ( "\n" "ghi" "jkl" )          # concatenation
        "abcdef
ghijkl"
"def" "abc" [3], 'a'                       # subscript into concatenation
        97
        97
quit                                      # no variables, yet
lexi_screen
$
```

Some operators are missing from the implementation: comma is supported at the **stmts** level; assignments, increment, and decrement can only be applied to variables; and conditions, unfortunately, cannot be supported. Consider the following expression:

```
a && b
```

a is recognized and evaluated during recognition. **b** is only supposed to be evaluated if **a** is true. **b** must be recognized, however, and since we evaluate *during* recognition, we cannot support this class of operators. Kernighan and Pike (1984) give a simple example of code generation in a desk calculator. Once we resort to generating code during recognition, we can then selectively execute the code and thus support conditional evaluation.

2.4 Variables: *sym.c*

A desk calculator is more fun if we can manipulate variables. If we restrict the variable names, e.g., to lower-case letters for integer variables and upper-case letters for string variables, we can build a very simple system with two preallocated value vectors. Arbitrary variable names are easier to use, though, and a certain leniency in variable typing does much to make our users happier. We will need a symbol table to store information about the **Identifier** tokens recognized during lexical analysis:

```
typedef struct symbol Symbol;
        struct symbol {
                char * s_name;
                int s_yylex;
                union { char * s_sval;
                        int s_ival;
                        } s_val;
                };

#define s_int   s_val.s_ival
#define s_str   s_val.s_sval
```

A **Symbol** has a dynamically saved name **.s_name** of arbitrary length, a token value **.s_yylex** to be returned by **yylex()**, and for variables a value. We record the current type of a variable in **.s_yylex** and we represent the current value as a **union**. Coding is simplified if we define simple component names to select the available alternatives. Since various parts of our system will need to know about symbols, we place the definitions in a header file *calc.h*.

Adding Names to the Grammar

Lexical analysis already calls a function **lexi_screen()** to deal with names. The following code appeared in the *lex* source *scan.l*:

```
alpha    [a-zA-Z_]
alnum    [a-zA-Z_0-9]
%%

{alpha}{alnum}*          {
#ifdef  DEBUG
                         Return(token(Identifier));
#else
                         return lexi_screen(yytext);
#endif
                         }
```

lexi_screen() receives a name and should return its non-zero token value. An action in **yyparse()** certainly requires access to the particular symbol; **lexi_screen()** must assign a pointer to the **Symbol** representing the name to **yylval**. We need to extend the types of values attached to tokens at the beginning of *calc.y* and define what we mean by an **Identifier**:

```
%{
#include "calc.h"
%}

%union { int y_int; char * y_str; Symbol * y_sym; }

%token   <y_sym> Identifier, Integer, String
%type    <y_sym> lval
%%

lval     : Identifier          /* $$ = $1; */
         | Integer             /* $$ = $1; */
         | String              /* $$ = $1; */
```

A variable can have three token values: **Identifier** does not yet have a value, **Integer** has an integer value, and **String** has a string value. A new non-terminal **lval** combines the three possibilities.

      Symbol is now part of the type definition of **yylval**. Therefore, *calc.h* must be included into the files generated from *scan.l* and *calc.y*. *lex* and *yacc* both copy code within %{ and %} unchanged. Objects depend not only on their sources but also on the included files. We must immediately record the new situation in our *Makefile*. Dependencies are cumulative, so a single line consisting only of targets and source suffixes:

```
pr:     calc.h
calc.o scan.o:  calc.h
```

Screening Names: *lexi_screen( )*

How do we store symbols? A simple, inefficient method is a linear list, represented either as a vector of **Symbol** elements or dynamically linked. System V provides **lsearch**(3) to maintain a vector, but a fixed maximum number of symbols sounds like a horrible idea. **hsearch**(3) supports a hash table scheme, the most efficient search technique, but **hsearch**( ) depends on a fixed initial allocation and does not provide sorted or at least sequential access to each symbol in turn; therefore, implementing a symbol table dump would be a bit complicated.

   tsearch(3) is probably the best choice. This family of library functions implements dynamically allocated binary search trees to store pointers to arbitrary information, and it provides sorted sequential access and even deletion. A search tree turns into an expensive version of a linear list if our symbols arrive sorted,† but for calculators this is not likely. A slight obstacle is the fact that the documentation of **tsearch**(3) in the System V Interface Definition (1986) is not terribly easy to understand, although the functions are easy to use! Here is **lexi_screen**( ):

```
char * calloc(), * strsave(), * tsearch();

int lexi_screen(name)
        register char * name;
{       register Symbol ** spp;
        Symbol s;
        static char * symbols;          /* tree */

        s.s_name = name;
        if (! (spp = (Symbol **) tsearch((char *) & s, & symbols, scmp)))
                fatal("no room");

        if (*spp == & s)
        {       if (! (*spp = (Symbol *) calloc(1, sizeof(Symbol))))
                        fatal("no room");
                (*spp) -> s_name = strsave(name);
                (*spp) -> s_yylex = Identifier;
        }
        yylval.y_sym = *spp;
        return yylval.y_sym -> s_yylex;
}
```

The search tree requires a pointer to its root node; for an empty tree, this must be a null pointer such as **symbols**. For declaration purposes, **tsearch**( ) returns a character pointer and requires three arguments: an arbitrary pointer value, which will be located or entered in the search tree;

---

† ...and the library version **twalk**(3) requires excessive amounts of automatic memory. There is a better way, consult Chapter 18 in Schreiner (1987).

the address of the root node pointer, where a pointer to the tree may be entered; and the address of a comparison function determining the order of elements when visited in **postorder**. In our case, the first argument will be a pointer to a **Symbol**, and the comparison function **scmp( )** will compare two such pointers according to the component **.s_name**:

```
static int scmp(a, b)
        register Symbol * a, * b;
{
        return strcmp(a -> s_name, b -> s_name);
}
```

Of course, each **Symbol** known to the search tree is dynamically allocated. However, while trying to locate a name, we use an automatic **Symbol**, the local variable **s** in **lexi_screen( )**, for comparison purposes. **s.s_name** is set to point to the **name** which **lexi_screen( )** is supposed to locate or enter, and **& s** is passed to **tsearch( )**.

tsearch( ) returns a pointer to that place in the search tree, where a pointer to the requested information, our **Symbol**, is stored. If **tsearch( )** returns a null pointer, we have either passed defective arguments, or there is no more room for a new search tree node. Here we can do little else but terminate our system.

When do we store a new name, i.e., when do we really need to allocate a new **Symbol**? We passed a pointer to a local variable **s** to **tsearch( )**. Pointers stored in the search tree, however, should point to dynamically allocated memory. If **tsearch( )** discovers the address of **s** in the search tree, we can be sure that we have just produced a new node. Only in this case do we create a new **Symbol**, save our **name**, and label it as an uninitialized **Identifier**. It pays to allocate the **Symbol** with **calloc(3)**: no matter what components we might still invent, they will all be initialized to zero.

Whether or not the **Symbol** is new, **lexi_screen( )** returns the current token value stored in the symbol, and passes a pointer to the symbol as attached value in **yylval**.

lexi_screen( ) is the first function concerned with symbol table management. There will probably be more, so we start a new source file *sym.c* and add it to *Makefile*:

```
calc    = calc.c scan.o sym.o
pr:     sym.c
sym.o: calc.h syn.i
```

The object *sym.o* depends on *calc.h* for the definition of **Symbol** and on *syn.i* for token values such as **Identifier**. *make* has built-in rules to compile an object from a C source. If we place **lexi_screen( )** into a new file, we obviously must erase the stub in *calc.y*.

Integer Assignment

With a symbol table in place, we can add variables to our desk calculator language. We only need to extend the grammar in *calc.y*. It turns out to be convenient to describe an integer expression **ie** in part as a simple integer expression **i**. We also need to add an operator table entry for the assignment operators, grouped from the right and lowest precedence, and add the **INC** operators **+ +** and **− −** to the list of unary operators with highest precedence:

```
%type    <y_int>  ie, i

%right   <y_int>  '=' PASGOP ASGOP        /* += etc. */
%left              '|'
...
%right   <y_int>  '!' '~' INC             /* ++ -- */
```

Assignment is added to **ie**, while simple integer references are moved to the new non-terminal **i**:

```
ie      : i                      /* $$ = $1; */
        | lval '=' ie            { integer($1), $$ = $1 -> s_int = $3; }
        | lval PASGOP ie         { $$ = $1 -> s_int = integer($1) + $3; }
        | lval ASGOP ie
            { switch($2) {
                case '|':    $$ = $1 -> s_int = integer($1) | $3; break;
                case '^':    $$ = $1 -> s_int = integer($1) ^ $3; break;
                case '&':    $$ = $1 -> s_int = integer($1) & $3; break;
                case '<':    $$ = $1 -> s_int = integer($1) << $3; break;
                case '>':    $$ = $1 -> s_int = integer($1) >> $3; break;
                case '-':    $$ = $1 -> s_int = integer($1) - $3; break;
                case '*':    $$ = $1 -> s_int = integer($1) * $3; break;
                case '/':    if ($3 == 0) response("?div by 0");
                             $$ = $1 -> s_int = integer($1) / $3; break;
                case '%':    if ($3 == 0) response("?mod 0");
                             $$ = $1 -> s_int = integer($1) % $3; break;
            } }
        | INC lval               { $2 -> s_int = integer($2);
                                   $$ = $1 == '+' ?
                                        ++ $2 -> s_int : -- $2 -> s_int;
                                 }
        | lval INC               { $1 -> s_int = integer($1);
                                   $$ = $2 == '+' ?
                                        $1 -> s_int ++ : $1 -> s_int --;
                                 }

i       : Iconstant              /* $$ = $1; */
        | Integer                { $$ = $1 -> s_int; }
        | se '[' ie ']'          { ... }
        | '(' ie ')'             { $$ = $2; }
```

i must pass the integer value of simple references such as an **Iconstant**. Since **lexi_screen( )** attaches a symbol table pointer to an **Integer**, i.e., a variable name, we need to pass the value **.s_int** from the **Symbol**.

How did the value get there in the first place? Our grammar does not permit an uninitialized **Identifier** as **i**, i.e., a new name cannot be used on the right-hand side of an integer assignment, which is probably a desirable state of affairs. Unfortunately, **yyparse( )** will return the message *syntax error* in this case.

Before a variable name can be referenced, a value must have been assigned to it. Consider typical formulations for assignment:

```
ie      : i                     /* $$ = $1; */
        | lval '=' ie           { integer($1), $$ = $1 -> s_int = $3; }
        | lval PASGOP ie        { $$ = $1 -> s_int = integer($1) + $3; }
        | INC lval              { $2 -> s_int = integer($2);
                                    $$ = $1 == '+' ?
                                            ++ $2 -> s_int : -- $2 -> s_int;
                                }
```

A new function **integer()** must arrange for a **Symbol** to describe an **Integer**, and it must return its current value. As the code above illustrates, **integer()** is used rather frequently, and it exactly solves the problem of managing integer variable values. Here is the function, also a part of *calc.y*:

```
static int integer(sp)          /* turn lval into Integer... */
        register Symbol * sp;   /* ...and return value */
{
        if (sp -> s_yylex != Integer)
                sp -> s_yylex = Integer, sp -> s_int = 0;
        return sp -> s_int;
}
```

If a variable is not yet an **Integer**, it is forced to have initial value zero. Together with our explanation of **lval** above, this has slightly surprising consequences. Here is a brief session with the current release of *calc*:

```
10 + 20, "axel" " was here"     # still?
        30
        "axel was here"
i                               # new name
        ? syntax error
i = ~0, ++ i, i --              # assignment, increment
        -1
        0
        0
++ j, k += 20                   # new names (!)
        1
        20
quit
        ? syntax error
^D
$
```

String Assignment

String variables are the next step. The implementation poses a few subtle problems: string values must be managed dynamically; turning **String** into **Integer** must be done carefully; and expressing concatenation without an explicit operator complicates the grammar extension a bit:

```
%type    <y_str> se, cat, s
%%


i        : ...
         | s '[' ie ']'          { ... }


se       : cat                   /* $$ = $1; */
         | lval '=' se           { $$ = strsave(Strcpy($1, $3)); free($3); }
         | lval PASGOP se        { $$ = strsave(Strcat($1, $3)); free($3); }


cat      : s                     /* $$ = $1; */
         | cat s                 { $$ = cat($1, $2); }
         | cat '+' s             { $$ = cat($1, $3); }


s        : Sconstant             /* $$ = $1; */
         | String                { $$ = strsave($1 -> s_str); }
         | '(' se ')'            { $$ = $2; }
```

Assignment is grouped from the right, i.e., the rule will be right recursive. Concatenation, however, is grouped from the left, i.e., its rule will be left recursive. Since there is no concatenation operator, we cannot specify associativity in the operator table. The solution is to insert an extra rule into the grammar to separate concatenation from assignment. Since concatenation has higher precedence, formulations for **cat** are 'closer' than formulations for string expressions **se** to simple string references **s**.

Index operations may be applied to concatenated string values, or to the result of a string assignment. However, *yacc* will complain about more conflicts unless we only permit a simple string reference **s** in front of index brackets. Effectively, we have to enclose a concatenation in parentheses if we wish to index into it.

If we reference a **String** variable, we pass a dynamic copy of its value, i.e., we copy **.s_str** using our function **strsave( )**. Assigning a string value to a variable really is a dynamic version of **strcpy**(3):

```
char * Strcpy(sp, cp)           /* string assignment */
        register Symbol * sp;
        register char * cp;
{       char * strsave();

        unset(sp);
        sp -> s_yylex = String;
        return sp -> s_str = strsave(cp);
}
```

Before a variable name can be referenced, a value must have been assigned to it. Consider typical formulations for assignment:

```
ie      : i                     /* $$ = $1; */
        | lval '=' ie           ( integer($1), $$ = $1 -> s_int = $3; )
        | lval PASGOP ie        ( $$ = $1 -> s_int = integer($1) + $3; )
        | INC lval              ( $2 -> s_int = integer($2);
                                  $$ = $1 == '+' ?
                                        ++ $2 -> s_int : -- $2 -> s_int;
                                )
```

A new function **integer( )** must arrange for a **Symbol** to describe an **Integer**, and it must return its current value. As the code above illustrates, **integer( )** is used rather frequently, and it exactly solves the problem of managing integer variable values. Here is the function, also a part of *calc.y*:

```
static int integer(sp)          /* turn lval into Integer... */
        register Symbol * sp;   /* ...and return value */
{
        if (sp -> s_yylex != Integer)
                sp -> s_yylex = Integer, sp -> s_int = 0;
        return sp -> s_int;
}
```

If a variable is not yet an **Integer**, it is forced to have initial value zero. Together with our explanation of **lval** above, this has slightly surprising consequences. Here is a brief session with the current release of *calc*:

```
10 + 20, "axel" " was here"     # still?
        30
        "axel was here"
i                               # new name
        ? syntax error
i = ~0, ++ i, i --              # assignment, increment
        -1
        0
        0
++ j, k += 20                   # new names (!)
        1
        20
quit
        ? syntax error
^D
$
```

String Assignment

String variables are the next step. The implementation poses a few subtle problems: string values must be managed dynamically; turning **String** into **Integer** must be done carefully; and expressing concatenation without an explicit operator complicates the grammar extension a bit:

```
%type   <y_str> se, cat, s
%%


i       : ...
        | s '[' ie ']'         { ... }

se      : cat                  /* $$ = $1; */
        | lval '=' se          { $$ = strsave(Strcpy($1, $3)); free($3); }
        | lval PASGOP se       { $$ = strsave(Strcat($1, $3)); free($3); }

cat     : s                    /* $$ = $1; */
        | cat s                { $$ = cat($1, $2); }
        | cat '+' s            { $$ = cat($1, $3); }

s       : Sconstant            /* $$ = $1; */
        | String               { $$ = strsave($1 -> s_str); }
        | '(' se ')'           { $$ = $2; }
```

Assignment is grouped from the right, i.e., the rule will be right recursive. Concatenation, however, is grouped from the left, i.e., its rule will be left recursive. Since there is no concatenation operator, we cannot specify associativity in the operator table. The solution is to insert an extra rule into the grammar to separate concatenation from assignment. Since concatenation has higher precedence, formulations for **cat** are 'closer' than formulations for string expressions **se** to simple string references **s**.

Index operations may be applied to concatenated string values, or to the result of a string assignment. However, *yacc* will complain about more conflicts unless we only permit a simple string reference **s** in front of index brackets. Effectively, we have to enclose a concatenation in parentheses if we wish to index into it.

If we reference a **String** variable, we pass a dynamic copy of its value, i.e., we copy **.s_str** using our function **strsave( )**. Assigning a string value to a variable really is a dynamic version of **strcpy**(3):

```
char * Strcpy(sp, cp)          /* string assignment */
        register Symbol * sp;
        register char * cp;
{       char * strsave();

        unset(sp);
        sp -> s_yylex = String;
        return sp -> s_str = strsave(cp);
}
```

unset( ) removes whatever value our variable might have had. The **Symbol** is then turned from **Identifier** to **String** and a copy of the dynamic argument of **Strcpy( )** is assigned as its value. **Strcpy( )** then returns the assigned value. The calling action produces a dynamic copy of the result and releases the original argument.

```
unset(sp)                           /* clear variable */
        register Symbol * sp;
{
        switch (sp -> s_yylex) {
        case String:
                free(sp -> s_str);
        }
        sp -> s_yylex = Identifier;
}
```

If **unset( )** finds a variable to be a **String** it releases its value. The value deposited by string assignment is returned to dynamic memory here.

strcat(3) concatenates its second argument to the end of its first one and returns the result. This operation is so similar to an operator assignment like + = that we really should support it. Our concatenation has no operator of its own, and assignment = must be interpreted as **Strcpy( )**. We are definitely stuck with a new concatenation operator such as + and concatenation assignment + =. Since − = has no reasonable meaning in the context of strings, + = is the only assignment operator used for strings and integers. This is why we have made it a special symbol **PASGOP** during lexical analysis.

Strcat( ) is a variation on the theme introduced by **Strcpy( )**. There are two very different cases: concatenating to a **String** and concatenating to something else.

```
char * Strcat(sp, cp)               /* concatenation assignment */
        register Symbol * sp;
        register char * cp;
{       char * strsave();

        if (sp -> s_yylex != String)
                return Strcpy(sp, cp);
        return sp -> s_str = cat(sp -> s_str, strsave(cp));
}
```

If we do not concatenate to a **String**, we are really performing simple assignment. Otherwise we build the concatenation, release its left constituent, assign a dynamic copy of the concatenation as new value of our variable, and return the concatenation as a result. It is important to note that **Strcpy( )** and **Strcat( )** are used exactly alike in an action.

We have built a concatenation before: in the action associated with string concatenation. For ease of maintenance it is very important to recognize and avoid code duplication. We turn the action into a new function **cat( )**, so that we can call the same code in three places. Our method of developing a larger system by successively extending a smaller one is dangerous in this respect. While we have decomposed *wish* into large, independent subsystems where code duplication is quite unlikely, we still must carefully monitor growth within each part.

Strcat( ) and **Strcpy**( ) suggest that later we might support C library functions for our desk calculator language. We have therefore placed them into a new file *lib.c*, together with **cat**( ). The function **unset**( ) logically belongs into *sym.c*, since it deals with variable values in the symbol table. We need to add *lib.c* to our *Makefile*:

```
calc   = calc.c lib.o scan.o sym.o
pr:    lib.c
lib.o: calc.h syn.i
```

One more important change is required. The previous release of *calc* supported only integer variables, i.e., a **Symbol** could only be an uninitialized **Identifier** or an **Integer** with a suitable value. Just as string assignment might be confronted with an **Integer**, integer assignment might now be applied to a **String**, and we must release its value. Every integer assignment, however, starts by calling our function **integer**( ). We simply need to call **unset**( ) unless we already have an **Integer**:

```
static int integer(sp)            /* turn lval into Integer... */
        register Symbol * sp;     /* ...and return value */
{
        if (sp -> s_yylex != Integer)
        {       unset(sp);
                sp -> s_yylex = Integer, sp -> s_int = 0;
        }
        return sp -> s_int;
}
```

We have avoided code duplication by creating **integer**( ). Here we gain the benefits (and this certain secure feeling): we always use the same code, and a single extension will apply to all possible cases.

Reserved Words

unset( ) changes a name back to being an **Identifier**, i.e., to the state immediately after the name was first assembled in **lexi_screen**( ) during lexical analysis. So far, **unset**( ) has always been used just prior to assignment, but it could be useful to support an *unset* statement in its own right. *unset* as a command is inspired by the shell and we might just as well add a *set* statement to display all currently known variables with their values:

```
%token         SET, UNSET
%%

stmt    : /* null */
        | SET                   { dump_sets(); }
        | unset

unset   : UNSET
        | unset lval            { unset($2); }
```

set and *unset* are added at the **stmt** level. Neither operation is plausible within an expression, and it would be overly restrictive to demand such a statement to be the only thing in an entire input **buffer**.

set cannot have arguments. *unset* should be allowed to apply to zero or more names, known as **Integer**, or **String**, or not at all. We see no reason to plague our user with silly comments about doing nothing at all, or misspelling. Arguments to *unset* are separated by white space. It would be tempting to allow commas as well, but we have already decided to delimit **stmt** by commas, so they are no longer available as delimiters within a single **stmt**.

We use left recursion to describe our sequence of names to be *unset*. Therefore, we can place the new token **UNSET**, i.e., the reserved word to head the statement, in the absolute part of the recursive explanation. This part is recognized first and leftmost. Lexical analysis will decide how **UNSET** is represented in the input.

unset() does not remove a name from the symbol table. It is tempting to use **tdelete**(3) and free dynamic memory, but we cannot be entirely sure that we are not deleting a name during syntax analysis which has already been recognized again by lexical analysis. **yyparse()** is allowed to be one input token ahead of **yylex()**. Our solution is more bullet-proof if we leave names behind in the symbol table even after our user has marked them as no longer active. If a new assignment is made to the name, it starts out as it should: as an **Identifier**.

How does **dump_sets()** show the symbol table? We must arrange to traverse the symbol table search tree using **twalk**(3), but the pointer **symbols** to the root of the tree is safely hidden inside **lexi_screen()**. If we move the pointer definition to be local to the entire file *sym.c*, we can easily implement **dump_sets()**:

```
#include <search.h>

static char * symbols;                 /* tree */

static dump1_set(spp, order)
        register Symbol ** spp;
        VISIT order;
{       register Symbol * sp = *spp;

        if (order == postorder || order == leaf)
        switch (sp -> s_yylex) {
        case Integer:
                reply("%s=%d", sp -> s_name, sp -> s_int);
                break;
        case String:
                reply("%s=\"%s\"", sp -> s_name, sp -> s_str);
        }
}

dump_sets()
{
        twalk(symbols, dump1_set);
}
```

twalk( ) takes a pointer to the root of a search tree – no, not a pointer to that pointer like **tsearch( )** – and a pointer to a function to be called at each node. The function, **dump1_set( )** in our case, is called with a pointer to the pointer stored in the search tree – yes, one level of indirection more than the comparison function – and with an indication of the traversal order. The **enum** type VISIT is defined in the public header *search.h*. Unfortunately, **twalk( )** believes in Knuth's original names (1968) for tree traversal disciplines: **preorder, postorder,** and **endorder. leaf** indicates a node without descendants, visited once during a call to **twalk( )**. All other nodes are visited three times.

We want to show variables in the order of the comparison function used to build the tree. This is *inorder* in modern terminology. We need to print information if **twalk( )** calls **dump1_sets( )** with a **leaf** or **postorder** node. **dump_sets( )** is supposed to show variables, i.e., the token type .s_yylex must be **Integer** or **String**. By not displaying **Identifier** we create the *unset* effect for our user. Control characters should probably be escaped when a **String** is displayed, but we are in good company if we do not bother.

Finally, we need to define the reserved words **set** and **unset** as representations for the tokens SET and UNSET. Section 2.2 indicated that we defer this problem to **lexi_screen( )**, since individual patterns inflate **yylex( )** unnecessarily. A few words could, of course, be discovered using **strcmp(3)** at the beginning of **lexi_screen( )**, but that would be neither general nor efficient.

Either we add reserved words to our search tree and mark them with special token values such as SET or UNSET, or we use a reserved word table and search just prior to looking at the search tree for user-defined symbols. If we are willing to read reserved words from a file during task initialization, we can add them cheaply to a search tree or to a table maintained using **hsearch( )**. We gain efficiency, but we need an extra file together with our task. If the reserved words are to be part of our compiled program, we need to store them in the same table that is used for searching purposes to avoid a space penalty at runtime.

This table can be kept sorted in the source, and we can use **bsearch(3)** to look for reserved words. A much better solution, however, is to add pointers into the table to our search tree. The pointers cause only a little space overhead, but they avoid a separate, usually unsuccessful, binary search prior to **tsearch( )**. For example, if we manage to balance the initial tree of reserved words, five comparisons will weed out 31 reserved words, and the next comparison can already distinguish up to 32 user-defined names.

Balancing the tree during initialization is, of course, the problem. We really should preprocess our source to maintain reserved words in preorder for a balanced, postorder-sorted tree. Schreiner (1987) offers a short cut, a function **tload( )** that accepts a sequence of pointers to sorted information and builds a search tree of minimal height. While this is only a balanced tree for certain amounts of information, it is still a reasonable initialization in all cases. **tload( )** is easy to use, and it adds little code to our program:

```
char * tload();
static char * symbols;                    /* tree */

static Symbol reserved[] = {              /* reserved words, sorted */
        { "set",          SET },
        { "unset",        UNSET },
        { (char *) 0 } };
static Symbol * next_reserved = reserved;
```

```
static Symbol * next_res()                /* move along reserved[] */
{
        return next_reserved -> s_name ?
                next_reserved ++ : (next_reserved = (Symbol *) 0);
}


int lexi_screen(name)
        register char * name;
{       register Symbol ** spp;
        Symbol s;

        if (next_reserved && ! tload(next_res, & symbols))
                fatal("no room");

        s.s_name = name;
        ...
```

tload( ) uses a function to obtain the sequence of information pointers. **next_res( )** first returns pointers to the reserved word symbols in order, and finally a null pointer. If **tload( )** cannot build a tree, it will return a null pointer. Our invariant for having built the initial tree is another null pointer: **next_res( )** advances **next_reserved** along the table **reserved[ ]** of reserved words, and finally sets it to null. This invariant is so cheap that we can make **lexi_screen( )** self-initializing.

    reserved[ ] does not really need to end with a null entry. If the vector is local to *sym.c* we could use its dimension to limit **next_reserved**; however, if we move **reserved[ ]** elsewhere, the dimension is no longer easily available and a null entry is a more robust mechanism.

    Using binary search trees from Schreiner (1987) has another benefit: this implementation uses binary threaded trees (Knuth, 1968) and offers a function **tpost( )**, with the same arguments as **twalk( )**, that performs precisely a postorder traversal. **tpost( )** operates iteratively and avoids the problems of **twalk( )** with pathological trees. **dump_sets( )** can be simplified:

```
static dump1_set(spp)
        register Symbol ** spp;
{       register Symbol * sp = *spp;

        switch (sp -> s_yylex) { ... }
}


dump_sets()
{
        tpost(symbols, dump1_set);
}
```

2.5 Environment Variables: *export*

The UNIX shells support variables for text substitution. Variable values can be set by assignment in the shell, and a built-in command like *export* is used to mark variables for export to a command called by the shell, or to display the marked variables. *env*(1) displays exported variables or runs a command with a modified set of exported variables. Since *env* is not built into the shell, it is a secure way to find out what environment is passed to a command.

When started, a UNIX program receives three arguments. The third argument is a pointer to a null-terminated vector of pointers to the exported variables. From C, the third argument is also available as a global variable **char ** environ**. A program can start another program through one of the **exec**(2) system calls. If no explicit arrangements are made, the values accessible from **environ** are exported to the other program.

From C, two functions are used to manipulate the environment, i.e., the set of exported values. **getenv**(3) takes a variable name as a string and returns a pointer to the (static) string value of the variable, if there is an exported variable of the desired name. **putenv**(3) includes its argument in the environment; the argument is a string consisting of a variable name and its text value, separated by =. The argument to **putenv**() must exist as long as necessary, i.e., preferably not in automatic storage.

It is interesting to interface our symbol table to the environment. We can look at imported values, manipulate them just like our own variables, or *unset* them. We can mark our own variables for export, and thus control the environment of a program that we might start from our calculator, or later from *wish*.

We need six new functions. **import**() should be called very early in our program, since it adds the environment variables as **String** variables to our symbol table. **export**() must be called just prior to using an **exec** system call, since it posts the current environment from the symbol table at **environ**. Our own versions of the functions **getenv**() and **putenv**() interact with the symbol table, not with the list at **environ**. A symbol is marked for export with **envset**() and if it is undefined it will become an empty **String**. Finally, **envunset**() will remove the mark. One more function turns out to be convenient: **dump_envs**() shows just the exported variables. Here is a session with the new release of *calc*:

```
$ env - user='axel was here' export=yes number=10 calc
export                          # reserved word: show all
        number=10
        user=axel was here
                                # "export" is reserved
a = 10, b = "text"              # assignments
        10
        "text"
set                             # show all
        a=10
        b="text"
        number="10"
        user="axel was here"
export a c                      # mark: a exists, c is new
c                               # now it's String
        ""
```

```
! env                           # escape to shell, call env
a=10
c=
number=10
user=axel was here
!
^D
$
```

First, *env* sets up exactly three variables for the environment. **export** is a reserved word and cannot be added to our symbol table. Without arguments, **export** shows the currently exported variables. Values are exported as strings and the double quotes are also omitted in the output of **export**. Our command **set** displays quotes to distinguish true strings.

c is just an **Identifier**. Using the name as an argument to **export** marks the name for export and turns it into an empty **String**.

Implementation

In *calc.h* we add an export bit to **Symbol**:

```
typedef struct symbol Symbol;
        struct symbol {
                ...
                unsigned s_export : 1;
                };
```

.s_export is set by **envset( )** for an exported symbol and cleared by **envunset( )**:

```
static int exported;                /* current number of s_export */

envset(sp)                          /* mark variable for export */
        register Symbol * sp;       /* might be Identifier */
{
        switch (sp -> s_yylex) {
        case Identifier:
                sp -> s_yylex = String;
                sp -> s_str = strsave("");
        }
        if (! sp -> s_export)
                sp -> s_export = 1, ++ exported;
}

envunset(sp)                            /* unmark */
        register Symbol * sp;
{
        if (sp -> s_export)
                sp -> s_export = 0, -- exported;
}
```

exported records how many symbols are currently exported. This makes building a new environment during **export( )** much simpler. It is tempting to clear **.s_export** when we clear a variable with our function **unset( )**, but this function is also called when a variable changes its type. Clearly, the export mark should survive such an operation. Instead, we call **envunset( )** when a variable is removed. Here are the changes to the grammar *calc.y*:

```
%token          EXPORT
%%


stmt    : /* null */
        | unset
        | EXPORT                ( dump_envs(); )
        | EXPORT exports


unset   : UNSET
        | unset lval            ( envunset($2), unset($2); )


exports : lval                  ( envset($1); )
        | exports lval          ( envset($2); )
```

EXPORT is a new addition to **reserved[ ]** in *sym.c*. The token is, of course, represented by the word **export**. By convention, we spell token names for reserved words just like the words themselves, but in upper case. Token names for classes of symbols such as **Identifier** start with an upper-case letter. Non-terminals are local to the *yacc* source and are written in lower case.

　　main( ) also needs to be extended. We need to call **import( )**, and we should provide an escape to the shell so that we can call *env* and check our results:

```
main()
(       char buf[BUFSIZ];

        import();
        setjmp(on_response);
        while (gets(buf))
        (       if (* buf == '!')
                        export(), system(buf+1), puts("!");
                else
                        lexi_buf(buf), yyparse();
        )
        return 0;
)
```

The remainder of an input line starting with **!** is executed as a command using **system**(3). We follow the typical UNIX convention, although **!** is a prefix operator and might well start a line within our calculator. By the way, Kernighan and Pike (1984) note that the library version of **system( )** might not be the function of choice in a dialog situation. They do provide an improved version. For our test driver, the standard **system( )** should suffice.

　　import( ) is easy: just call our own version of **putenv( )**. Since **import( )** must be called once and early, we can move our reserved word initialization. **tload( )** builds a tree from scratch and it must be called before we add to the tree. We can modify the previous invariant to prevent **import**( ) from being called more than once:

```
import()                               /* import initial environment */
                                       /* call once and first */
{       extern char ** environ;
        register char ** ep = environ;

        if (! next_reserved)
                fatal("import twice");
        else if (! tload(next_res, & symbols))
                fatal("no room");

        while (* ep)
                putenv(* ep ++);
        environ = (char **) 0;         /* flag export() */
}
```

export( ) is a variation on the usual theme of tree traversal. If an old environment exists, we release it first. **import**( ) sets the original **environ** to null, since we can most certainly not release it to dynamic memory. **export**( ) then allocates a new environment vector, fills it during a postorder traversal from the symbol table, terminates the vector with a null pointer, and posts it as new **environ**. As the example session above shows, this is where **system**( ) and other functions look.

```
export()                               /* export current environment */
{       char ** ep;
        extern char ** environ;

        if (ep = environ)
        {       while (* ep)
                        free(* ep ++);
                free(environ);
        }
        if (ep = environ = (char **) malloc((exported + 1) * sizeof(char *)))
        {       tpost(symbols, export1);
                * environ = (char *) 0, environ = ep;
        }
        else
                fatal("no room");
}
```

export1( ) does all the work for a single exported symbol. With **malloc**(3) and **sprintf**(3) it builds a dynamic copy of the required text, and it posts the text while advancing **environ** along the vector. **environ** is corrected after the tree traversal by **export**( ).

```
static export1(spp)
        Symbol ** spp;
{       register Symbol * sp = * spp;
        register char * cp;
        char * itoa();
        extern char ** environ;

        if (sp -> s_export)
        {       switch (sp -> s_yylex) {
                case String:
                        cp = sp -> s_str;
                        break;
                case Integer:
                        cp = itoa(sp -> s_int);
                        break;
                default:
                        return;
                }

                if (* environ = malloc(strlen(sp -> s_name) + strlen(cp) + 2))
                        sprintf(* environ ++, "%s=%s", sp -> s_name, cp);
                else
                        fatal("no room");
        }
}
```

Environment values are supposed to be strings. Therefore, we need a function **itoa( )** to convert our **Integer** values into static strings:

```
char * itoa(i)                     /* integer to string conversion */
        register int i;
{       static char buf[sizeof(int)*3 + 1];

        sprintf(buf, "%d", i);
        return buf;                /* static result */
}
```

A static result is quite sufficient, since we paste it into the final text anyway.

Speaking of static values: what happens if **export( )** is called and an exported symbol is changed, or even **unset**, subsequently? Nothing, fortunately. Following **export( )**, the environment is in dynamic memory and disjoint from the symbol table. This is why **export( )** should be called immediately before the environment is sent to another program.

Starting another program happens less frequently than changing variable values in our desk calculator. **putenv(3)** is not exactly convenient or efficient to update the original environment with each assignment to exported variables. This is why we replace the library function for our program and introduce **import( )** and **export( )**. Thus far, we have no use for **getenv( )**. If the library function is called somewhere in *wish*, it will look at the current state of **environ**, i.e., it will find no environment values immediately after **import( )**, and it might find values from a previous **export( )** which are no longer current. Since building **getenv( )** for our symbol table is so simple, we certainly should do it:

```
char * getenv(name)                     /* find name in symbol table */
        register char * name;
{       register Symbol ** spp;
        Symbol s;
        char * itoa();

        s.s_name = name;
        if ((spp = (Symbol **) tfind((char *) & s, & symbols, scmp))
            && (* spp) -> s_export)
                switch ((* spp) -> s_yylex) {
                case Integer:
                        return itoa((* spp) -> s_int);
                case String:
                        return (* spp) -> s_str;
                }
        return (char *) 0;
}
```

tfind(3) is another search tree function. It takes the same arguments as **tsearch**(3), but it does not enter an object into the tree. If the desired information cannot be found, **tfind( )** will return a null pointer, and **getenv( )** then returns unsuccessfully.

     putenv( ) is used by **import( )** and must make symbol table entries. During **import( )** these are probably all new, but if **putenv( )** is called elsewhere, it should act just like an assignment in our desk calculator:

```
int putenv(buf)                         /* add "name=value" to symbol table */
        char * buf;
{       register char * cp;
        register Symbol * sp;

        if (cp = strchr(buf, '='))
        {       *cp++ = '\0';
                switch ((sp = enter(buf)) -> s_yylex) {
                case Integer:
                case String:
                        unset(sp);
                case Identifier:
                        break;
                default:
                        return 1;
                }
```

```
                    sp -> s_yylex = String;
                    sp -> s_str = strsave(cp);
                    envset(sp);
                    cp[-1] = '=';
                    return 0;
            }
            return 1;
    }
```

The argument to **putenv( )** must contain = separating name and value, otherwise we should not enter the information. Just like **putenv**(3), our replacement will return zero for a successful call, and non-zero otherwise.

We terminate the name temporarily by a null byte and look for it in the symbol table. If it is a variable, it needs to be **unset( )**; if it is an **Identifier**, we are still happy. Anything else should presumably not be overwritten in our table. The variable is entered as a **String** and marked for export. We use **envset( )**, of course, so that there is a single function maintaining the **exported** invariant. Before **putenv( )** terminates successfully, we replace the = sign, just in case...

How does **putenv( )** look for a name in the symbol table? This is exactly what **lexi_screen( )** does, but **lexi_screen( )** returns information in **yylval**, and **putenv( )** should not cause a foreign value there to be overwritten. Therefore, we move the table lookup to a new function **enter( )** which is called by **lexi_screen( )** and **putenv( )**:

```
        static Symbol * enter(name)            /* search or enter */
                register char * name;
        (       register Symbol ** spp;
                Symbol s;
                ...
                return *spp;
        }


        int lexi_screen(name)
                register char * name;
        (
                yylval.y_sym = enter(name);
                return yylval.y_sym -> s_yylex;
        }
```

Once again, we had to turn part of a function into a new function to avoid code duplication.

Finally, **dump_envs( )** is yet another tree walk. It is almost identical to **dump_sets( )**; however, we ignore symbols where **.s_export** is not set, and we use a slightly different output format. Instead of a new tree walk, we could call **export( )** and simply print the values accessible from **environ**, but this would be less efficient.

Module Structure

Where do all the new functions live? **itoa( )** clearly is a candidate for a library function, i.e., it is added to *lib.c*.

The other functions need to be placed according to an information hiding principle. **envset( )** and **envunset( )** maintain a variable **exported** which is used by **export( )** and should not be known to (m)any other functions. These three functions, therefore, belong together into a single source file, and **exported** should be **static** in that file.

export( ), however, pulls in **export1( )** and **symbols** for the tree walk. **symbols** is the information hidden by *sym.c*. Either we export this information from the module or we add our functions to *sym.c*. A variable can be exported from a module by making it global and not **static** in the file, or by adding functions to the module which provide a more controlled access. **export( )** would be happy with the *value* of **symbols**, i.e., it is not going to change the symbol table. However, **getenv( )**, through **tfind( )**, needs the *address* of **symbols**. While **tfind( )** does not change the tree, it is built to the same argument conventions as **tsearch( )** which does.

If we want to hide **exported** and **symbols**, we cannot really separate the environment functions from the symbol table functions. Since *sym.c* thus far is a short file, it is the natural place to put the environment functions.

2.6 Macros

The C preprocessor demonstrates how useful a macro facility is: we can give names to constants or frequently used sequences of text; we can tailor our own names for reserved words or operators; and if the macros permit parameters, we can use macros as inline functions.

Our symbol table provides a mapping from names to text. **String** variables can be viewed as the stuff macros are made of. Input to our lexical analysis consists of lines, or rather buffers, and we have already designed **lexi_buf( )** with a macro facility in mind. In this section we will put the two together.

Defining Macros

The first step is to support macro definitions. While the symbol table is the logical place to store the definitions, **String** variables are not very good candidates for macros themselves. If a macro name is discovered in the input, it is removed and the replacement text is put into its place. If the unadorned name of a **String** variable acts as a macro call, we could never use the variable again. $ in the shell circumvents exactly this problem. It flags a name for text replacements while unadorned names are left alone. The C preprocessor, however, replaces unadorned names, and it uses a special definition syntax for introducing replacements.

Our definition syntax must be designed for recognition more or less prior to lexical analysis. Either we let **lexi_buf( )** handle the problem, just like the C preprocessor uses **#** to flag preprocessor lines, or we add a pattern to **yylex( )**, where an entire input line contains a macro definition:

```
^{white}*"def"{white}+{alpha}{alnum}*({white}.*)?$ { lexi_def(yytext); }
^{white}*"undef"{white}+{alpha}{alnum}*{white}*$   { lexi_undef(yytext); }
```

If a line contains **def**, a name, and optionally a replacement text, all surrounded by white space, **lexi_def**( ) will be called to make a macro definition. Similarly, **lexi_undef**( ) will be called for lines containing **undef** and a name.

Note that **undef** allows only a single name, while **unset** allows many. It would not be very hard to extend the pattern and **lexi_undef**( ) to cover that possibility, but we would depart from the preprocessor flavor.

We should continue to maintain *scan*, i.e., the **DEBUG** version of lexical analysis. Since we cannot conditionalize the patterns, we either make the function calls dependent on **DEBUG** not being defined, or we add fake functions for debugging.

We provide a way to display macro definitions: **def** without an argument can be specified to execute the customary tree walk. Either we add a pattern for a line just containing **def**, and call the tree walk from lexical analysis, or we add **def** as a reserved word, and add a suitable formulation to the *yacc* source. The latter solution is, of course, less restrictive, since it permits **def** to be used just like any other information statement.

```
%token          DEF
%%


stmt     : /* null */
         | DEF                      { dump_defs(); }
```

lexi_def( ) receives a line containing the macro definition. It must extract the macro name and the replacement text, and add both to the symbol table. Extracting the name is an operation which **lexi_undef**( ) also needs to perform, and we turn it into a separate function:

```
#include <ctype.h>

static char * name_def(lp)              /* ^ white* word white+ name white* */
        register char ** lp;            /* *lp: ^; advanced past name */
{       register char * name;

        for (name = *lp; isspace(*name); ++ name) ;     /* white* */
        do ++ name; while (! isspace(*name)) ;          /* word */
        do ++ name; while (isspace(*name)) ;            /* white+ */
        for (*lp = name; *++*lp && ! isspace(**lp); ) ; /* name */
        if (**lp)                                       /* white* */
                *(*lp)++ = '\0';                        /* terminate name */
        return name;
}
```

name_def( ) has two results: it returns a pointer to the name and terminates the name with a null byte; and it points ***lp** to the beginning of the replacement text, or to a null byte if there is no such text. Initially, ***lp** must point to the line to be analyzed. We could use **strtok**(3) or **sscanf**(3) to take the line apart, but the solution above is just as simple and more compact.

lexi_def( ) lets **name_def**( ) untangle its input line and uses **enter**( ) to put the macro name into the symbol table. If an **Integer** or a **String** of the same name is found, it needs to be unexported and its value released. If a macro is to replace a reserved word, we do not permit the operation. Otherwise we can dynamically store the replacement text as **.s_str**:

```
lexi_def(line)
        char * line;
{       register Symbol * sp;

        sp = enter(name_def(& line));
        switch (sp -> s_yylex) {
        case Integer:
        case String:
                envunset(sp);
        case 0:
                unset(sp);
        case Identifier:
                sp -> s_yylex = 0;                      /* 0 is no token */
                sp -> s_str = strsave(strcat(line, "\n"));
                break;
        default:
                response("?reserved");
        }
}
```

Macro names never are tokens for syntax analysis. Since a token value cannot be zero, we set
.s_yylex to zero to uniquely identify a macro. **unset( )** must be modified to release **.s_str** in this
case too. **putenv( )** might overwrite a macro definition and must treat a macro just like a **String**.
All other uses of **.s_yylex** are compatible with this choice. Macro names cannot be marked for
export. **putenv( )** turns them into string variables, and our grammar cannot call **envset( )** for a
macro, since its name is not available as a token.

   lexi_undef( ) is much simpler than **lexi_def( )**. If we find the desired macro name, we
turn it back into an **Identifier** using **unset( )**:

```
lexi_undef(line)
        char * line;
{       register Symbol ** spp;
        Symbol s;

        s.s_name = name_def(& line);
        if ((spp = (Symbol **) tfind((char *) & s, & symbols, scmp))
            && (*spp) -> s_yylex == 0)
                unset(*spp);
}
```

We use **tfind**(3) to search for the macro name because there is no point to enter a name into the
symbol table just as we try to remove its meaning. **undef** should only apply to macros, so our
user must use **unset** to remove variables. We choose not to complain about unsuccessful **undef**
attempts because if there is no macro, we need not remove one to achieve the **undef** effect.
However, we then skirt the issue of spelling errors.

   lexi_def( ) and **lexi_undef( )** must be part of *sym.c*, since the functions need to access
information hidden in this module. With the functions in place, we can already compile a new
release of *calc* to test macro definitions:

```
$ calc
def a b
def b c
def
        a       b
        b       c
def a c                     # redefinition
def                         # check
        a       c                       # redefinition
        b       c
undef b
def
        a       c                       # redefinition
a
lexi_macro
$
```

Commenting Macros

The basic mechanisms work, but a comment becomes part of the replacement text. This is not only inefficient, it would also be a source of trouble later, when the comment is inserted for a macro call and not removed by lexical analysis. Either we demand **def** and **undef** lines to be uncommented, or we add two more patterns based on the *lex* context operator / and on the fact that in the case of two patterns recognizing the same text, *lex* will act on the first one:

```
^{white}*"def"{white}+{alpha}{alnum}*({white}[^#\n]*)?/"#".*"\n"         |
^{white}*"def"{white}+{alpha}{alnum}*({white}.*)?$ { lexi_def(yytext); }

^{white}*"undef"{white}+{alpha}{alnum}*{white}*/"#"        |
^{white}*"undef"{white}+{alpha}{alnum}*{white}*$   { lexi_undef(yytext); }
```

A definition such as

```
def a "text with # mark"
```

will now only extend to #, but this might be preferable to the previous situation. Macros do not know about calculator syntax, and they could take the comment convention quite literally.

Probably the best of both worlds is to store comments, after all, and to tack a newline on the end of the text in **lexi_def( )**. The newline terminates a possible comment, and it gets silently ignored once the replacement text is scanned. While we waste some space in the symbol table, we have no restrictions on the contents of the replacement text this way.

Using Macros

lexi_screen( ) returns the token value **.s_yylex** for a word passed to it. We arrange for **yylex( )** to call our replacement mechanism **lexi_macro( )** in this case:

```
{alpha}{alnum}*          { register int i;
#ifdef  DEBUG
                             Return(token(Identifier));
#else
                         if (i = lexi_screen(yytext))
                             return i;
                         lexi_macro();
#endif
                         }
```

lexi_macro( ) knows that **yylval.y_sym** points to the macro definition in the symbol table, courtesy of **lexi_screen( )**, and it must arrange for **input( )** to start reading the replacement text. This really means pushing the **Stream** stack already designed for this purpose:

```
typedef struct stream Stream;
        struct stream { char * buf, * bp; Stream * prev; };

static Stream _in, * in = & _in;

#ifndef DEBUG_LINE
static lexi_macro()
{       register Stream * sp;
        char * malloc(), * strsave();

        if (! (sp = (Stream *) malloc(sizeof(Stream))))
                fatal("no room");
        sp -> buf = sp -> bp = strsave(yylval.y_sym -> s_str);
        sp -> prev = in, in = sp;
}
#endif
```

We still maintain our *scan* program for testing lexical analysis – **lexi_macro( )** cannot exist during testing.

Who pops the stack? If things go wrong, lexical analysis is aborted and started on an entirely new buffer by a fresh call to **lexi_buf( )**. If there is a replacement stack active, we need to release it first. **lexi_buf( )** is extended:

```
lexi_buf(buf)
        register char * buf;
{       extern int yyprevious;
        char * strcat();

#ifndef DEBUG_LINE
        register Stream * sp;

        while (sp = in -> prev)
                free(in -> buf), free(in), in = sp;
#endif
        in -> buf = in -> bp = strcat(buf, "\n");
        NLSTATE;
}
```

This is, however, not the normal course of events. *lex* arranges for a function **yywrap( )** to be called once **input( )** returns zero to indicate end of input. **yywrap( )** is the logical place to pop the input stack:

```
yywrap()
{       register Stream * sp;

        if (sp = in -> prev)
        {       free(in -> buf), free(in), in = sp;
                return 0;
        }
        return 1;
}
```

Let's look at the new release:

```
$ calc
def a b
b = 3; a                  # simple call
        3
        3
def a b +
a 2; b                    # continue text out of macro
        5
        3
a = 2                     # continue token out of macro
        ?syntax error
```

Tokens cannot be continued out of a macro: **input( )** must return zero before **yywrap( )** will be called. This, however, terminates assembly of a token such as + =, even if we permit + and = to be separated by white space.

If we want to continue tokens, we would have to call **yywrap( )** from within **input( )**. In this case, however, our **unput( )** mechanism might have to push characters scanned in a replacement text back into a *previous* buffer... It seems wise to settle for not supporting token continuation.

Macro Parameters: *macro( )*

With simple text replacement in place, we can think about more powerful macros. If a macro name is immediately followed by a left parenthesis in the input, we replace the name together with a comma-separated list of argument texts enclosed in parentheses. The argument texts are substituted for parameter marks in the replacement text.

For implementation purposes this means that the input pointer must be positioned past a balancing right parenthesis in the current input buffer.† Arguments must be substituted in the replacement text model from the symbol table, before the result is pushed as the next input buffer. The implementation can be accomplished local to **lexi_macro( )**:

```
static lexi_macro()
{       register Stream * sp;
        register char * mp;
        char * malloc(), * strsave(), * macro();

        mp = macro(& in -> bp, yylval.y_sym -> s_name, yylval.y_sym -> s_str);
        if (! mp)
                response("?bad macro");
        if (! (sp = (Stream *) malloc(sizeof(Stream))))
                fatal("no room");
        sp -> buf = sp -> bp = strsave(mp);
        sp -> prev = in, in = sp;
}
```

macro( ) is a new function with three arguments: the current input position, to discover and move past arguments; the macro name; and the replacement text model. If all goes well, **macro( )** returns a pointer to a static copy of the expanded replacement text, and it advances the input pointer.

macro( ) can live in a new file *macro.c*, since it is a general-purpose function. We do not need parameter names in the macro definition, since we follow languages such as *m4* or the shell and let **$1** through **$9** refer to arguments and **$0** refer to the macro name itself. The latter is dangerous: if the macro name appears in its own replacement text, and if the caller of **macro( )** supports resubstitution, we have infinite recursion. **lexi_macro( )** itself does not resubstitute, but our scanning mechanism as such does. On recursion it will run out of memory and terminate the task through **fatal( )**:

---

† ...i.e., a macro call must be contained in an input buffer, or in the replacement text of another macro. It cannot be concatenated.

```
$ calc
def a $0
a                    # some time goes by...
                     # ...much more on a big machine...
no room
$
```

$0 is not really the culprit – recursion during resubstitution is. Non-recursive resubstitution, however, is quite useful: a macro can reference another one and will receive the current information when the macro is called. We should not suppress the facility just because it might be abused.

Expanding parameters and bypassing an argument list amounts to parsing an argument list. We need to find a closing parenthesis or a comma, and before that we need to account for balanced parentheses, and character and string constants. This part of the **macro()** algorithm is best encapsulated as a separate function **span()** which can be characterized by the following table:

	expected delimiter			
input	, or)	)	'	"
default	*loop*	*loop*	*loop*	*loop*
\	+ *next*	+ *next*	+ *next*	+ *next*
)	*return*	*return*	*loop*	*loop*
,	*return*	*loop*	*loop*	*loop*
(	*span*)	*span*)	*loop*	*loop*
'	*span* '	*span* '	*return*	*loop*
"	*span* "	*span* "	*loop*	*return*

loop means to keep searching. + *next* accounts for the fact that \ hides the meaning of the following character for the purposes of **span()**. Other characters can be concealed by recursively calling **span()** with a different delimiter. Here is the implementation:

```
static jmp_buf on_error;         /* macro() returns NULL */

static char * span(arg, del)      /* find matching delimiter */
       register char * arg;       /* begin of search */
       char del;                  /* delimiter: ) ' " or \0 for , or ) */
{      register int ch;           /* current */

       while (ch = * arg ++)
       {      switch (ch) {
              case '\\':
                     if (! * arg ++)
                            goto error;
              default:
                     continue;
```

```
                              case '(':
                                      if (del != '"' && del != '\'')
                                              arg = span(arg, ')') + 1;
                                      continue;
                              case ')':
                                      if (del == ')')
                                              goto done;
                              case ',':
                                      if (del == 0)
                                              goto done;
                                      continue;
                              case '\'':
                                      if (del == '"')
                                              continue;
                                      break;
                              case '"':
                                      if (del == '\'')
                                              continue;
                              }
                              if (del == ch)
                                      goto done;
                              arg = span(arg, ch) + 1;
                      }
        error:  longjmp(on_error, 1);
        done:   return arg - 1;
        }
```

Unbalanced parentheses or constant delimiters cause **span**( ) to go astray. We might be entangled in recursion. The easiest way to get out is through a **longjmp**(3).

Now we can replace a parameter by an argument text. **parm**( ) needs to know where to copy the argument text to, the name of the macro so that **$0** can be replaced, the beginning of the argument list so that **$1**, etc., may be found, and the actual parameter number in question. The number must be zero or positive, but it can be larger than the actual number of arguments present. If an argument cannot be found, **parm**( ) silently substitutes an empty text. In any case, **parm**( ) returns the position past the copied text; the caller is responsible for enough space to be available.

```
        static char * parm(bp, name, in, n)      /* copy argument for parameter */
                char * bp;                       /* result area */
                char * name;                     /* macro name */
                register char * in;              /* input area */
                int n;                           /* index */
        {       register char * cp;

                if (n == 0)                      /* $0 */
                {       while (*bp++ = *name++)
                                ;
                        return bp - 1;           /* position past copied value */
                }
```

```
        if (*in == '(')                 /* $i */
        {       cp = span(++ in, 0);    /* [in..cp-1] is replacement */
                while (--n > 0)
                {       if (*cp == ')') /* no more arguments */
                                return bp;
                        cp = span(in = cp+1, 0);
                }
                while (in < cp)
                        *bp++ = *in++;
        }
        return bp;
}
```

The pieces are in place. **macro()** has two tasks: first it copies the replacement text and uses **parm()** to insert arguments as required; if all goes well, and if there is an argument list, the input pointer must be advanced beyond it – another little task for **span()**:

```
char * macro(inp, name, text)           /* expand call */
        char ** inp;                    /* *inp at ( or next character */
        char * name;                    /* macro name */
        char * text;                    /* replacement text */
{       static char buf[BUFSIZ];
        register char * bp, ch;

        if (setjmp(on_error))
                return (char *) 0;

        for (bp = buf; ch = *bp++ = *text++; )
                if (ch == '$')
                        if (! *text)
                                continue;
                        else if (isdigit(*text))
                                bp = parm(--bp, name, *inp, *text++ - '0');
                        else
                                bp[-1] = *text++;

        if (**inp == '(')
                *inp = span(*inp + 1, ')') + 1;         /* past */

        return buf;
}
```

macro() is responsible for receiving the **longjmp()** if something goes wrong in **span()**. We return a null pointer in this case. A trailing $ is silently ignored. $ not followed by a digit quotes the next character, i.e., $$ will represent a single $ in the macro expansion.

A slight blemish is the fact that **macro()** returns a result in static storage, and does not check for buffer overflow.

Testing a Library Function

macro( ) is a genuine new library function, perhaps to be used in other projects. It pays to supply a simple test driver within the source file *macro.c*:

```
#ifdef  TEST

main()
{       char buf[BUFSIZ], * mp, * bp = buf;

        for (;;)
        {       fputs("(args) ", stdout), fflush(stdout);
                bp = buf;
                if (! gets(buf))
                        break;
                mp = macro(& bp, "name", "\
                        $$0 \"$0\"\n\
                        $$1 \"$1\"\n\
                        $$2 \"$2\"\n\
                        $$3 \"$3\"\n\
                        $$4 \"$4\"\n\
                        $$5 \"$5\"\n\
                        $$6 \"$6\"\n\
                        $$7 \"$7\"\n\
                        $$8 \"$8\"\n\
                        $$9 \"$9\"");
                puts(mp ? mp : "{null}");
                puts(bp);
        }
        return 0;
}

#endif
```

If we define **TEST** and compile *macro.c*, we can at least verify that the arguments are extracted correctly. Here is a sample session:

```
$ macro
(args) ((1,2),'(3',"4)",\()past
                        $0 "name"
                        $1 "(1,2)"
                        $2 "'(3'"
                        $3 ""4)""
                        $4 "\("
                        $5 ""
                        $6 ""
                        $7 ""
                        $8 ""
                        $9 ""
past
(args) ^D
$
```

Clearly, **macro( )** is quite reasonable about C syntax!

Adding parameters to macros in our calculator is now only a matter of linking the right files. **lexi_macro( )** is part of *scan.l* since it accesses the **Stream** data type and the input buffer stack. **lexi_macro( )**, however, calls **macro( )**. For the calculator to be loaded correctly, we need to add the object *macro.o* to its load list. Here are the extensions to the *Makefile*:

```
calc    = calc.o lib.o macro.o scan.o sym.o
T       = scan scanl macro calc
pr:     macro.c

# macro test program

macro:  macro.c        ; $(CC) $(CFLAGS) -o $@ -DTEST macro.c
                         rm -f macro.o
```

A sample session now is almost fun:

```
$ calc
def strcpy $1 = $2
def strcat $1 += $2
b = "new"; strcpy(a, b); b="\nline"; strcat(a, b)
        "new"
        "new"
        "
line"
        "new
line"
^D
$
```

2.7 Functions

strcat( ) or **strcpy( )** and other functions can be defined as macros. Macros, however, do not introduce new functionality and they do not check validity of their arguments themselves. Consider:

```
def strcpy a = b
strcpy("abc", "def")
        ?syntax error
```

The error message refers to the assignment attempt, not to the argument of **strcpy( )**.

Principles

What would it take to make a function like **strcpy( )** or a value like **SIGINT** accessible to our calculator? We need to define a **%token** value, add a word to **reserved[ ]**, add a formulation to the grammar, and specify an action which calls the desired function. Here are some examples:

Tokens in *calc.y*:

```
%token SIGint, ATOI, CHDIR, EXIT, GETPID
%token ISALPHA, ITOA, KILL, STRCAT, STRCPY
%%
```

Reserved words in *sym.c*:

```
static Symbol reserved[] = {
        { "SIGINT",     SIGint },
        { "atoi",       ATOI },
        { "chdir",      CHDIR },
        { "exit",       EXIT },
        { "getpid",     GETPID },
        { "isalpha",    ISALPHA },
        { "itoa",       ITOA },
        { "kill",       KILL },
        { "strcat",     STRCAT },
        { "strcpy",     STRCPY },
        ...
```

Formulations in *calc.y*:

```
i       : SIGint                      { $$ = SIGINT; }
        | GETPID '(' ')'             { $$ = getpid(); }
        | EXIT '(' ie ')'            { $$ = exit($3); }
        | ISALPHA '(' ie ')'        { $$ = isalpha($3); }
        | KILL '(' ie ',' ie ')'    { $$ = kill($3, $5); }
        | ATOI '(' se ')'           { $$ = atoi($3), free($3); }
        | CHDIR '(' se ')'          { $$ = chdir($3), free($3); }
```

```
s       : ITOA '(' ie ')'                    { $$ = strsave(itoa($3)); }
        | STRCAT '(' lval ',' se ')'
                { $$ = strsave(Strcat($3, $5)), free($5); }
        | STRCPY '(' lval ',' se ')'
                { $$ = strsave(Strcpy($3, $5)), free($5); }
```

It does not exactly look difficult, at least as long as we stay away from tricky functions and manage dynamic strings properly. We also need to provide the right header files: *signal.h* for **SIGINT**, and *ctype.h* for **isalpha(3)**. The result certainly adds a new dimension to our calculator, especially if we want to use it as a command language:

```
$ calc
def cd chdir("$1")
cd(/)
        0
! echo *
bin boot dev dos etc lib lost+found mnt tmp usr xenix
!
def cd chdir(HOME)
cd
        0
! pwd; sleep 100 & echo $!
/usr/axel
963
!
kill(963, 9)
        0
isalpha(HOME[1])
        2
kill(getpid(), SIGINT)

$
```

Nice, but expensive... We could now start our favorite text editor and add as much to the *calc* sources as we can type and copy, but we would soon run into several problems. **SIGint** hints at the definite problem of naming conflicts between a reasonable approach to token names and system constant names that we cannot change. Functions such as **atoi(3)** and **chdir(2)**, or **strcat()** and **strcpy()**, are not really different if viewed as a combination of formulations and associated actions. However, if we add each value and function as an individual formulation, our grammar will quickly grow beyond limits which are hard-wired into *yacc*.

Designing a Name Table

For screening purposes, i.e., as part of the vector **reserved[ ]**, we need a textual representation and the token name of each value and function to be built into the calculator. For recognition, i.e., as additional formulations in the grammar, we need token names only for each class of things that are used in an identical fashion. For execution, i.e., within the action associated with the formulation for a token name representing a class of values or functions, we need to distinguish the class members.

Values can, of course, be retrieved from the symbol table, and they start out as part of **reserved[ ]**. A function is part of a class if it has identical argument and result types as all members of the class. From **reserved[ ]** we can obtain a pointer to the individual function, and the formulation is designed to call the function through the pointer and perform whatever preparations or cleanup may be required. The following name table contains the essential information for the example above:

```
# "name"        %token          etc.
#--------------------------------------------- reserved word
export          EXPORT          -
#--------------------------------------------- value
#include <signal.h>
SIGINT          Ivalue
version         Svalue          "calc\0401.0"
#--------------------------------------------- system call
chdir           I_s
exit            I_i
getpid          I_
kill            I_i_i
#--------------------------------------------- library function
atoi            I_s
strcat          S_ls_s          Strcat
strcpy          S_ls_s          Strcpy
itoa            S_i
#--------------------------------------------- library macro
#include <ctype.h>
isalpha         I_i             #if
```

The table is line and field oriented. Lines beginning with **#** are comments except, perhaps, for **#include** statements. Fields are separated by white space. If a string like **version** requires white space, it must be escaped.

The first field in each line of the table contains the text for **reserved[ ].s_name**, i.e., the representation of each function and value name. Clearly, we should not require the name table to be sorted, even if **reserved[ ]** must be.

The second field contains the token name. For values we invent new token names like **Ivalue** and **Svalue**. For functions, the token name describes the calling conventions: **I** or **S** designates the result type, **i** or **s** denote integer or string arguments, **ls** denotes a string **lval**, i.e., a variable which will receive a string value. We distinguish functions from other token names by separating the constituent parts with underscores.

Sometimes we need more information. For a line describing a value we need the actual value. If the value is defined in a system header file, the actual value often has the same macro name as the word stored in **reserved[ ].s_name**, i.e., the first field of the line can serve as reserved word for the value and as actual value. For a line describing a function we need the actual function name – once again usually just the reserved word for the function.

The third field can contain an explicit value or a function name. **isalpha( )** shows that there might be yet another possibility: if we try to build a macro into the calculator as a function, our implementation must provide a function calling the macro, and the function name should appear as third field. This is only necessary, if we really are confronted with a macro, therefore, we put **#if** in the third field, and a fourth field could contain the name of the calling function. We would usually derive the calling function name by turning the first letter of the macro name in the first field into upper case.

export shows the last possibility for a table entry: statement keywords may also be invented here. They are really no different from values, but the value field can be left uninitialized, indicated by − in the third field.

Implementing the Name Table: *mky*

The name table is not only a documentation aid to get our thoughts (and Section 1.2 of this book) organized. It is really a small language to define concisely the entire content of **reserved[ ]** and to describe supporting information such as **%token** names or extra formulations, all in one place. Sections 1.2 and 1.3 demonstrate that we have just laid the groundwork for a virtual explosion of words and features in our calculator. Unless we tightly control description and implementation of the features, if at all possible in a single place, we will certainly get lost in a multitude of bits and pieces of code spread all over.

We need to generate mechanically directly from the name table whatever code we require to support the name table. The name table language was designed on the fly, simply by writing down what we need to know about each kind of reserved word, but it was designed with mechanical source generation in mind.

awk(1) (Aho, Kernighan and Weinberger, 1988) is a text-processing language ideally suited for this type of problem. *awk* reads a line, splits it up into fields, and selects actions based on pattern matching and logical conditions.

awk patterns are quite similar to those used in *lex*(1). **BEGIN** introduces an action to be executed prior to any input line, **END** introduces an action to be executed once all lines have been read.

awk actions are written in a C-like language where variables need not be declared and can accept numeric and string values. Actions access the fields of the current input line as **$1**, etc., and they can write to standard output as well as files.

Dynamic strings alone are very convenient, but *awk* additionally supports arrays. Strings are used as array indices, i.e., we have a content-addressed storage mechanism. Only unique indices are stored, of course, and a **for-in** statement retrieves exactly the index values of an array.

awk is ideally suited for our code generation problem. Each line of the name table creates an entry in **reserved[ ]**, but only unique token names should be added to the grammar. For each class of functions we must design exactly one formulation.

The entries in **reserved[ ]** must be sorted. Our *awk* program writes them to standard output and we pipe the result through *sort*(1). Since **reserved[ ]** will contain values from include files, function names, and names for macro calling functions, we need to make sure that all relevant declarations are available when **reserved[ ]** is compiled. We cannot write the declarations to standard output, since they would get shuffled by *sort*, but we can write them to a separate file *extern.i* to be included when **reserved[ ]** is compiled.

Our *awk* program stores token names in an array. Once the entire name table has been read, we can write unique **%token** statements and formulations for function calls. Unfortunately, **%token** must precede the first **%%** in the *yacc* source and the formulations are best placed right before the second **%%** to avoid accidental redefinition of the start symbol of the grammar.

We could, of course, write two more files and collate them together with the other *yacc* source into yet another file for processing by *yacc*, but there is an easier way. If we let the name table precede the *yacc* source in the same file *calc.y* (the name table does contain token definitions, after all), our *awk* program can extract the name table and insert the required lines in a single pass. The result is written to a single new file *calc.i* which then becomes the *yacc* source. Here are the changes to *Makefile*:

```
pr:     mky
calc.c y.tab.h: calc.i  ; $(YACC) $(YFLAGS) calc.i
                            mv y.tab.c calc.c
calc.i extern.i reserved.i: calc.y mky  ; mky < calc.y > reserved.i
sym.o: calc.h syn.i extern.i reserved.i
```

mky is a shell script containing the *awk* program. **reserved[ ]** remains in *sym.c* so that the object *sym.o* depends on the initialization in *reserved.i* and the declarations in *extern.i*. However, we move **reserved[ ]** to the end of *sym.i* to avoid potential clashes between include files required for initialization and the code of our symbol table module.

The overall structure of *mky* is simple once we have decided on the information flow:

```
:       Bourne Shell
#       mky < calc.y extern.i calc.i > reserved.i
        PATH=/bin:/usr/bin

awk '

        ...
' | sort
```

The shell script starts with **:** to request that the Bourne Shell is used as a processor. We also normalize **PATH** just to make sure that we invoke only public commands. We use the script to read standard input, write sorted standard output, and write to the files *calc.i* and *extern.i*. The system is easier to maintain if we name the files in a single place. Therefore, we import the file names from shell script arguments into *awk* variables in the **BEGIN** action:

```
awk '
BEGIN { E = "'${1:-extern.i}'"        # extern declarations
        C = "'${2:-calc.i}'"          # yacc source file
        Q = "'\''"                    # single quote
        L = "abcdefghijklmnopqrstuvwxyz"
        U = "ABCDEFGHIJKLMNOPQRSTUVWXYZ"
        section = 0
}
```

Admittedly, this looks like a gruesome assembly of quotes, but it is necessary. Single quotes delimit the *awk* program as argument to *awk*. Double quotes surround string constants within the program. If we want to pass the shell variable value **$1** through the command line into the program, we need first a double quote to start the string constant which the value will become inside the program. Next we need a single quote to suspend quoting of the *awk* command argument. We are now back in normal shell text substitution and can reference the value **$1**; we supply *extern.i* as a default, if the value is not set or is null. A single quote resumes quoting of the *awk* argument. We are now at the end of the text of a string constant in the *awk* program, and we close the constant with a double quote.

Obviously, we can get this right† at most once per shell variable value. Therefore, **$1** is assigned to the *awk* variable **E**. Single quotes are tricky enough to merit assigning one to an *awk* variable **Q**; the graphic details are left to the patient reader.

mky needs to know which part of the source *calc.y* it is working on. For *yacc*, the source is partitioned using %%, and we simply extend this convention to cover our name table. A variable **section** is maintained in the *awk* program according to the following architecture in *calc.y*:

section	input	action
0	`/* ... */` `%%`	copied to *calc.i*
1	`name table` `%%`	processed by *awk*

2	`%union ...`
	
	`%%`
		copied to *calc.i*
		%token added
		then %% copied

3	`buffer : ...`
	
	`%%`
		copied to *calc.i*
		formulations added
		then %% copied

4	`#ifdef ...` `#endif`	copied to *calc.i*

section is changed at %% and controls code generation for the collected token names. Here is the corresponding architecture of *mky*:

```
/^%%/ { if (++ section == 3)
        {       ... emit %token statements ...        > C
                print "%%"                            > C
        }
        else if (section == 4)
        {       ... emit formulations ...             > C
                print "%%"                            > C
        }
        next
}


section != 1    { print > C ; next }          # copy
```

† ...maybe even for a value containing white space?

```
/^#include/      { print > E ; next }        # copy #include

/^#/             { next }                     # ignore comments
/^[    ]*$/      { next }                     # ignore empty lines

{ ... remember token names ...
   ... emit initializers for reserved[] ...
   ... emit declarations for reserved[] ...  > E

}
```

Program design is derived directly from the input structure. This successful technique was developed by Jackson (1975). Of course, several files can still be presented to *awk* as a single, partitioned input if we use a pipeline fed by a list of *cat*(1) and *echo*(1) commands.

awk splits a line and compares it with all patterns in sequence. Every match selects the associated action in turn. **next** ends selection and resumes the process with the next input line and the first pattern. This can be used as an elegant control structure reminiscent of a **switch** in C, but it sometimes forces an illogical arrangement of the actions, especially, if we need to pay a little attention to efficiency. A new version of *awk* supports function definitions which could help to circumvent the problem.

In our program, collection of the name table happens near the end of *mky*. We need to distinguish the various kinds of input lines and assemble the necessary information. To simplify code maintenance, we move the information from fields to variables, and we avoid code duplication by supplying defaults and rejoining the program mainline in the next action.

```
NF < 2 {
        print NR ": two fields required" > "/dev/tty"
}


{       name = $1; token = $2    # name token
}


token !~ /^._/ {
        symbol[token] = ""
        if (NF < 3)            # name token            value := name
                value = name
        else                   # name token value
                value = $3
        if (value == "-")      # name token -
                printf "{ \"%s\",\t%s },\n", name, token
        else
                printf "{ \"%s\",\t%s,\t(long) %s },\n", name, token, value
        next
}
```

So far, we have complained about a missing token name, and we have written initializers for reserved words and built-in values. If the token name does not have an underscore as second character, it describes a reserved word or a value. In **symbol[ ]** we maintain a list of the unique token names. A new name is added by using it as an index for **symbol[ ]** and assigning an arbitrary element value at this index.

```
token ~ /^I/ {                       # name I_...
        typ = "int"; class[token] = "i"
}

token ~ /^S/ {                       # name S_...
        typ = "char *"; class[token] = "s"
}

{       if (NF == 2)                 # name class            fun := name
                fun = name
        else                         # name class fun
                fun = $3
}

fun !~ /^#if/ {                      # name class fun
        printf "%s %s();\n", typ, fun                          > E
        printf "{ \"%s\",\t%s,\t(long) %s },\n", name, token, fun
        next
}
```

Integer and string functions require slightly different processing. We remember a result type in **typ** and we simplify later processing by storing the type as element value at the token name as index for **class[ ]**. If we do not need to accommodate a macro, we can simply write a function declaration to *extern.i*, i.e., to the file name in **E**, and an initializer to standard output.

Macros are bit trickier, since we have to build a calling function, the calling function must pass parameters, and string parameters must be declared. A good example is the macro **mvaddstr( )** from the *curses*(3) library. The name table entry would be

```
mvaddstr           I_i_i_s #if
```

and *extern.i* needs to contain

```
#ifdef  mvaddstr
int Mvaddstr(v1, v2, v3)
        char * v3;
{       return mvaddstr(v1, v2, v3); }
#else
int mvaddstr();
#define Mvaddstr            mvaddstr
#endif
```

to account for all possibilities, including that **mvaddstr( )** is not a macro at all.

Building the calling function name is the easy part. Either the name is specified as a fourth field, or we turn the first character of the macro name into upper case (and we assume it is in lower case). *awk* supports substring and character search operations, and we can piece the function name together:

```
{
        if (NF == 3)              # name class #if        fun := Name
                fun = substr(U, index(L, substr(name,1,1)), 1) substr(name,2)
        else                      # name class #if fun
                fun = $4

        n = split($2, v, "_"); pass = ""
        if (v[2] == "")
                n = 1
        if (n > 1)
        {       pass = "v1"
                for (i = 2; i < n; ++ i)
                        pass = pass ", v" i
        }
```

The parameter list is derived from the token name. **split**( ) takes a string apart and stores the pieces as vector elements beginning with index one. We need to split at underscores. The result type is **v[1]** and parameter types would be **v[2]** to **v[n]**, where **n** is returned by **split**( ). A slight complication is a token name such as **I_** which describes an integer function without an argument, but causes **split**( ) to return 2.

We are ready to write to *extern.i*. Admittedly, it looks like busy work, but we write the *awk* code only once to process whatever macros we might desire.

```
        printf "#ifdef\t%s\n", name                              > E
        printf "%s %s(%s)\n", typ, fun, pass                     > E
        for (i = 1; i < n; ++ i)
                if (v[i+1] == "s")
                        print "\tchar * v" i ";"                 > E
        printf "{\treturn %s(%s); }\n", name, pass               > E
        print "#else"                                            > E
        printf "%s %s();\n", typ, name                           > E
        printf "#define\t%s\t%s\n", fun, name                    > E
        print "#endif"                                           > E
        printf "{ \"%s\",\t%s,\t(long) %s },\n", name, token, fun
        next
}
```

All information has been collected. It is time to write the code near the beginning of *mky* which is responsible for generating %*token* statements and formulations. Recall that **symbol[ ]** uses token names for reserved words and values as indices, and that **class[ ]** uses token names for functions as indices, with the element values indicating the result type. Here are the %*token* statements:

```
/^%%/ { if (++ section == 3)
        {       for (token in symbol)
                        print "%token\t<y_sym>\t" token > C
                for (token in class)
                        print "%token\t<y_sym>\t" token > C
                print "%%"                              > C
        }
```

This was the easy part of course. Making the formulations is harder (remember all the quotes in the *yacc* source!), and writing the actions is even more busy work.

```
else if (section == 4)
{       head["i"] = "\t\t{ $$ = (* (int (*)()) $1 -> s_any)("
        tail["i"] = ");"
        head["s"] = "\t\t{ $$ = strpass((* (char * (*)()) $1 -> s_any)("
        tail["s"] = "));"

        for (token in class)
        {       n = split(token, v, "_")
                if (v[2] == "") n = 1;

                rule = ""
                call = ""
                free = ""
                if (n > 1)
                {       if (v[2] ~ /^l/) rule = " lval"
                        else rule = " " v[2] "e"
                        call = "$3"
                        if (v[2] == "s") free = " free($3);"
                }
                for (i = 2; i < n; ++ i)
                {       rule = rule " " Q ","  Q
                        if (v[i+1] ~ /^l/) rule = rule " lval"
                        else rule = rule " " v[i+1] "e"
                        call = call ", $" (2*i + 1)
                        if (v[i+1] == "s")
                                free = free " free($" (2*i + 1) ");"
                }

        print class[token] "\t: " token " " Q "(" Q rule " " Q ")" Q    > C
        print head[class[token]] call tail[class[token]] free " }"      > C
        print "stmt\t: " token "\t{ dump_class(" token "); }"           > C
                }
                print "%%"                                              > C
        }
        next
}
```

The key is to piece the result together from carefully designed parts: **rule** is the parameter list in the formulation, **call** is the parameter list within the action, and **free** handles calls to **free**(3) to release string values which are no longer needed.

    rule is composed of a comma-separated list of non-terminals permitting integer expressions **ie**, string expressions **se**, and variables **lval** as arguments for a function. The formulation explains a simple integer value **i** or a simple string value **s** depending on the return type of the function. It should now be clear, how we hit on the strange composition of our token names.

call is composed of a comma-separated list of references to the attached values **$3, $5,** and so on. **$1** refers to the value attached to the token name for the function. All other references are to the delimiters.

free contains one call to **free**(3) for each value attached to a string expression **se** specified as an argument.

A certain amount of glue keeps the pieces together. **head[ ]** contains the beginning of an action, and **tail[ ]** contains the end of the function call. Actions for **i** and **s** are different, therefore, we store the necessary pieces as array elements and derive the index from the result type stored as element value of **class[ ]** for the current **token**. Here are typical results, edited to show the parts:

```
%token   <y_sym> S_ls_s         /* Strcat, Strcpy */
%token   <y_sym> I_i            /* isalpha, exit */
%%


s        : S_ls_s '(' lval ',' se ')'          /* rule */
         { $$ = strpass((* (char * (*)()) $1 -> s_any)(   /* head["s"] */
                        $3, $5                 /* call */
                             ));               /* tail["s"] */
                        free($5);              /* free */
                        }
stmt     : S_ls_s        { dump_class(S_ls_s); }

i        : I_i '(' ie ')'                      /* rule */
         { $$ = (* (int (*)()) $1 -> s_any)(   /* head["i"] */
                        $3                     /* call */
                             );                /* tail["i"] */
                        }
stmt     : I_i           { dump_class(I_i); }
```

We can add a few help facilities at little extra cost. A new statement **const** executes a tree walk **dump_const**( ) to display built-in values. For each token name describing a function class we add the token name as a **stmt** to request another tree walk **dump_class**( ) to display all function names of the class. The actual statement is any function name from the class, specified without an argument list. The tree walks, of course, are easy exercises with **tpost**( ) and are added to *sym.c*.

Some of the library functions return null pointers to indicate failure. Our dynamic string management is not designed to handle null pointers. Therefore, we have introduced **strpass**( ), a version of **strsave**( ) which prevents null pointers from being propagated:

```
static char * strpass(s)
        register char * s;
{
        if (! s)
                response("?null");
        return strsave(s);
}
```

Initializing a Union

mky generates many initializers for **reserved[ ]**. Depending on the token value **.s_yylex**, very different values must be stored to be retrieved by the actions: **Ivalue** requires an integer value; **Svalue** requires a string constant stored in static memory, i.e., a C string constant; integer function names require pointers to the actual function with **int** as returned type; and string function names require pointers to functions returning the type **char ***.

Our **Symbol** already has a **union** component to store integer or string variable values, etc. We can extend the **union** to cover the new cases, but C does not permit initializing arbitrary alternatives within the **union** at compile time.

A subtle technique circumvents the restriction: we can initialize the first alternative within a **union**. This is already supported by some C compilers, and it is part of the new ANSI standard. We only need to make sure that this first alternative can be used to store all required values, and that we are able to retrieve the values correctly in the corresponding actions.

Pointers can be converted to any required pointer type by means of a cast, and pointers are normally sufficient to store and retrieve integer values with suitable casts. It is important to note that not every implementation of C can store pointers as integer values. XENIX/286 can serve as a crash test for portability. **int** values have 16 bits, **long** values have 32 bits, and pointer sizes vary according to the 'memory model'. Small memory model pointers have 16 bits, large pointers have 32 bits, and middle memory pointers to functions have 32 bits, while data pointers still have 16 bits!

We have placed a new alternative **.s_any** with type **long** first in the **union**. *mky*, therefore, casts all value initializations to **long**, and as we saw above, the **head[ ]** part of the actions casts back as required. Here are the actions for the constant values:

```
%token          Ivalue, Svalue
%%


i       : Iconstant            /* $$ = $1; */
        | Integer              { $$ = $1 -> s_int; }
        | Ivalue               { $$ = (int) $<y_sym>1 -> s_any; }


s       : Sconstant            /* $$ = $1; */
        | String               { $$ = strsave($1 -> s_str); }
        | Svalue               { $$ = strsave((char *) $<y_sym>1 -> s_any); }
```

mky supplies typed **%token** statements for **Ivalue** and **Svalue**. *yacc* does permit multiple **%token** statements for the same token name, but it does not permit more than one to be typed. If we hide the special meaning of **Ivalue** and **Svalue** from *mky*, we need to define the formulations in the *yacc* source proper, i.e., we need to supply untyped **%token** statements together with the formulations. Fortunately, we can force a reference to an attached value to have a specific type by using the notation **$<y_sym>1**.

Casting back and forth is a kludge, admittedly, but a portable solution to a sticky problem. If an older C compiler does not initialize a **union**, we can introduce a new data type **RSymbol**, where the **union** component is replaced by a **struct** with **.s_any** as the only component. As long as **Symbol** and **RSymbol** are maintained with identical layouts, the difference cannot be noticed once the pointers are extracted from the binary search tree. The software available with this book can be conditionally compiled with either technique and **assert**(3) is used to check on plausible layouts.

2.8 Conclusion

This chapter presented the development of a desk calculator. Particular emphasis was placed on a general purpose, extensible design. The calculator was built through a series of releases with less and less restricted functionality. Each release resulted from adding more functionality to the previous release.

Major building blocks, such as lexical analysis or macro expansion, have their own test drivers, which were upgraded if the building blocks were extended.

A special table language was developed to permit a simple representation of the name table for reserved words, built-in values, and built-in functions. It is quite easy to change the name table.

What We Have

The calculator can be connected to another program using just a few functions: **import( )** must be called early on to let the calculator take control of the environment variables; **export( )** must be called just prior to using **system**(3) or one of the **exec**(2) system calls to arrange for current environment variables to be passed; **getenv**(3) and **putenv**(3) are emulated by the calculator; **lexi_buf**(*buf*) is called to pass a buffer *buf* to lexical analysis; **yyparse( )** is then called to execute the calculator on the buffer.

There must be room for a newline to be added to the end of the buffer. The buffer itself could contain newline characters, but statements must be delimited by semicolons or commas, and comments and the macro control statements **def** and **undef** are line oriented.

The calculator will respond through some functions in the style of **printf**(3): **reply( )** is used to display the result of a statement, dump statements such as **set** may call **reply( )** more than once; **yyerror( )** and **response( )** indicate errors and should not return; **fatal( )** indicates a severe error and should lead to task termination.

What We Have Done

The calculator consists of several source files which are designed to provide a module structure. Certain constant information is passed from one module to another through intermediate files.

A *Makefile* controls system construction, program listings, and removal of temporary files.

A header file *calc.h* provides information common to all modules, i.e., the definition of an element of the symbol table.

Lexical analysis is implemented through *scan.l*, the source for a scanner generated by *lex*. This module encapsulates appearance of the desk calculator language, e.g., comments, white space, constants, names, etc.

The scanner contains the hooks for a macro facility. Macros are stored within the symbol table, but macro parameter substitution is handled by functions contained in *macro.c*. This module would be reworked if, for example, we decided to support parameter names.

All aspects of the symbol table are managed through functions in *sym.c*. While this module contains the name screening mechanism, the table of predefined names is imported from the grammar source. Environment and macro definition handling concerns the symbol table and is also part of *sym.c*. Changes to symbol table organization can be accomplished entirely in this module; changes to the initial content of the symbol table are made in the grammar source.

A few miscellaneous library functions are collected in *lib.c*. This file is the logical place to put access functions for library functions, e.g., **Strcat( )** for **strcat**(3), etc.

The grammar source *calc.y* is to be preprocessed by *mky* before *yacc* can be used to create the actual module. *mky* extracts information about reserved symbols for the screener, and generates **%token** statements for reserved words and rules for function calls to the source seen by *yacc*. The grammar source is changed to add built-in functions and values, or to support new statements in the calculator.

What We Have Not Done

Development by extension, as demonstrated for *calc* and perhaps more common than industry might care to admit, requires careful version control and thorough testing so that no features are destroyed during extension. Version control can be accomplished through systems like *sccs* or *rcs*, but it is questionable if such general systems would be applied during a small development with deliberate temporary steps such as *calc*. The sources available with this book show our (trivial) approach to version control and unification.

Schreiner and Friedman (1985) discuss an approach to test organization: test sources are kept and run under control of a shell script. If comprehensive sources are developed concurrently with the actual system, availability of all previous features can easily be verified for each new release. The method essentially breaks down, however, for screen-oriented programs, since their output cannot easily be captured and monitored by mechanical means. Our implementation is deliberately organized around tables – we can only lose features through ambiguities silently resolved by *lex*, or through problems reported as conflicts by *yacc*.

calc is not programmable, i.e., we do not support decision making through comparison and logical operators in conjunction with statements such as **if** or **while**.

We abstained from adding tricks to the lexical analysis and macro mechanisms: file inclusion and conditionalization seem quite feasible and would add a certain flair of decision making, but this would obscure the essential aspects of our system. Since lexical analysis is buffer oriented, we could have added labels to the grammar and redirected lexical analysis based on computational results – a mechanism similar to *goto* in the shell of UNIX version 6.

Neither solution to decision making, however, would be well structured and integrated into the calculator design. Kernighan and Pike (1984), and to a lesser degree Schreiner and Friedman (1985), show how a system designed for immediate mode calculations is converted to storing its programs for subsequent execution – the conventional approach for implementing control structures. While the conversion is not complicated, it does require a certain amount of code and would have lengthened this chapter considerably.

## CHAPTER THREE

Introduction to *curses*
cdc

3.1 Getting Acquainted

curses(3) refers to a function library, originally extracted from William Joy's text editor *vi*(1) by Ken Arnold at Berkeley. The library provides functions to control a very large number of alphanumeric terminals: output characters to any point on the screen in a number of video modes, input and decode key presses, and manage their echo. *curses* hide peculiar aspects of a particular terminal from the programmer, and try to minimize the number of characters sent to the terminal screen at the expense of program size and processor time.

The term *curses* encompasses two major software components and, unfortunately, two similar implementations providing not quite the same functionality. Terminals are described by entries in a database, which is implemented either as a single ASCII file */etc/termcap*, or as a tree of binary files at */usr/lib/terminfo*. The database entry is used by the *curses* functions to handle screen control and input decoding for a specific terminal while keeping the functionality totally portable.

termcap and *terminfo*

A database entry is selected by a symbolic terminal name normally reminiscent of the manufacturer's product number, e.g., **vt100nam** for a VT-100 terminal from Digital Equipment Corporation with automatic wraparound turned off. The terminal name usually must be set in the environment variable **TERM** when a *curses* program such as *vi* is started.† The database entry describes everything *curses* need to know about the terminal, e.g., escape sequences for cursor motion or erasing the screen, and escape sequences sent by whatever function keys the terminal might have.

termcap(7) entries denote these capabilities with two-letter names. Only some names are known to *vi* and *curses*. Other names could be added by specific application programs. XENIX, for example, defines special key names for a spreadsheet. In the interest of portability, however, even *termcap* should be viewed as a black box of information.

terminfo(7) files are precompiled using *tic*(1). In the source for a database entry, capabilities are specified using short names inspired by ANSI standards such as X3.64-1979 for termi-

---

† *vi* is not implemented with *curses*, but this editor hints at most things that can be done with *curses*, and it is always used to exercise new terminal descriptions in the database.

nal escape sequences. A program accesses a compiled database entry with the header file
term.h which defines long variable names for the capabilities. There is a very large number of
capabilities which might be defined for a terminal, and programmers essentially cannot add
their own.

Access to *termcap* is slow, since the database file has to be searched sequentially and the
capabilities within a database entry must be decoded and sorted out. Access to *terminfo* is much
faster, since only a single file has to be opened and read in, and no decoding is required.

Building a correct and efficient description for a new terminal, especially from scratch,
is quite difficult. Fortunately, most existing terminals are already known to *termcap* and
terminfo. Only newly developed terminals or emulations might require designing a new entry,
and even then it would usually evolve from an existing one. We will, therefore, take the database for granted.

Different *curses*

There are two versions of *curses* extant. While they have a lot of functions and functionality in
common, they do differ in at least one rather significant aspect. The older version of *curses* uses
termcap and is distributed with systems derived from Berkeley UNIX. The newer version is
based on *terminfo* and is available on System V. Multiple universe systems such as the Pyramid,
also known as Nixdorf's Targon/35, provide both brands of *curses*, implicitly selected within
each universe. Other systems, e.g., XENIX and SUN, also provide both brands, but one is the
default and the other one requires a certain amount of gimmickry during compilation and loading.

As a rule of thumb, if the file */etc/termcap* exists on a system, *termcap curses* are still
likely to be used. The directory */usr/lib/terminfo* is indicative for *terminfo curses*. When writing
a new program, the fact that *termcap curses* generally do not support explicit attributes such as
A_UNDERLINE could probably be used to conditionalize application program sources with
respect to each library. If the header file *curses.h* defines this constant, it is likely to belong to
terminfo curses.

If *curses* are only used for output operations, there are few differences between the two
implementations. However, if we get input from the terminal through *curses*, and especially if
we want to handle function keys, *terminfo curses* work significantly better and are much easier to
use.

Rather than worrying about backward compatibility, in this book we are interested in
programming with all features of a modern implementation of *curses* and with their systems
programming implications. Providing complete portability would amount to extending *termcap*
curses to support all that has been improved in *terminfo curses*. It is much easier to install the
newer version to begin with, as many vendors have done.

We will, therefore, stick to System V *terminfo curses*, just call them *curses*, and no
longer outline the differences. A *curses* application that is conditionalized for both implementations is shown in Chapter 13 in Schreiner (1987). UNIX terminal programming, which would be
required to extend *termcap curses*, is discussed in Rochkind (1985), and a keyboard decoder
could be extracted from Rochkind (1988).

3.2 Output

Usually, *curses* assume that **stdin** and **stdout** are connected to a terminal. Once **initscr**( ) is called, *curses* take over all aspects of terminal control. To return to a sane state afterwards, **endwin**( ) definitely should be called before the program terminates, and even then some things might have to be reset with other *curses* function calls. If **endwin**( ) is missing, it might be necessary to reset the terminal by typing **stty sane** (even without any echo) and terminate this command with *control*-J, i.e., a true newline character, since *curses* may have turned off terminal echo and the mapping of *return* to *newline* upon input.

We really should intercept some signals, and even a call to **exit**(2), to protect our unsuspecting victims:

```
#include <curses.h>
#include <signal.h>

exit(code)
        register int code;
{
        endwin();
        fflush(stdout), fflush(stderr);
        _exit(code);
}

main()
{

        initscr();
        signal(SIGINT, exit);
        ...
        return 0;       /* implies exit(0); */
}
```

Of course, if we rely on the original **exit**( ) to flush and close other output streams, we would have to do this ourselves before we call **_exit**(2) to terminate the task. **exit**( ) must not return!

A *nroff* Viewer: *nv*

Let us briefly look at the absolutely no-frills version of a viewer for *nroff*(1). If the output from *nroff* is passed through *col*(1), we should only receive visible characters plus the following:

space	space forward
backspace	space backward, overtype
tab	move to tab position
return	move to left margin
newline	move down and to left margin
shift-out	start bold font
shift-in	end bold font

Furthermore, a quick test using *od*(1) might reveal that *nroff* represents font two (italic) by the sequence *underscore backspace character*, and possibly font three (bold) by overtyping. Here is our viewer:

```
main()
{       register int ch, c2;
        FILE * inp;
        int x, y;

        if (! (inp = popen("PATH=/bin:/usr/bin col", "r"))
            || ! freopen("/dev/tty", "r", stdin))
                perror("input"), fflush(stderr), _exit(1);

        initscr();
        signal(SIGINT, exit);

        for (;;)
        {       switch (ch = getc(inp)) {
                case EOF:
                        refresh(), exit(0);
                case ' ':
                case '\b':
                case '\t':
                case '\r':
                        break;
                default:
                        if ((c2 = inch() & A_CHARTEXT) == '_')
                                addch(A_UNDERLINE | ch);
                        else if (c2 == ch)
                                addch(A_STANDOUT | ch);
                        else
                                break;
                        continue;
                case '\n':
                        getyx(stdscr, y, x);
                        if (++ y < LINES)
                                break;
                        refresh(), getch(), erase();
                        continue;
                case '\16':
                        standout();
                        continue;
                case '\17':
                        standend();
                        continue;
                }
                addch(ch);
        }
}
```

Before we start *curses* by calling **initscr( )** and setting up for a possible *interrupt* signal, we use **popen**(3) to insert *col* as a preprocessor for our standard input. Thus we make sure that we only receive the characters mentioned above, and we can also reconnect our own standard input with */dev/tty* so that *curses* can read from the terminal keyboard.

In the main loop we read a character from *col* and pass it to **addch( )**, which will arrange to output the character and advance the current position. **addch( )** knows how to cope with visible characters, *backspace*, *tab*, *newline*, etc., but we need to fiddle with video attributes. **standout( )** will emphasize subsequent output until **standend( )** restores normal conditions.

If we need to investigate overtyping, we can call **inch( )** to receive the character in the current output position. This character may already have an attribute, which can be removed with the mask **A_CHARTEXT**. An attribute for a single character can just be added as the character is passed to **addch( )** for output.

initscr( ) starts us out at the top of an empty screen, i.e., at row zero and column zero, but eventually a *newline* will get us past the bottom of the screen. **LINES** is a variable defined in *curses.h*, and initialized by **initscr( )**, indicating the number of rows on the screen. Similarly, **COLS** contains the number of columns. **getyx( )** is a macro returning the current position within a window to the variables specified as arguments (no pointers required here). **stdscr** references the window setup by **initscr( )**, which is as large as the terminal screen, and which our functions have all been using implicitly.

So far we have happily painted on **stdscr** using **addch( )**, but nothing has been sent to the terminal. **refresh( )** finally unleashes the *curses*. The physical terminal screen is made to look like **stdscr** while transmitting as little as possible. Next, **getch( )** waits for a single character from the keyboard. **erase( )** fills **stdscr** (but not yet the terminal screen) with blanks and sets the current position back to the top left corner. Now we are ready to start over.

curses and the Environment

We can use the *nroff* viewer for a few interesting experiments. Clearly, if the environment variable **TERM** is not set, *curses* are at a loss. Assume that *nv* is our viewer, and that *nv.c* is the corresponding source file:

```
$ env TERM= nv < nv.c
Sorry, I don't know how to deal with your '' terminal.
Memory fault - core dumped
$ adb nv core
* $c
_endwin()        from _exit+0x15
_exit() from __ec_quit+0x70
__ec_quit(0x42, 0x47, 0x4196, 0x47)       from _initscr+0x73
_initscr()       from _main+0x79
_main(0x1, 0x40a4, 0x47, 0x40ac, 0x47)  from __start+0x5e
__start()        from start0+0x7
* $q
$ env TERMINFO=/usr/lib/terminfo TERM=vt50 nv < nv.c
...
$
```

The memory fault can result from calling **endwin()** without having executed **initscr()** success-fully. If we supply our own **exit()**, we really need to maintain a private flag to store this invari-ant.

TERMINFO can be set to point to the root of the *terminfo* directory tree. This way we can use private terminal descriptions. *tic* also checks this variable when storing a compiled data-base entry.

vt50 is a very old terminal. If we fool **initscr()** into setting up for this terminal, our viewer will have the fewest frills ever (not even attributes), and the screen will scroll by half pages.

initscr() also checks the environment for the variables **COLUMNS** and **LINES**. If they are found, they overwrite the physical screen dimensions defined in *terminfo*. You might check the following:

```
$ nv < nv.c                   # view a regular file
...
$ env LINES=10 nv < nv.c      # limit screen height
...
$ env COLUMNS=40 nv < nv.c    # try to limit screen width
...
$
```

Limiting the number of screen lines should work correctly. Limiting the number of columns, however, will probably result in something resembling double-spaced output with the text lines still taking up the full screen. If *terminfo* claims that the terminal automatically inserts newlines to continue long output lines onto new physical screen lines, *curses* will not insert newlines after 40 columns. If you can, make a new terminal description without the **am** (*automatic* m*argin*) capability, and run the last test again. This time, *curses* will insert newlines and the output looks more reasonable. The moral is, of course, that **COLUMNS** and **LINES** should only be set in a physical windowing environment, e.g., on a BLIT terminal.

curses and the Database

Apart from supporting a rudimentary window concept, which we will start to study in Section 3.4, *curses* are very useful to solve two sticky problems: the library minimizes the amount of output actually sent to a terminal screen, and it integrates this with reading input and decoding function keys.

The key to output minimization is, of course, to keep track of what is on the physical terminal screen, to collect and buffer what is supposed to be there, and to update the physical screen only if the program explicitly requests it. Keeping track requires memory, on the order of two bytes per character in each window, and updating while minimizing output requires CPU time for comparisons and evaluation of the cost of various outputs achieving the same effect. The simple *nroff* viewer uses about 60 KB on XENIX, and viewing the file *nv.c* requires about 1.6 seconds of user CPU time more than the 0.6 seconds system time taken up by *cat* on a 286 sys-tem.

If space and CPU time is at a premium, and if we are not too concerned with terminal modes, output volume, and input decoding, we can still query the *terminfo* or *termcap* data-base for *escape* sequences and make our programs independent of specific terminal types.

For example,

```
$ tput clear
```

is highly probable to clear the terminal screen and could be used in a shell script. *tput*(1) outputs the value of certain *terminfo* capabilities as standard output. The following program is more likely to clean up, even if the terminal screen should be flashing foreign characters or not at all:

```
#include <curses.h>
#include <term.h>

#define OUT(s)  if (s) tputs(s, lines, put)

static int put(ch)
        register int ch;
{
        return putc(ch, stderr);
}

main()
{
        system("PATH=/bin:/usr/bin stty sane");
        setupterm((char *) 0, 2, (int *) 0);
        OUT(exit_alt_charset_mode);
        OUT(exit_attribute_mode);
        OUT(clear_screen);
        return 0;
}
```

stty sane is a fairly portable way to restore sensible terminal parameters. **setupterm( )** initiates access to *terminfo*; the arguments shown above rely on a suitable default for **TERM**. References to the capabilities **exit_alt_charset_mode, exit_attribute_mode, clear_screen**, and **lines** are set up in the header file *term.h*, and **tputs( )** should be called as shown to output the strings with sufficient padding for older terminals.

Our window shell is built around the features that *curses* have to offer, and we will not pursue bare access to the database further. A programming example for *termcap* can be found in Schreiner (1986), an improved version of *tputs* for *termcap* appears in Schreiner (1987), and Rochkind (1988) presents his own window system based (among others) on *termcap* and *terminfo*.

3.3 Input

Getting input is more difficult than just displaying output. The System V terminal driver has a bewildering variety of option settings, and even after *curses* have filtered out the few really necessary ones, there is still room for considerable confusion. Let us briefly look at a no-frills drawing program, primarily designed to illustrate a few more *curses* features.

A Drawing Program: *doodle*

The user of *doodle* is presented with an empty screen. Visible characters are echoed as they are typed, arrow keys move the cursor around, and if the terminal has function keys such as *insert character* or *delete line*, they would do just that. Here is the main loop of *doodle* as a typical example for cursor control:

```
y = x = 0;
for (;;)
{       switch (refresh(), ch = getkey()) {
        case KEY_A1:    -- y, -- x;             break;
        case KEY_UP:    -- y;                   break;
        case KEY_A3:    -- y, ++ x;             break;
        case KEY_LEFT:
        case '\b':
        backspace:              -- x;           break;
        case KEY_B2:    y = LINES/2, x = COLS/2; break;
        case KEY_RIGHT:         ++ x;           break;
        case KEY_C1:    ++ y, -- x;             break;
        case KEY_DOWN:  ++ y;                   break;
        case KEY_C3:    ++ y, ++ x;             break;
        case KEY_HOME:  y = x = 0;              break;
        case KEY_LL:    y = LINES-1, x = 0;     break;
        case KEY_DL:    deleteln();             continue;
        case KEY_IL:    insertln();             goto where;
        case KEY_DC:    delch();                continue;
        case KEY_IC:    insch(' ');             continue;
        case KEY_CLEAR: clear();                goto where;
        case KEY_EOS:   clrtobot();             goto where;
        case KEY_EOL:   clrtoeol();             goto where;
        default:
                if (ch == erasechar())
                        goto backspace;
                if (ch == killchar())
                        exit(0);
                if (! isascii(ch) || ! isprint(ch) && ! isspace(ch))
                        continue;
                addch(ch);
        where:  getyx(stdscr, y, x);
        }
        if (x >= 0 && x < COLS && y >= 0 && y < LINES
            && (x != COLS-1 || y != LINES-1))
                move(y, x);
        else
                getyx(stdscr, y, x);
}
```

If **refresh**( ) is called, the physical cursor appears wherever **initscr**( ) or **move**( ) and other output functions have last put the logical cursor in **stdscr**. The *curses* input function **getch**( ) reads a character from the keyboard. We will see below how we can arrange for **getch( )** to decode function keys into values such as **KEY_HOME**. Right now, we would reach the **default** part of the **switch** and put visible characters or control characters such as *newline* and *tab* to **stdscr**. The macro **getyx( )** records the new cursor position in **y** and **x** since **addch( )** might have interpreted a control character and moved much more than just a character to the right. We are ready to continue reading.

erasechar( ) and killchar( ) return the current *erase* and *kill* characters set for the terminal. We interpret **erasechar( )** as a motion to the left and **killchar( )** as a request to terminate *doodle*. A simple call to **exit( )** is sufficient to clean things up, since we are using the same **exit( )** function as in the *nroff* viewer *nv*.

The terminal might have a number of function keys which our user would expect to result in cursor motion. *curses* defines special values for these function keys (outside the range of **char**) which **getch( )** returns under certain conditions. **KEY_HOME** and **KEY_LL** (*lower left*) are fairly obvious, the other names are derived from the following keypad:

A1	UP	A3
LEFT	B2	RIGHT
C1	DOWN	C3

Implementation of cursor motion sounds simple: since we keep track of the cursor position in **y** and **x**, we change those values as required and call **move( )** to accomplish the cursor motion. If we try to move off-screen, however, **move( )** will cheerfully record the new cursor position in **stdscr**, and subsequent **addch( )** operations would fail until we have used **move( )** to get back onto the screen. It is best if we limit the cursor ourselves to the area defined for **stdscr**. Also, we do not permit the cursor to reach the bottom right corner of the screen, since some terminals consider that spot their funny bone. If we have messed up the intended cursor position, we use **getyx( )** to restore the original position from **stdscr**.

curses support typical intelligent terminal operations such as *delete line* or *insert character* within windows – even if the physical terminal cannot directly perform these operations. There is a perhaps confusing duplicity between function keys that might be decoded by **getch( )** and *curses* output functions:

KEY_CLEAR	clear( )	clear screen
KEY_EOS	clrtobot( )	erase: cursor to end of screen
KEY_EOL	clrtoeol( )	erase: cursor to end of line
KEY_DL	deleteln( )	delete line under cursor
KEY_IL	insertln( )	insert blank line under cursor
KEY_DC	delch( )	delete character at cursor
KEY_IC	insch(ch)	insert character at cursor

We have chosen to call the corresponding output function for each such function key in *doodle* so that we can test the various features. It should be clear, however, that this is a programming decision that we can make when using *curses*; the correspondence of input and output is not built into the library itself.

curses have several ways to fill a window with blanks. **erase( )** fills **stdscr** with blanks and the next **refresh( )** will output those blanks to the physical screen. **clear( )** calls **erase( )** and additionally sets **clearok( )** to TRUE. In this case, the physical screen is erased through an escape sequence, if possible, and the new contents of **stdscr** are written onto an empty screen. **clear( )**

is a very visible signal on the physical screen and should be used to alert the user to reading an entire new screen. **erase**( ) is preferable if we wish to keep the screen change visually quiet.

Terminal State Control

Well, does *doodle* perform as advertised? *doodle* clearly assumes that function keys are decoded, and that any input through **getch**( ) is unbuffered and without echo on the terminal screen. If we build the loop above into the typical *curses* frame shown earlier, and used for *nv*, we see two equal output characters for each key press. Depending on the terminal type, function keys will cause several characters to be echoed instead of effecting a cursor motion! To experiment with various terminal state controls, we add the following main program:

```
#include "main.h"

MAIN
{       register int ch, y, x;

        initscr(), on_screen = 1;
        signal(SIGINT, exit);

        OPT
        ARG 'c': PARM                   /* -c 0/1: cbreak */
                if (atoi(*argv)) cbreak(); else nocbreak();
                NEXTOPT
        ARG 'e': PARM                   /* -e 0/1: echo */
                if (atoi(*argv)) echo(); else noecho();
                NEXTOPT
        ARG 'i':                        /* -i: idlok TRUE */
                idlok(stdscr, TRUE);
        ARG 'k':                        /* -k: keypad TRUE */
                keypad(stdscr, TRUE);
        ARG 'l':                        /* -l: leaveok TRUE */
                leaveok(stdscr, TRUE);
        ARG 'm':                        /* -m: map keys */
                mflag = 1;
        ARG 'r': PARM                   /* -r 0/1: raw */
                if (atoi(*argv)) raw(); else noraw();
                NEXTOPT
        ARG 's':                        /* -s: scrollok TRUE */
                scrollok(stdscr, TRUE);
        ARG 't':                        /* -t: no typeahead */
                typeahead(-1);
        OTHER

                ;
        ENDOPT

        y = x = 0;
        ...
```

main.h is a header file described in Schreiner (1986), with extensions in Schreiner (1987), which provides a set of macros **OPT**, **ARG**, **OTHER**, **ENDOPT**, **PARM**, and **NEXTOPT**, to decode a 'standard' UNIX command argument list similar to **getopt**(3). The main program supports options to set terminal modes as follows:

`-c0`	`nocbreak()`	(default)
`-c1`	`cbreak()`	single character input
`-e0`	`noecho`	no character echo
`-e1`	`echo`	(default)
`-i`	`idlok(stdscr, TRUE)`	hardware insert/delete line allowed
`-k`	`keypad(stdscr, TRUE)`	decode function keys
`-l`	`leaveok(stdscr, TRUE)`	no need to correct cursor
`-r0`	`noraw()`	(default)
`-r1`	`raw()`	single character input, no signals
`-s`	`scrollok(stdscr, TRUE)`	window scrolls up
`-t`	`typeahead(-1)`	no line-breakout optimization

For the *stdio* function **getchar**(3), the terminal default of **echo**() and **nocbreak**() means that a full line (up to newline or *control*-D) must be typed before a single character is delivered to the calling program. This is necessary to implement the erase and kill keys for intra-line editing.

The *curses* function **getch**() operates by default with **echo**() and **cbreak**(). It really has no choice because *curses* need to know the exact contents of the terminal screen. If **echo**() is turned on, key presses cause the terminal screen to change. *curses* need to know immediately, among other things to limit the range of string input functions like **getstr**() and to be able to prevent the physical screen from being scrolled once a newline is input in the bottom row of the screen. So **getch**() operates with **echo**() and **cbreak**(),† and each character typed is immediately available to the program. Even the end of input indication *control*-D is echoed and passed as a character.

Once we set **noecho**(), the customary default **nocbreak**() applies, and things behave a bit more as we should expect. Now, characters are available to the program only once a line is completed with newline or *control*-D. For cursor handling, we really require **noecho**() and **cbreak**() to receive each character immediately and without a screen echo.

In **raw**() mode, each character is also immediately handed to the program. This time, however, signals are no longer interpreted by the terminal driver. Therefore, if a *curses* program is run in **raw**() mode, we have to make absolutely sure that we provide a reliable exit. If we make a mistake, the user needs a second terminal to kill a run-away task. **raw**() and **cbreak**() are mutually exclusive states, and the function calls influence each other.

Function keys are decoded once **keypad**() is set to TRUE. By default, this is not the case, since *curses* need to turn off terminal echo and once again read keys as they are pressed to decode function keys. In short, **keypad**() implies **noecho**() and **cbreak**(), although this is not

---

† Actually, **noecho**() is set during **getch**() – as can be verified by running *stty*(1) from another terminal. **getch**(), however, outputs its own echo and the net effect is about the same.

mentioned in the manuals. It is probably wise not to rely on this too much. For sensible operation, *doodle* should be called as follows:

```
$ doodle -e0 -c1 -k     # noecho(), cbreak(), keypad(,TRUE)
```

Fortunately, the other options are easier to explain. **idlok()**, when set to TRUE, lets *curses* use the ability of a terminal to insert and delete lines. This can be visually displeasing in certain applications, hence it is by default set to FALSE – inefficiency is preferable over visual noise.

leaveok(), when set to TRUE, permits *curses* to leave the physical cursor wherever it ends up following a screen update. By default, this is not allowed; after all, we usually want the physical cursor to be at the position of the window cursor. For a cursor manipulation program such as *doodle*, setting **leaveok()** to TRUE is a very bad idea.

By default, **scrollok()** is also FALSE: if we press newline at the bottom of a window such as **stdscr**, the window contents must not be scrolled up. This option is usually changed only to implement a line-oriented terminal simulation. We shall see an example in Section 3.4.

typeahead() normally applies to file descriptor zero, i.e., to standard input. During **refresh()**, *curses* check if anything has been typed at the file descriptor set by **typeahead()**. If so, **refresh()** terminates early, without updating the entire screen, and the *curses* program continues – presumably by reading that input. A subsequent call to **refresh()** will then automatically complete the screen update.

If we call **typeahead(−1)**, i.e., if we turn checking off, we will notice a change in *doodle*. Function key presses are now handled one by one. If we press a few quickly in a row, the cursor will execute each single one. By default, a quick sequence of, for example, left arrows will make the cursor hesitate and then jump to whatever endpoint is reached by the sequence.

Turning checking off is perhaps preferable. *curses* do not process function keys particularly swiftly; partially because this simply cannot be done with the UNIX terminal driver. Our users might well prefer to see the progress of the cursor move, even if it is slow, rather than seeing nothing and then a quick jump.

Key Mapping

doodle is designed to work with a large number of function keys. Without arrow keys and **KEY_HOME**, we cannot get back to the top left corner of the screen. Not all terminals, however, support function keys as *terminfo* would like them to. *terminfo* does not even provide sensible names for keys such as **HELP** or **CANCEL** which can be found on rather popular terminals.

To test *doodle* on various terminals, we need to influence key decoding. We replace the call to **getch()** with a new function **getkey()**, and add a global variable **mflag** set under control of the option −m to selectively turn key mapping on. **getkey()** is based on **getch()**, but it uses a key translation table:

```
static int getkey()
{       static struct map { int in, out; } map[] = {
                { KEY_HOME,     KEY_A1 },
                { KEY_PPAGE,    KEY_A3 },
                { KEY_LL,       KEY_C1 },
                { KEY_NPAGE,    KEY_C3 },
                { KEY_F(1),     KEY_IC },
                { KEY_F(2),     KEY_DC },
                { KEY_F(3),     KEY_DL },
                { KEY_F(4),     KEY_HOME },
                { KEY_F(5),     KEY_CLEAR },
                { KEY_F(6),     KEY_EOS },
                { KEY_F(7),     KEY_EOL },
                { KEY_F(8),     KEY_LL },
        0 };
        register int ch = getch();
        register struct map * mp;

        if (mflag)
        {       for (mp = map; mp -> in && mp -> in != ch; ++ mp)
                        ;
                if (mp -> in)
                        ch = mp -> out;
        }
        return ch;
}
```

map[] corrects the situation on an IBM PC enhanced keyboard, where keys like **KEY_HOME** are sent by the corners of the keypad, and where we have numbered function keys available. We use the numbered keys to represent some of the special keys that *doodle* requires.

map[] does something that could be accomplished in two other ways. The main loop of *doodle* could refer directly to the keys which map[] uses to represent the missing keys, or the terminal description in *terminfo* could be changed to sacrifice function keys in favor of the missing keys. Neither alternative is preferable, however. Clearly, *terminfo* should not be changed for the benefit of a single program. Other programs might require the numbered keys while caring less about movement keys. If the numbered keys are hardwired into the main loop of *doodle*, the program will still not work on a very dumb terminal.

map[] and **getkey()** encapsulate a virtual keyboard model for the application *doodle* and provide one hardware instance based on the *terminfo* entry for the IBM PC. In Section 4.7 we shall load different keyboard maps selected by **TERM** and provide application-specific keyboard descriptions that can even be dynamically tailored.

3.4 Windows

Just like the *stdio* library is built around the **FILE** data type, the central concept in *curses* is a **WINDOW**. A **WINDOW** has a number of attributes, mostly kept as unpublished components of the **WINDOW** structure data type defined in the header file *curses.h*.

```
short _cury, _curx;       current position
short _maxy, _maxx;       size in rows, columns
short _begy, _begx;       physical position of top left
```

There is a macro **getyx()** to determine the current position within a window, but only recently†
have macros **getmaxyx()** and **getbegyx()** been defined to determine size and physical position of
a **WINDOW**. We should make sure to use the macros only:

```
#ifndef getbegyx
#define getbegyx(win,y,x) ((y) = (win) -> _begy, (x) = (win) -> _begx)
#endif
#ifndef getmaxyx
#define getmaxyx(win,y,x) ((y) = (win) -> _maxy, (x) = (win) -> _maxx)
#endif
```

Macro parameters should always be enclosed in parentheses in the replacement text of a macro
to avoid precedence clashes. *curses* macros tend to leave something to be desired. If you are
planning to use pointers to **WINDOW** pointers, you might consider redefining **getyx()** or invent
some other macros.

Clearly, we should not access components of the **WINDOW** structure explicitly at all, and
we should definitely not make assignments to them, since this is information hidden by *curses*.
However, we often do need read access to the information. Macros like **getyx()** prevent write
access, and defining macros like **getmaxyx()** ourselves at least localizes the intrusion into hidden
information. The following macros are usually more convenient:

```
#define begy(win)        ((int) (win) -> _begy)
#define begx(win)        ((int) (win) -> _begx)
#define cury(win)        ((int) (win) -> _cury)
#define curx(win)        ((int) (win) -> _curx)
#define maxy(win)        ((int) (win) -> _maxy)
#define maxx(win)        ((int) (win) -> _maxx)
```

The cast is not necessary, but it keeps the macros from being usable as targets of assignments,
and it should not cause extra code to be generated.

initscr() creates two windows which may be referenced using the constants **stdscr** and
curscr. All other windows must be dynamically created through **newwin()** or **subwin()**, and
released with **delwin()**.

stdscr is a constant reference to a window as large as the screen of the terminal identified through the **TERM** environment variable. The variables **LINES** and **COLS** provide simple
access to **maxy(stdscr)** and **maxx(stdscr)**. Just like the simple *stdio* functions **putchar**(3),
puts(3), and **printf**(3) implicitly reference **stdout**, the simple *curses* functions **addch()**,
addstr(), and **printw()** write to **stdscr** and implicitly influence the current position of this window.

curscr technically is another constant **WINDOW*** which symbolizes the current contents
of the physical terminal screen. We shall see that only very few *curses* functions may be applied
to **curscr** to force special effects such as a complete replot of the screen. Unfortunately,

---

† *curses* for System V release 3.

cury(curscr) and **curx(curscr)** do not return the physical cursor position – this would be extremely handy for some fancy footwork with multiple processes writing to the same screen.

A Screen Calculator

Section 2.8 pointed out that our desk calculator has a very small interface to the outside world. It was carefully designed so that interaction can be managed in various ways. In this section we connect the calculator to a simple screen handler based on *curses* to illustrate the basic principles.

Section 2.8 lists the interfacing requirements for the calculator: **import()** must be called to control the environment; **lexi_buf()** passes an input line to the scanner; **yyparse()** executes the calculator on the buffer; usually the calculator will report back through one or more calls to **reply()**; and if things go wrong, we hear about it through **response()**, **yyerror()**, or even **fatal()**. Section 3.2 has shown the basic design of a *curses* program.

If we put things together, we should receive a look-alike to the last release developed in Section 2.7, i.e., a calculator that reads an input line through the screen and responds on subsequent lines. The support functions and the main program are the first step towards our window shell. Therefore, we start a new module *wish.c*:

```
#include <curses.h>
#include <setjmp.h>
#include <signal.h>
#include <varargs.h>

static jmp_buf on_response;              /* restart command */

response(va_alist)                       /* respond and restart */
        va_dcl                           /* fmt, val... */
{       register va_list ap;
        register char * fmt;

        va_start(ap);
        fmt = va_arg(ap, char *), _reply(fmt, ap);
        va_end(ap);

        longjmp(on_response, 1);
}
```

A portable way to receive a variable number of arguments is provided through the header file *varargs.h*. The parameter list must be **va_alist** and it must be declared as **va_dcl**. Individual parameters such as **fmt** can then be retrieved by means of an argument list pointer **va_list ap**.

As before, we will channel all output through a single function. **va_alist**, however, cannot be passed as an argument. Therefore, we introduce a new output function **_reply()** which receives an output format **fmt** and a pointer **ap** to the rest of our argument list.

The call to **_reply()** exhibits a subtle portability problem in C. **fmt** is retrieved from our own argument list with the macro **va_arg()**. The macro call influences the value of **ap**. We really must introduce the variable **fmt**, since the order of argument evaluation is not defined in C. If we do not evaluate the macro call prior to evaluating the entire argument list for **_reply**(), the pointer argument **ap** could have the wrong value.

The other communication functions follow the same pattern. They all receive a variable argument list and pass it to **_reply**():

```
reply(va_alist)                         /* respond and continue */
        va_dcl                          /* fmt, val... */
{       register va_list ap;
        register char * fmt;

        va_start(ap);
        fmt = va_arg(ap, char *), _reply(fmt, ap);
        va_end(ap);
}


yyerror(s)                              /* calculator error */
        register char * s;
{
        response("?%s", s);
}
```

_reply() must work much like **printf**(): it receives a format and a pointer to the list of arguments to be converted. Corresponding to the **printf** family, there is a set of library functions **vprintf**(), **vfprintf**(), and **vsprintf**() which accept a format and an argument list pointer, both possibly preceded by a **FILE** pointer or a character buffer. *curses* provide an output function **printw**() with the same arguments as **printf**(), but they do not support something like the **vprintf** family. Fortunately, it is easy to build a poor man's equivalent:

```
#include "wish.h"


static _reply(fmt, ap)                  /* show response */
        register char * fmt;
        register va_list ap;
{       char buf[CLEN];

        vsprintf(buf, fmt, ap);
        printw("\t%s\n", buf);
}
```

We use **vsprintf**() to format our message in a reasonable buffer,† and show the buffer on the terminal screen with **printw**(). A tab precedes the output to distinguish it from input.

CLEN is the buffer size. This value could be tuned if necessary. We start a new definition file *wish.h*, where we will collect this kind of information. Access macros for **WINDOW** components, described at the beginning of this section, are also added to this file.

While we are learning about *varargs.h*, we might as well add a solid version of **fatal**(). We do not know if this function is only called when *curses* own the terminal screen. Therefore, we introduce an invariant **on_screen** and a function **crt_off**(), and we are ready to code **fatal**():

---

† It appears to be customary not to check for overflow.

```
        static char on_screen;                    /* set if initscr() */

        crt_off()                                 /* get off screen */
        {
                if (on_screen)
                        endwin(), on_screen = 0;
        }

        fatal(va_alist)                           /* message and quit */
                va_dcl
        {       register char * fmt;
                register va_list ap;

                crt_off();
                va_start(ap);
                fmt = va_arg(ap, char *);
                if (fmt && * fmt)
                        vfprintf(stderr, fmt, ap), putc('\n', stderr);
                va_end(ap);
                exit(1);

        }
```

crt_off() is responsible for cleaning up the screen well enough so that stream i/o can be used again. We can refine this function as required, and we can build a counterpart **crt_on**() if needed. **crt_off**() is also called when our program terminates normally:

```
        exit(code)
        {
                crt_off();
                fflush(stdout), fflush(stderr);
                _exit(code);
        }
```

Finally, **main**() initializes everything and manages the dialog with our calculator. In true UNIX fashion we want to quit on end of input. Section 3.3 has explained, why we will receive the customary *control*-D as part of the buffer read with **getstr**():

```
        main()
        {       char buf[CLEN];

                import();

                if (signal(SIGINT, SIG_IGN) != SIG_IGN)
                        signal(SIGINT, exit);

                initscr(), on_screen = 1;
                echo(), nocbreak();
```

```
setjmp(on_response);
for (;;)
{        getstr(buf);
         if (*buf == ('D' & 31))
                 break;
         lexi_buf(buf), yyparse();
}


return 0;
}
```

Here we have also coded the signal interception correctly: even in an interactive program it is not nice to connect **SIGINT** unconditionally to the intercept function. If our user has arranged to ignore a signal, we are really obliged to leave well enough alone.

import( ) sets up the environment checked by our replacement for **getenv**( ). Since **initscr**( ) queries the environment for the terminal type, we must call **import**( ) prior to **initscr**( ).

Does this first release of *wish* work? Well... almost. The dialog dutifully starts at the top of the screen and proceeds downward. Tab characters and newline characters are interpreted correctly by **printw**( ) and *curses*. However, once we reach the bottom of the screen, newlines are no longer effective, and further output and echo is written along the bottom line. The terminal's 'funny bone' is not written to, and further conversation takes place in the twilight zone below the bottom right of the terminal. An interrupt aborts the program and restores sanity to the terminal.

We forgot to set the **scrollok**( ) condition. While we are changing **main**( ), let us also connect the interrupt signal **SIGINT** to the **response**( ) mechanism and introduce **SIQQUIT** as an orderly way to quit the program. An interactive program should acknowledge an interrupt and return to program command level; the *quit* signal (usually caused by *control-*\) could then act as a stronger interrupt to terminate execution.

```
static trap(sig)                         /* signal intercept */
        register int sig;
{
        signal(sig, trap);
        response("?signal %d", sig);
}


main()
{       ...
        if (signal(SIGINT, SIG_IGN) != SIG_IGN)
                signal(SIGINT, trap);
        if (signal(SIGQUIT, SIG_IGN) != SIG_IGN)
                signal(SIGQUIT, exit);

        initscr(), on_screen = 1;
        echo(), nocbreak();
        scrollok(stdscr, TRUE);
        ...
```

We build a general intercept function **trap( )** which arranges for the signal to be caught again and reports the signal number. This way, **trap( )** can be connected to any signal.

With **scrollok( )** set, *curses* act just like the stream-oriented interface used in the last chapter. There are a few differences. Unless we set **idlok( )**, scrolling is painfully slow. *control*-D has a visible echo. Editing activities, i.e., the echo of the *erase* and *kill* keys, may look different, especially at the bottom of the screen. If not at the bottom of the screen, the cursor will wrap around to a new line even if the terminal does not have an autowrap feature. If we get to the bottom right of the screen with a long input line, there is no more echo on that line. If an input line is long enough, we more or less silently overrun our input buffer. If we cause an interrupt, **trap( )** reports receiving it, but the terminal echo is gone for good. Most of these effects are pleasant and show *curses* hard at work. The interrupt problem can be circumvented by calling **echo( )** from **trap( )**.

A Window Calculator

curses do not only handle **stdscr** and **curscr**. Input and output functions like **getch( )** and **addch( )** in reality are macros calling functions such as **wgetch( )** and **waddch( )** which reference an output window explicitly by means of an extra first argument.

initscr( ) allocates one such window, designated by **stdscr**, and the simple input and output macros pass **stdscr** to the corresponding functions. **newwin( )** can be called to allocate a new window:

```
static WINDOW * cur;                    /* i/o window */

static _reply(fmt, ap)                  /* show response */
{       ...
        wprintw(cur, "\t%s\n", buf);
}

main()
{       int top = 10, left = 20, lines = 5, cols = 40;
        ...
        initscr(), on_screen = 1;
        echo(), nocbreak();

        if (! (cur = newwin(lines, cols, top, left)))
                fatal("no window");
        scrollok(cur, TRUE);

        setjmp(on_response);
        for (;;)
        {       wgetstr(cur, buf);
                ...
```

newwin( ) takes dimensions and origin of a window and returns a pointer to a **WINDOW** data structure. This pointer plays the same role as **FILE** in the *stdio* library: it identifies the input or output connection for the various *curses* functions. As the example shows, it takes very little to confine our calculator to a small area in the center of the screen. Scrolling is now limited to the **cur** window, and the output from a *set* command is rather interesting to watch, especially if we make our window a bit larger.

Windows cannot be larger than **stdscr** and their allocation by **newwin( )** requires dynamic memory. **newwin( )** returns a null pointer, if the desired window cannot be created. It is fairly simple to arrange for our calculator to run in several windows on the same screen. We shall return to this topic in Chapter 4.

3.5 Boxes and Subwindows

Really professional windows have borders. *curses* provide a function **box( )** that will draw on the outermost rows and columns of a window. Used alone, this function does not help much. By default, **newwin( )** starts us out in the top left corner. If we call **box( )**, the cursor remains unchanged† and **wgetstr( )** will read the first input line right on top of the border. Eventually, the border will disappear through scrolling.

We are in trouble even if we follow each input and output function with a new call to **box( )**. Automatic end of line wrapping happens at the right edge of the window, i.e., right on top of our border. Scrolling happens if we emit a newline on the bottom row of the window – once again on top of the border.

It is a good idea to let *curses* handle things like autowrap and scrolling, since our own code would probably be less elegant, and it would certainly duplicate portions of *curses*. What we need is a way to have the box in one window and the dialog in a smaller window just inside. To help us conserve dynamic memory, *curses* provide **subwin( )** for just such a purpose:

```
main()
{       int top = 10, left = 20, lines = 5, cols = 40;
        ...
        if (! (cur = newwin(lines, cols, top, left)))
                fatal("no window");
        box(cur, 0, 0), wrefresh(cur);
        if (! (cur = subwin(cur, maxy(cur)-2, maxx(cur)-2,
                       begy(cur)+1, begx(cur)+1)))
                fatal("no window");
        scrollok(cur, TRUE);
        ...
```

subwin( ) takes an existing window pointer, dimensions, and origin for a new window. The dimensions cannot exceed those of the original window. The origin is absolute on the physical screen, not relative to the existing window, but we can use our macros **begy( )** and **begx( )** to arrange for relative positioning. If all goes well, **subwin( )** returns a pointer to the new subwindow.

---

† ...maybe.

Here we allocate a window with five lines, draw the box, and use **wrefresh( )** to show the box on the terminal screen. (Yes, thus far we have quietly relied on **wgetstr( )** to refresh the window implicitly, just before new input is read!)

Since we will no longer touch the box, we have assigned the subwindow pointer to **cur**, effectively losing any access to the surrounding window. The rest of the program can remain unchanged, and scrolling works just fine inside the box.

Unfortunately, subwindows are not quite windows in good standing. The manual *curses*(3) specifies that a subwindow must be freed with **delwin( )** before the original window can be destroyed using **delwin( )**. This otherwise innocent statement can only be taken as a strong hint that a subwindow shares memory with the original window. A slight extension to our program lets us demonstrate the problem:

```
main(argc, argv)
        int argc; char ** argv;
(       int lines = atoi(argv[1]), ... ;
        WINDOW * out;

        ...
        if (! (out = cur = newwin(lines, cols, top, left)))
                fatal("no window");

        ...
        for (;;)
        (       wgetstr(cur, buf);
                if (strcmp(buf, ".") == 0)
                (       touchwin(out), wrefresh(out);
                        continue;
                )
                ...
```

Now we save the pointer to the border window **out** and arrange to refresh this window once an input line contains a single period. For testing, we make the number of lines in the calculator window selectable from the command line. If zero is passed as a dimension to **newwin( )** or **subwin( )**, the functions will extend the dimension to the border of the physical screen or the surrounding window.

Things work just fine with a five-line window. If, however, we start out with a bigger window, and refresh the border window after the subwindow has scrolled, the call to **wrefresh(out)** appears to scroll the interior *down* by one line! A careful look at the definition of **WINDOW** in *curses.h* reveals that the window content is stored as a vectorized matrix:

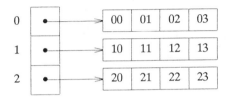

Scrolling simply means rotating the pointers to the line vectors. A subwindow will share a part of each line vector, but since it need not start at the left edge of the surrounding window, it has its own pointers to the line vector parts. Scrolling a subwindow, therefore, will result in a scrambled appearance when the surrounding window is refreshed.

touchwin( ) must be called prior to **wrefresh**( ): *curses* establish no internal connection between a subwindow and its surrounding window, otherwise the **delwin**( ) calls could be implied. If there is no connection, however, changing the subwindow does not mark the surrounding window as having been changed. If a window is not marked as having been changed somewhere, **wrefresh**( ) has no effect. **touchwin**( ) marks an entire window as changed.

As a footnote on testing software you might like to test this version of *wish* with various sizes for the calculator window. If there are five lines originally, the interior contains three lines. An input cycle normally affects exactly three lines, i.e., the pointer rotation from scrolling returns to the original state. The scrambling effect can only be seen on a larger window.

An Alternate Frame: *frame.c*

At long last, *curses* from release 3 of System V provide a portable way to get to line drawing characters. Constants like **ACS_ULCORNER** are defined in such a way that they will be displayed as a plus sign on a dumb terminal, and as the upper left corner from the line drawing character set if there is one.

Earlier *curses* might still provide a way to professional lines and corners, at least for a specific terminal. If **A_ALTCHARSET** is defined in *curses.h*, it can be passed just like an attribute to **addch**( ), together with a character code to be displayed. The catch is to select the character code in a portable fashion. Here is a kludge for the XENIX console:

```
#include <curses.h>

#if     defined(M_XENIX) && defined(A_ALTCHARSET) && ! defined(ACS_VLINE)
#       include <term.h>
#       define  _ACS_(a,b) (enter_alt_charset_mode ? A_ALTCHARSET | a : b)
#else
#       define  _ACS_(a,b) b
#endif
#ifndef ACS_VLINE
#       define  ACS_VLINE        _ACS_('3','|')
#       define  ACS_HLINE        _ACS_('D','-')
#       define  ACS_ULCORNER     _ACS_('Z','+')
#       define  ACS_URCORNER     _ACS_('?','+')
#       define  ACS_LLCORNER     _ACS_('a','+')
#       define  ACS_LRCORNER     _ACS_('Y','+')
#endif
#define ACS_V2LINE      _ACS_(':',':')
#define ACS_H2LINE      _ACS_('M','=')
#define ACS_UL2CORNER   _ACS_('I',':')
#define ACS_UR2CORNER   _ACS_(';',':')
#define ACS_LL2CORNER   _ACS_('H',':')
#define ACS_LR2CORNER   _ACS_('<',':')
```

The XENIX C compiler defines **M_XENIX** to identify itself. If the attribute **A_ALTCHARSET** is also defined and the special character **ACS_VLINE** is not, we base the selection for the special characters on the *terminfo* capability **enter_alt_charset_mode**. If this string value is not a null pointer, i.e., if a value was assigned to **smacs** in the *terminfo* entry for the terminal, we define the alternate character for the character value '**3**' as a vertical line character.

Which real characters correspond to the desired alternate characters is the kludge: **M_XENIX** is characteristic of the XENIX C compiler, not of the XENIX console. By relying on **enter_alt_charset_mode**, we cannot be entirely sure that we will get the correct appearance. If the terminal name is **ansi**, we could be more certain, but that would require a string comparison.

The capability names for *terminfo* are not part of *curses*. They must be obtained from an extra header file *term.h* which is quite large.

Given the special character names, we could write a replacement for **box()**. More flexible, however, are perhaps the following two functions:

```
int wframe(wp, nrows, ncols, y, x)            /* draw a frame */
        register WINDOW * wp;
{
        return box(wp, nrows, ncols, y, x, ACS_VLINE, ACS_HLINE,
                ACS_ULCORNER, ACS_URCORNER, ACS_LLCORNER, ACS_LRCORNER);
}

int wframe2(wp, nrows, ncols, y, x)           /* draw a double frame */
        register WINDOW * wp;
{
        return box(wp, nrows, ncols, y, x, ACS_V2LINE, ACS_H2LINE,
                ACS_UL2CORNER, ACS_UR2CORNER, ACS_LL2CORNER, ACS_LR2CORNER);
}
```

wframe() adds a single-line frame to a window with the top left corner given in window coordinates, and with dimensions interpreted as for **newwin()**. Line drawing character sets usually contain double lines as well, and we define **wframe2()** to draw a double-lined frame. Both functions are based on an internal function **box()** that takes care to leave the cursor unchanged:

```
static int box(wp, nr, nc, y, x, v, h, ul, ur, ll, lr)  /* draw fancy box */
        register WINDOW * wp;
{       register int i = ERR;
        int wy, wx;

        getyx(wp, wy, wx);

        if (! nr) nr = wp -> _maxy - y; /* extend to border */
        if (! nc) nc = wp -> _maxx - x;
        nr += y-1, nc += x-1;           /* last one */

        if (mvwaddch(wp, y, x, ul) != ERR && mvwaddch(wp, y, nc, ur) != ERR
            && mvwaddch(wp, nr, x, ll) != ERR)
        {       if (wp -> _begy + nr != LINES-1 || wp -> _begx + nc != COLS-1)
                        mvwaddch(wp, nr, nc, lr);
```

```
                        for (i = x + 1; i < nc; ++ i)
                                mvwaddch(wp, y, i, h), mvwaddch(wp, nr, i, h);
                        for (i = y + 1; i < nr; ++ i)
                                mvwaddch(wp, i, x, v), mvwaddch(wp, i, nc, v);
                        i = OK;
                }
                wmove(wp, wy, wx);
                return i;
        }
```

wframe( ) and **wframe2**( ) are general functions which we might well use in other projects. We therefore place them in their own file *frame.c* so that they may be added to a private library.

3.6 Scrolling

Executing a *set* command in our calculator usually produces a large amount of output since all environment variables will be shown as well. If we watch the output in the current version of *wish*, at least on XENIX, we actually see all variable values scroll past. Since we have not used **wrefresh**( ), that should certainly come as a surprise.

The fine print in the System V Interface Definition (1986) hints at a possible explanation. *curses* provide a function **scroll**( ) to cause a window to scroll up one line. **scroll**( ) is supposed to try to use the terminal's own scrolling capability. This might be conveniently implemented by letting scrolling imply something like **refresh**( ). If **scrollok**( ) is set, adding a newline character to the bottom line of a window could conceivably behave just like **scroll**( ), so...

The really funny part is that − once again on XENIX − adding the newline will refresh the state *prior* to scrolling, while calling **scroll**( ) will *not* imply a screen refresh. In both cases, only the next call to **wrefresh**( ) shows the lines actually scrolled. For *wish* this does not matter. The next call to **_reply**( ) will add another newline, cause a scroll operation, and implicitly refresh again. The final call to **wgetstr**( ) also needs to refresh before it can read a new buffer. All in all, we see the environment variables fly, but by now a certain uneasy feeling might accompany the 'movie'.

It seems wise to call **scroll**( ), rather than writing a newline in **_reply**( ). Following that, we should only see the tail end of a series of calls to **_reply**( ), since now only **wgetstr**( ) implies a screen refresh. Therefore, we add pagination to **_reply**( ):

```
        static int nscroll;                     /* count down to more */

        static _reply(fmt, ap)                  /* show response */
                register char * fmt;
                register va_list ap;
        {       char buf[CLEN];

                if (-- nscroll == 0)
                {       scrollok(cur, FALSE);
                        mvwaddstr(cur, maxy(cur)-1, 0, "more? "), wrefresh(cur);
                        nscroll = wgetch(cur) == 'q' ? 0 : maxy(cur) - 2;
                        wmove(cur, maxy(cur)-1, 0), wclrtoeol(cur);
                }
```

```
                scrollok(cur, TRUE);
                vsprintf(buf, fmt, ap);
                waddch(cur, '\t'), waddstr(cur, buf);
                if (cury(cur) == maxy(cur)-1)
                        scroll(cur), wmove(cur, maxy(cur)-1, 0);
                else
                        waddch(cur, '\n');
        }

        main()
        {       ...
                for (;;)
                {       wgetstr(cur, buf);
                        nscroll = maxy(cur);
                        ...
```

Once a new input line has been read, we permit **maxy(cur)** scroll operations, i.e., we let at most the current content of the window be scrolled up. If there are more calls to _reply( ), we ask if our user wants to see **more?**.

Since the answer might contain a newline, and since we are certainly at the bottom of the window at this point, we turn scrolling off during the query, so that we can reliably erase query and answer with **wclrtoeol( )**. The query, however, might be interrupted, and we would get through **trap( )** and **response( )** back to _reply( ) and past the query. This is why we turn scrolling back on even if the query does not get entered in the first place.

Replies initially proceed from the top of the window on down. As long as we have not reached the bottom line, we output a newline to get to the next line for fresh input or another reply. Once we reach the bottom, we call **scroll( )** to avoid spurious physical output, and explicitly position to the bottom left corner of **cur**.

Preventing Autowrap

Have we now successfully controlled the 'visual noise' from implicit refresh operations provoked by outputting newline characters? Unfortunately... not quite. If scrolling is turned on, a long output line will be broken at the right edge of **cur** and continued onto the next line. If this happens at the bottom of a window, an implicit refresh operation happens even if our output no longer contains newlines! If we answer **q** once _reply( ) asks if we wish to see **more?**, the window might flicker on a few long lines and finally settle for the tail end of a series of replies.

It can be argued whether or not a terminal simulation in a window should really provide automatic wraparound at the right margin. We can prevent the effect by setting **scrollok( )** normally to **FALSE** and managing all newline effects explicitly. Output beyond the right margin on the bottom line of the window is then quietly thrown away.

Input, however, is still very quietly accepted – without an echo once we reach the right margin on the bottom line. The visually most acceptable solution is perhaps the following:

```
static _reply(fmt, ap)                  /* show response */
        register char * fmt;
        register va_list ap;
{       char buf[CLEN];

        scrollok(cur, FALSE);
        if (-- nscroll == 0)
        {       mvwaddstr(cur, maxy(cur)-1, 0, "more? "), wrefresh(cur);
                nscroll = wgetch(cur) == 'q' ? 0 : maxy(cur) - 2;
                wmove(cur, maxy(cur)-1, 0), wclrtoeol(cur);
        }
        vsprintf(buf, fmt, ap);
        waddch(cur, '\t'), waddstr(cur, buf);

        scrollok(cur, TRUE);
        if (cury(cur) == maxy(cur)-1)
                scroll(cur), wmove(cur, maxy(cur)-1, 0);
        else
                waddch(cur, '\n');
}
main()
{       ...
        for (;;)
        {       scrollok(cur, TRUE);
                wgetstr(cur, buf);
                nscroll = maxy(cur);
                ...
```

This time we use **scrollok**( ) not as a program state, but as a qualifier right before each input or output operation. Even a signal cannot bother us now. Input is accepted with scrolling enabled. Output is produced with scrolling (and thus autowrap) disabled. Following a reply, we move down using a newline, or we scroll explicitly.

So far, the solution only prevents autowrap if output is produced on the bottom line of the window. If a very long output line starts above the bottom line, it will still wrap around to the next line, but it cannot cause an implicit refresh. We can erase the autowrapped part with the following change:

```
        static _reply(fmt, ap)            /* show response */
        {       ...

                vsprintf(buf, fmt, ap);
                y = cury(cur);
                waddch(cur, '\t'), waddstr(cur, buf);

                scrollok(cur, TRUE);
                if (cury(cur) > y)
                        wmove(cur, y+1, 0), wclrtobot(cur);
                else if (cury(cur) == maxy(cur)-1)
                        scroll(cur), wmove(cur, maxy(cur)-1, 0);
                else
                        waddch(cur, '\n');
        }
```

We record the current output line in **y**. If we have moved down during output, we cannot have been at the bottom of the window, so we position explicitly to the beginning of the autowrapped part and erase the unwanted text with **wclrtobot( )**. At the bottom of the window, *curses* have prevented autowrap as discussed above.

Summary

Windows in *curses* are simple to use, at least at first glance. Four versions of most input and output functions provide equivalent service for **stdscr**, or for a window dynamically created through **newwin( )** or extracted with **subwin( )**. For example:

addch(ch)	add to stdscr
mvaddch(y, x, ch)	move and then add
waddch(wp, ch)	add to window wp
mvwaddch(wp, y, x, ch)	move and then add
getch()	receive in stdscr
mvgetch(y, x)	move and then receive†
wgetch(wp)	receive in window wp
mvwgetch(wp, y, x)	move and then receive†

If we want to see window contents, we need to use **refresh( )** or **wrefresh( )**. Unless we operate entirely within one window, we will have to use **touchwin( )** prior to the refresh operation, to encourage *curses* to consider the entire window changed.

Things get tricky once we scroll, mostly because of subtle 'features' in the scrolling, refreshing, and input editing algorithms. If we do not care about 'visual noise', i.e., if we are willing to wait for a lot of output to slowly crawl across a larger window on a heavily loaded system, we can use **scroll( )** or allow newline output with impunity. If we want to avoid the visual noise

---

† Moving in combination with input affects echo or subsequent output, but not necessarily the physical cursor position prior to input.

entirely, we can only use **scroll( )**, and we must suppress autowrap by not permitting scrolling under most circumstances.

Once we scroll a subwindow, we need to refresh the subwindow immediately after refreshing its original window. This is best accomplished using **wnoutrefresh( )** on the original window followed by **wrefresh( )** on the subwindow. Copying the subwindow back into the original window will most likely invite disaster.

This section has certainly shown that it pays not to duplicate code. We were easily able to experiment with various scrolling mechanisms, but only because we had a single output routine **_reply( )** and a single input call within **main( )**. Window states inadvertently form a finite state automaton, and it certainly helps if we have a clear idea of all possible transitions, so that we can maintain the states correctly.

3.7 A *curses* Desk Calculator: *cdc*

It turns out that not all *curses* functions behave as the System V Interface Definition (1986) would like them to. Some do not seem to work at all. Others have rather subtle side effects, such as an interrupt during some input functions turning off terminal echo, or **getstr( )** moving the cursor even if echo is turned off. We have found a special version *cdc* of the calculator to be quite handy, which supports interactive access to just about all *curses* functions. Implementing *cdc* is mostly straight forward, but we need to look at some of the more subtle aspects.

Window Variables

We start out with the desk calculator from Chapter 2. Since very many *curses* functions use a window pointer as an argument, we need to add such a data type to our system. Obviously, we would like a variable to have a window pointer value if, for example, the result from **newwin( )** is assigned to it. Here are the necessary extensions to the *yacc* source *calc.y*:

```
%union { int y_int; char * y_str; Symbol * y_sym; WINDOW * y_win; }

%token   <y_sym> Window
%token           Ivaluep, Wvaluep, w_I

%type    <y_win> we, w


...
%left            ARROW                    /* -> */
%%

stmt    : /* null */
        | we                     { reply("0x%lx", (data_p) $1); }

i       : ...
        | Ivaluep                { $$ = * (int *) $<y_sym>1 -> s_any; }
        | w ARROW w_I            { $$ = (* (int (*)()) $<y_sym>3 -> s_any)($1); }
```

```
lval    : Identifier          /* $$ = $1; */
        | Window              /* $$ = $1; */

we      : w                   /* $$ = $1; */
        | lval '=' we         { if ($1 -> s_yylex != Window)
                                {     unset($1);
                                      $1 -> s_yylex = Window;
                                }
                                $$ = $1 -> s_win = $3;
                              }

w       : Window              { $$ = $1 -> s_win; }
        | Wvaluep             { $$ = * (WINDOW **) $<y_sym>1 -> s_any; }
        | '(' we ')'          { $$ = $2; }
```

The type of attached values needs to be extended. An attached value can now be a **WINDOW ***. Of course, this requires that *curses.h* is included during compilation.

A variable in the symbol table can have a window pointer as a value. In this case it has the token value **Window**. The symbol table structure in *calc.h* needs to be extended with a new alternative **.s_win**:

```
typedef struct symbol Symbol;
        struct symbol {
                ...
                union { long s_aval;     /* first; >= any pointer */
                        WINDOW * s_wval;
        ...
        #define s_win    s_val.s_wval
```

Of course, now we have to include *curses.h* wherever we include *calc.h*. Unfortunately, *curses.h* cannot be included more than once, so it is not wise to include *curses.h* at the beginning of *calc.h*.

Since we want to access window components, we need a new operator **ARROW** with very high precedence for structure selection. The component names will be added to the symbol table with our generator program *mky*, but we need to write an explicit formulation for the **ARROW** operation. Therefore, we define component names as a token **w_I**.

Now we are ready to add to the rules. A window expression **we** is another **stmt**; the attached value is a window pointer value. **reply()** will show the value using hexadecimal digits to help our user keep track of new windows. Unfortunately, pointer values cannot always be cast as integer values and displayed with **printf()** integer format elements. Casting as **long** and displaying a long value is more portable, but XENIX requires different casts for data and text pointers depending on the memory model. We add the following to *calc.h*:

```
                                         /* pointer casts for display */
#ifdef  M_I86SM                          /* 8086 small model */
#       define  text_p  long)(unsigned
#       define  data_p  long)(unsigned
#else
#ifdef  M_I86MM                          /* 8086 middle model */
#       define  text_p  long
#       define  data_p  long)(unsigned
#else
#       define  text_p  long
#       define  data_p  long
#endif
#endif
```

Unlike string values, window pointer values cannot be destroyed at the statement level. It is up to the user to manage properly all window pointers. Without a large coding effort, we have no chance to reclaim all unused window memory or to prevent illegal access to *curses* functions. *cdc* is supposed to simulate real use of *curses* as well as possible – ignoring the stray pointer problem is about par for the course.

The **ARROW** operation combines a simple window expression **w** with a component name **w_I** and produces an integer value. The cast in the associated action is perhaps exciting:

```
      | w ARROW w_I          ( $$ = (* (int (*)()) $<y_sym>3 -> s_any)($1); }
```

Access to the value is, of course, by means of a function stored with the reserved word. The function address in the generic component **.s_any** is cast as a pointer to a function returning an **int** value, and the function is called with the window pointer value as an argument.

Window variables are a new kind of **lval**, i.e., they can be assigned to. Of course, we need to check that **unset()** does not get confused by the new token value. It is best to check every use of **.s_yylex** in the symbol table module *sym.c*. It turns out that **lval** can be exported. For **Window** variables, such a request is best silently ignored.

Window expressions are designed just like integer or string expressions. A window expression **we** can be a simple window expression **w** or the assignment of a window expression value to a variable. This is where a symbol is turned into a **Window**. The assignment action follows the pattern established for integers and strings. If the symbol is not a **Window**, it must be **unset()** and turned into a **Window**. Then the pointer value can be stored in **.s_win**.

Finally, a simple window expression **w** can be a reference to a **Window** variable, i.e., to the value stored as **.s_win**. It can also be a window expression in parentheses. In this way we can assign a window pointer and look at a component within a single expression.

Lastly, we need access to the constants **stdscr** and **curscr** defined by **initscr()**. These values, however, cannot be stored as constants in the symbol table, since they are declared **extern** in *curses.h*. We can store pointer values to those external pointers, so that the action for **Wvaluep** can get to the appropriate values.

Ivaluep is introduced to take care of a similar problem with the *curses* values **LINES** and **COLS**. These values are initialized by **initscr()** and we can once again only store pointers to the variables within *curses* in the symbol table.

The *lex* source in *scan.l* requires but one change. A pattern to recognize an **ARROW** needs to be added.

scan.l must include *calc.h* during compilation, since the type for attached values makes a reference to **Symbol**. This type now also references **WINDOW** and we include *curses.h*. Unfortunately, **ECHO** is now defined twice: *curses.h* pulls in the information to control the terminal driver, where **ECHO** is a flag, and *lex* defines **ECHO** as an action to copy **yytext[ ]** to standard output. Undefining **ECHO** just before *curses.h* is included corrects the problem. In an extreme case we could fake a definition for **WINDOW** without including *curses.h*, since a pointer to a structure can be used without the structure definition.

Extending the Symbol Table Manager

Scanning with the editor for all uses of **.s_yylex** helps: in all cases we need to consider possible new token values. **Window** can show up wherever **Integer** and **String** are referenced. **Ivaluep** and **Wvaluep** are new concepts similar to **Ivalue** integer built-in values.

This is where **switch** statements help, because they provide a nice table control structure. It turns out that **unset()** was robust to begin with and need not be changed. New **cases** must be added to the dump functions **dump1_set()** for variables and **dump1_const()** for built-in values.

Windows cannot be in the environment. This is a place where several functions cooperate to implement a single feature. We have, however, carefully avoided code duplication. If we keep **envset()** from turning **.s_export** on for a **Window**, it can never become part of the environment. It can be argued whether or not we should provide an error message in this case. We chose not to.

Adding the Functions

If we had not automated the tedious task of adding functions already in Section 2.7, now would certainly be the time to do it! *curses* simply has too many functions to even consider doing it by hand.

mky already takes care of some aspects. Adding attribute or key constants, or even things like **stdscr** or **COLS** does not require any new code. Here are some typical name table entries:

```
#include <curses.h>
#include "wish.h"

version        Svalue       "cdc\0401.0"

A_ATTRIBUTES   Ivalue
KEY_DOWN       Ivalue

COLS           Ivaluep      &COLS
LINES          Ivaluep      &LINES

curscr         Wvaluep      &curscr
stdscr         Wvaluep      &stdscr

addch          I_i          #if
addstr         I_s          #if
```

No new ideas thus far. *mky* even handles a few simple *curses* macros correctly. Alas, the following entries illustrate slight complications on the way to *cdc*:

```
_begx          w_I
_begy          w_I


begx           I_w              #if
begy           I_w              #if


erasechar      C_
newwin         W_i_i_i_i
getyx          I_w_li_li        Getyx


copywin        I_w_w_i_i_i_i_i_i
```

w_I clearly is a special case. A function must be built to accept a window pointer and return the component value. Here is a typical result from *extern.i*:

```
static int _Begx(wp) WINDOW * wp; { return wp -> _begx; }
static int _Begy(wp) WINDOW * wp; { return wp -> _begy; }
```

Window pointer values can be function arguments. This poses a slight problem if the 'function' is a macro and we have to build a calling function. Fortunately, parameters were already allowed to be strings and we just need to add another case. Here is a typical result:

```
#ifdef  begx
int Begx(v1)
        WINDOW * v1;
(        return begx(v1); }
#else
int begx();
#define Begx      begx
#endif
```

erasechar() could really return an integer value. Unfortunately, *curses.h* defines it **extern** with **char** as return type. To avoid a declaration clash, we need to introduce a character return type in *extern.i*, but we can then handle it just like an integer value.

newwin() shows that we need to support **WINDOW *** as a return value. Now we get new elements for **head[ ]** and **tail[ ]**, since we need to build a new class of actions. Here is the grammar part that applies to **newwin()**:

```
w       : W_i_i_i_i '(' ie ',' ie ',' ie ',' ie ')'
              { $$ = (* (WINDOW * (*)()) $1 -> s_any)($3, $5, $7, $9); }
stmt    : W_i_i_i_i   { dump_class(W_i_i_i_i); }
```

Functions like **getstr()** are variations on the theme introduced by **strcat()**. The resulting string value must be assigned to a variable, i.e., we need to write a function **Getstr()** which will receive a symbol table pointer argument rather than a string.

getyx() introduces the last complication, at least as far as supporting *curses* in the desk calculator grammar is concerned. This time we assign to integer variables. It turns out that the rules are already correctly generated by *mky*, since from the point of view of the grammar, the parameter specifications _ls_ and _li_ both require **lval** in the formulation. A function **Getyx**() is then expected to perform the actual assignment.

copywin() demonstrates the power of *mky*. This entry in the name table requires no new technology anymore, but the rule certainly would be tedious to write.

Processing a File

A first release of *cdc* is now very easy to put together. If we are content to write our *curses* calls into a file, we can specify the file as an argument to *cdc* and essentially turn the desk calculator loose:

```
#define USAGE(x)        fatal("cdc [-o file] file...")

static char on_screen;              /* set if initscr() */
static FILE * ofp;                  /* -o out */

MAIN
{       char obuf[BUFSIZ];

        import();

        if (signal(SIGINT, SIG_IGN) != SIG_IGN)
                signal(SIGINT, exit);

        OPT
        ARG 'o': PARM                   /* -o outfile */
                if (ofp) fclose(ofp);
                if (! (ofp = fopen(*argv, "w")))
                        fatal("%s: cannot create", *argv);
                setvbuf(ofp, _IOLBF, obuf, sizeof obuf);
                NEXTOPT
        OTHER
                USAGE(cdc.1);
        ENDOPT

        initscr(), on_screen = 1;

        if (argc)
                do
                        file(*argv);
                while (++ argv, -- argc);
        else
                USAGE(cdc.1);

        return 0;
}
```

The **MAIN** macros (Schreiner, 1987) take care of the ugly details of parsing the command line. It might be nice to see a log of inputs and replies and so we open a log file and arrange for line buffering. *cdc* thus far is a very typical filter. Following option processing, the actual work for each argument file is done by a function **file( )**:

```
static jmp_buf on_response;              /* restart calculator */

static file(fnm)
        register char * fnm;
{       register FILE * fp;
        char buf[CLEN], * bp;

        if (strcmp(fnm, "-") == 0)
                USAGE(cdc.1);
        else if (! (fp = fopen(fnm, "r")))
                fatal("%s: cannot open", fnm);

        if (ofp)
                fprintf(ofp, "# file: %s\n", fnm);

        setjmp(on_response);
        while (fgets(buf, sizeof buf, fp))
        {       if (ofp)
                        fputs(buf, ofp);

                bp = buf + strlen(buf) - 1;
                if (*bp != '\n')
                        fatal("%s: line too long", fnm);
                *bp = '\0';

                if (*buf == '!')
                        System(buf+1);
                else
                        lexi_buf(buf), yyparse();
        }

        fclose(fp);
}
```

This code, too, is taken right from a textbook on filters. We open the input file, exclude the case of − as a file name, i.e., of processing standard input in place of a file, and start reading lines. Each line is copied to the log file, if any, and then the trailing newline is clipped. If there is a shell escape, we let a new function **System( )** handle it. Otherwise we can fire up our calculator.

The calculator responds by calling the same functions as before, and everything is channeled eventually into **_reply( )**:

```
static _reply(fmt, ap)                    /* show response */
        register char * fmt;
        register va_list ap;
{
        if (ofp)
                fputs("#\t", ofp),
                vfprintf(ofp, fmt, ap),
                putc('\n', ofp);
}
```

If we compile at this point, a few entry points are found to be missing. This comes as no surprise, since *mky* had to be instructed through the name table to let a few *curses* functions be intercepted so that we could assign to variables. A typical example is the **getstr** group:

```
Mvwgetstr(wp, y, x, sp)
        register WINDOW * wp;
        int y, x;
        register Symbol * sp;
{       char buf[CLEN], * strsave();
        int n;

        n = mvwgetstr(wp, y, x, buf);
        unset(sp);
        sp -> s_yylex = String;
        sp -> s_str = strsave(buf);
        return n;
}
```

Here is another example, the **getyx** group:

```
static preget(y, x)
        register Symbol * y, * x;
{
        unset(x);
        x -> s_yylex = Integer;
        unset(y);
        y -> s_yylex = Integer;
}

Getyx(wp, y, x)
        register WINDOW * wp;
        register Symbol * y, * x;
{
        preget(y, x);
        return getyx(wp, y -> s_int, x -> s_int);
}
```

Endwin() is simply implemented as a call to **exit**(), and **Initscr**() calls **response**() to complain about being called twice.

Excursion to the Shell

We have arranged to pass lines beginning with **!** to the shell for execution. This is usually accomplished by a call to **system**(3). Therefore, we support **system**( ) as a built-in function, too. We need to connect the call to our own function, however, since we must **export**( ) the environment and persuade *curses* to release the terminal screen to the shell:

```
System(s)                                /* fix export and screen */
        register char * s;
{       register int n;

        crt_off();
        export(), n = system(s);
        crt_on("Press return to continue");
        return n;
}
```

crt_off( ) has already been introduced as part of our own **exit**( ) and **fatal**( ). Here is the inverse function. If **crt_on**( ) is called with a string argument, it will print it as a prompt, wait for the user to reply, and then turn the terminal screen back over to *curses*:

```
crt_on(s)                                /* get back on */
        register char * s;               /* prompt */
{
        clearok(curscr), on_screen = 1;
        if (s)
        {       static FILE * tty;

                fprintf(stderr, "\r\n%s ", s);

                if (! tty && ! (tty = fopen("/dev/tty", "r")))
                        fatal("/dev/tty: cannot open");
                clearerr(tty);
                for (;;)
                        switch (getc(tty)) {
                        case EOF:
                        case 'D' & 31:
                        case '\r':
                        case '\n':
                                return;
                        }
        }
}
```

clearok(curscr) is one of the few operations that can be performed with **curscr**. It instructs *curses* to clear and repaint the terminal screen from scratch upon the next **refresh**( ). Prior to that we prompt the terminal and read a reply. By using */dev/tty* we can make sure that we do not interfere with any buffering mechanisms elsewhere. We read from the terminal up to a line termination or to an end of input indication. Since we do not know what state the terminal is in, we also accept **\r** as an end of line. **clearerr**(3) is called to clear any end of file condition left from a previous call to **crt_on**( ).

Simulating the Cursor

How do we read statements from the terminal and provide a faithful simulation of *curses* at the same time? We saw in the preceding sections that the statements can be read in a window and the replies can be scrolled. However, the terminal has only one physical cursor. Statements and replies will pretty much trap that cursor in the dialog window, and our simulation will be far off when it comes to *curses* input functions, where the current (user) cursor position is quite important.

There appears to be no completely portable way to fiddle with the physical cursor. We would like to remember its position right after our user executes one of the **refresh** functions, and we would like to place the cursor at that position just before any input function. Things would be very simple, if **getyx(curscr, y, x)** would always return the physical cursor position. Unfortunately, this is not the case.

As a first approximation, we can note the current cursor position once **refresh**( ) or **wrefresh**( ) are called. While **wnoutrefresh**( ) does not move the physical cursor, since no output is sent to the terminal, it still decides where the cursor will be after the next **doupdate**( ) operation. These considerations lead to the following code:

```
static struct { int y, x; }
        last = { -1, -1 },          /* user's last wnoutrefresh() */
        phys = { -1, -1 );          /* user's physical cursor */

static notecursor(wp)               /* note user's physical cursor */
        register WINDOW * wp;
{
        if (wp)
                phys.y = begy(wp) + cury(wp),
                phys.x = begx(wp) + curx(wp);
        last.y = -1;
}


Doupdate()
{
        if (last.y != -1)
                phys = last, last.y = -1;
        return doupdate();
}


Refresh()
{
        return Wrefresh(stdscr);
}
```

```
Wnoutrefresh(wp)
        register WINDOW * wp;
{       register int n;

        clip(wp);
        n = wnoutrefresh(wp);    /* returns random value?? */
        last.y = begy(wp) + cury(wp);
        last.x = begx(wp) + curx(wp);
        return n;
}

Wrefresh(wp)
        register WINDOW * wp;
{       register int n;

        clip(wp);
        n = wrefresh(wp);          /* returns random value?? */
        notecursor(wp);
        return n;
}
```

phys is the physical cursor; **last** tracks the last window passed to **wnoutrefresh()**. Any physical output operation, i.e., **doupdate()** or **wrefresh()**, reflects its result in **phys** and clears **last**.

We will run a dialog in the last **cline** lines of the terminal screen in a command window **cur**. If there is a dialog, or if file commands are to be echoed to the dialog area, **cur** should not be wiped out by user operations. Therefore, we must keep **wnoutrefresh()** and **wrefresh()** from writing on that part of the screen occupied by **cur**. We have added calls to the following function **clip()** which does just that:

```
static WINDOW * cur;                /* i/o window */
static int cline;                   /* -c cmdlines */
static char vflag;                  /* -v: verbose */

static clip(wp)                     /* clip cur out of wp */
        register WINDOW * wp;
{       register int y;

        if (vflag && wp)
        {       wp -> _clear = 0;
                for (y = maxy(wp); begy(wp) + -- y >= begy(cur); )
                        wp -> _firstch[y] = wp -> _lastch[y] = -1;
        }
}
```

clip() is not quite portable because we access hidden components of the **WINDOW** structure. The components can be found by reading the header file *curses.h*. We clear the **clearok()** flag **._clear** so that the terminal screen is not physically erased. We set **_firstch[ ]** and **_lastch[ ]** to

-1 in all those lines of **wp** that cover lines in **cur**. The vector elements indicate the changed part of each line, and we pretend that there was no change in the overlapping area.

vflag is introduced to keep things honest. We still call all *curses* functions directly to avoid any inconsistencies which we might otherwise introduce. If **vflag** is not set, **clip**() will not introduce any side effects to protect **cur**.

Unfortunately, *curses* must implicitly refresh the terminal screen if input is read with echo turned on. These implicit refresh operations must be curtailed by **clip**() and tracked by **notecursor**() just like the explicit calls above:

```
#define getcursor(wp)    (state.s_noecho || notecursor(wp))


Mvgetch(y, x)
        register int y, x;
{
        return Mvwgetch(stdscr, y, x);

}


Mvwgetch(wp, y, x)
        register WINDOW * wp;
        int y, x;
{       int ch;

        clip(wp);
        ch = mvwgetch(wp, y, x);
        getcursor(wp);
        return ch;

}
```

Eight† input functions must be protected in this fashion: the four versions of **getch** and the four versions of **getstr**.

Now we know more or less how the user's calls on *curses* influence the physical cursor. One operation cannot be simulated. If **leaveok**() is set to **TRUE**, *curses* may leave the physical cursor at the end of a refresh operation wherever it is convenient. Cursor movement then is optimized and our simulation may well be too conservative in calculating the cursor position.

Simulating the Terminal State

What do we do with the cursor coordinate information in **phys**? Basically, we should use it to reposition the physical cursor just before executing commands, and restore the cursor to the command window, if any, just before reading the next command.

However, the cursor is not the only problem. The terminal driver has only one current state. Various *curses* functions like **echo**(), **cbreak**(), or even **nodelay**(), influence the terminal driver state. As long as user function calls are processed, this is the desired state, but it may do very funny things to our attempts at reading statements from the terminal inbetween. We are

---

† We cannot support the variable length argument lists of the **scanw** and **printw** families.

led to maintaining separate terminal states just as we maintained a separate user cursor position:†

```
static struct {                         /* user          command */
        int s_typeahead;                /* typeahead(n) typeahead(0) */
        unsigned s_cook : 2;            /* 1: cbreak()  0: nocbreak() */
                                        /* 2: raw() */
        unsigned s_noecho : 1;          /* noecho()      echo() */
        unsigned s_nonl : 1;            /* nonl()        nonl() */
        unsigned s_nointrflush : 1;     /* ...(,FALSE)  ...(,TRUE) */
        unsigned s_nodelay : 1;         /* ...(,TRUE)   ...(,FALSE) */
} state;

#define user_nl(flag)   (! state.s_nonl && (flag == TRUE ? nl() : nonl()))

static user_state(flag)                 /* volatile state monitor */
        int flag;                       /* TRUE: user, FALSE: command */
{       static int old = FALSE;         /* initially in command state */
        static WINDOW * cursor;         /* fake physical cursor move */
        register int cy, cx;

        if (flag == old)
                return;
        old = flag;

        user_nl(flag);
        if (flag == TRUE)
        {       if (state.s_typeahead) typeahead(state.s_typeahead);
                ...
                if ((cy = phys.y) < 0 || (cx = phys.x) < 0)
                        return;
        }
        else
        {       if (state.s_typeahead) typeahead(0);
                ...
                cy = begy(cur) + cury(cur), cx = begx(cur) + curx(cur);
        }

        if (! cursor)
                cursor = newwin(1, 1, 0, 0);

        mvwin(cursor, cy, cx);
        cursor -> _firstch[0] = cursor -> _lastch[0] = -1;
        wrefresh(cursor);
}
```

† The function **newterm( )** can be used to set up further terminal connections in one *curses* program. **set_term( )** is then used to switch between the terminals. This approach, however, would probably cause our screen to flicker. Another pair of functions, **savetty( )** and **resetty( )**, does not save and restore enough of the terminal state for our faithful purposes.

user_state(FALSE) restores our dialog situation; **user_state(TRUE)** will put the terminal into the proper state for the simulation. It turns out that **nodelay( )** is supposed to be window specific, but at least on our test system this is not the case. All input and output option settings now need to influence the state structure. Here is an example:

```
Cbreak()        { state.s_cook = 1; return cbreak(); }
Nocbreak()      { state.s_cook = 0; return nocbreak(); }
```

Once again we also call the *curses* function directly, to make sure the simulation is faithful as long as we do not interfere with a dialog. It helps to support a function **sane( )** to restore default conditions to a messed-up terminal:

```
Sane()                              /* set default conditions */
{
        Typeahead(0);
        Nocbreak();
        Echo();
        Nl();
        Intrflush(stdscr, TRUE);
        Nodelay(stdscr, FALSE);
}
```

user_state( ) positions the physical cursor according to the desired state. We use a one character window **cursor** for the necessary **wrefresh( )** operation. With **mvwin( )**, the window is positioned at the user's cursor position as recorded in **phys** or in the command window **cur**. Because **mvwin( )** marks the window as changed, we reset the changed range before calling **wrefresh( )**. This way, only the physical cursor is positioned on the terminal and no other information is changed.

Running the Dialog

What about the dialog? It turns out that our discussion of scrolling in Section 3.6 was entirely sound, even for this simulation. We just need to add calls to **user_state( )** to protect **refresh** and input operations:

```
static _reply(fmt, ap)              /* show response */
        register char * fmt;
        register va_list ap;
{       char buf[CLEN];
        int y;

        scrollok(cur, FALSE);
        if (-- nscroll == 0)
        {       user_state(FALSE);
                mvwaddstr(cur, maxy(cur)-1, 0, "more? "), wrefresh(cur);
                nscroll = wgetch(cur) == 'q' ? 0 : cline - 2;
                wmove(cur, maxy(cur)-1, 0), wclrtoeol(cur);
```

```
                    user_state(TRUE);
            }
            vsprintf(buf, fmt, ap);
            ... see Section 3.6 ...
```

Yes, we can call **wrefresh(cur)** since **cur** is small and does not overlap the user's area on the terminal screen. This will only confuse the issue, if the user has called **wnoutrefresh( )** but not **doupdate( )** on the same line. Here is the creation of **cur** in **main( )**:

```
        MAIN
        {       ...
                OPT
                ARG 'c': PARM                   /* -c cmdlines */
                        cline = atoi(*argv);
                        NEXTOPT
                ...
                ARG 'v':                        /* -v: input file echo */
                        vflag = 1;
                OTHER
                        USAGE(cdc.1);
                ENDOPT

                initscr(), on_screen = 1;
                nonl();

                if ((cline < 3 || cline >= LINES)
                    && (cline = LINES/3) < 3
                    && (cline = 3) >= LINES)
                        fatal("screen too small");

                if (! (cur = newwin(cline, COLS, LINES - cline, 0)))
                        fatal("no window");

                if (argc)
                        do
                                file(*argv);
                        while (++ argv, -- argc);
                else
                        terminal();

                return 0;
        }
```

terminal( ) is a new function which does the actual dialog management. It is more or less a copy of the main program from Section 3.6, but we add a shell escape and a way to recall the last non-blank input line by typing **!!**. Of course, we need to call **user_state( )** in the right places:

```
static terminal()
{       static char old[CLEN];          /* history */
        char buf[CLEN];

        if (ofp)
                fputs("# terminal\n", ofp);

        ++ vflag;                       /* flag get functions */

        setjmp(on_response);
        if (signal(SIGINT, SIG_IGN) != SIG_IGN)
                signal(SIGINT, trap);

        for (;;)
        {       user_state(FALSE);
                scrollok(cur, TRUE);
                do
                        wgetstr(cur, buf);
                while (strlen(buf) == 0);
                if (strcmp(buf, "!!"))
                        strcpy(old, buf);
                else
                        strcpy(buf, old),
                        mvwaddstr(cur, cury(cur)-1, 0, buf),
                        waddch(cur, '\n'),
                        wrefresh(cur);
                nscroll = cline;
                if (*buf == ('D' & 31))
                        break;
                if (ofp)
                        fputs(buf, ofp), putc('\n', ofp);
                if (*buf == '!')
                        System(buf+1);
                else
                        user_state(TRUE),
                        lexi_buf(buf), yyparse();
        }

        if (signal(SIGINT, SIG_IGN) != SIG_IGN)
                signal(SIGINT, exit);

        -- vflag;
}
```

We should not connect **SIGINT** to **trap**() while **on_response** no longer points to an active procedure. A **longjmp**() at the wrong moment might have unfortunate consequences.

file() must process statements from file arguments. **file**() now calls **user_state**(), since file and terminal processing might be intermixed. We have taken care that **user_state**() leaves well enough alone as long as the desired state has not changed.

As an optimization, we only correct the state of **nl**() with **user_nl**() around a refresh operation. **nonl**() prevents mapping of *return* to **\n** during terminal input and of **\n** to *return* followed by *newline* during terminal output. Because of its surprise effect on input, **nonl**() is not the default, but it lets *curses* do a better job of output optimization.

```
static file(fnm)
        register char * fnm;
{       register FILE * fp;
        char buf[CLEN], * bp;

        if (strcmp(fnm, "-") == 0)
                return terminal();
        else if (! (fp = fopen(fnm, "r")))
                fatal("%s: cannot open", fnm);

        if (ofp)
                fprintf(ofp, "# file: %s\n", fnm);

        if (setjmp(on_response))
        {       user_state(FALSE);
                scrollok(cur, FALSE);
                mvwaddstr(cur, maxy(cur)-1, 0, "more? ");
                touchwin(cur), wrefresh(cur);
                if (wgetch(cur) == 'q')
                        exit(1);
                wmove(cur, maxy(cur)-1, 0), wclrtoeol(cur);
        }
        while (fgets(buf, sizeof buf, fp))
        {       if (vflag)
                {       user_nl(FALSE);
                        scrollok(cur, TRUE);
                        waddstr(cur, buf), wrefresh(cur);
                        nscroll = cline;
                }
                if (ofp)
                        fputs(buf, ofp);

                bp = buf + strlen(buf) - 1;
                if (*bp != '\n')
                        fatal("%s: line too long", fnm);
                *bp = '\0';

                if (*buf == '!')
                        System(buf+1);
                else
                        user_state(TRUE),
                        lexi_buf(buf), yyparse();
        }

        fclose(fp);
}
```

We can add logic to echo file statements to the dialog area if **vflag** is set. If it is not, we at least show the dialog area if an error happens, i.e., if we return to **file( )** from **response( )**. In this case we give the user an opportunity to terminate *cdc* gracefully.

Conclusion

Clearly, *cdc* is an aside, at least as far as building the window shell is concerned. The program, however, makes two important contributions to our problem. It is a very useful interactive testbed for *curses* functions in general, and the simulation shows a number of subtle specifics.

curses have bugs, or perhaps 'features', which especially tend to bother casual users. *cdc* supports executing *curses* calls one at a time to study their effect. We found the simulation faithful enough to untangle numerous sticky problems.

We have not concealed two known *curses* bugs in *cdc* as a reminder for the uninitiated: the interrupt interception in **trap( )** does not reset **echo( )**, and **exit( )** does not reset **nodelay( )**. If **getstr( )** is interrupted with a signal, echo will be lost. If **nodelay( )** is not set back to FALSE prior to exiting *cdc*, the terminal can no longer be used. We did discover these and other *curses* bugs by using *cdc*, and it seemed unreasonable to conceal them.

## CHAPTER FOUR

A View Manager
vm.c

4.1 Design

Section 1.4 described the finished view manager and its module architecture. In this chapter we study design and implementation and try to motivate the solution. Once again, a recurring theme is extensibility. The view manager should support a variety of applications, as long as each application does not require more than our basic functionality of line input and scrolled output within a resizable window. This pattern, however, fits multi-file viewing, listening to processes, and perhaps interaction with other programs, multi-file editing, etc.

We start with a very simple basic idea. Beginning in Section 3.4 we saw how we can confine our desk calculator to part of a terminal screen. The logical next step is to manage several calculator windows, more or less independently, on different parts of the screen, move them around, change their size, let them overlap, etc.

At any given time there is one 'current' calculator window. Only by an explicit action can another calculator window become current and listen to our input. Clearly, the current window has to lie on top of all the others and be completely visible. Since we anticipate overlap, it is best to surround each calculator window by a frame.

A certain amount of order on our screen seems desirable. We want to be able to hide unused calculators. Either we permit moving them mostly off-screen, or we just keep *icons* as place markers around. A calculator now has three more or less independent parts: the icon version when not in use, the frame, and its interior. This is where the concept of a *view* and the data structure **View** described in Section 1.4 are born.

Should each view have its own independent calculator? Or should all calculators share the same symbol table? While this is an interesting topic to pursue, it definitely leads into more compiler construction and symbol table management, and we will not deal with it here. We stick to a single, common symbol table and consider the views more or less as a way to get more communication areas onto a single terminal.

We will probably erase and redraw icons, frames, and interiors quite often. The only way to make something appear back on top of the terminal screen is to call **wrefresh( )** for some window. While we can erase a window by filling it with blanks, other windows appear from underneath only if they are refreshed. We need to track the order in which views are brought to the top to update the terminal screen correctly once a view is removed. The easiest way to remove a calculator probably is to fill the entire terminal screen with blanks and then redraw all icons, frames, and interiors beginning with the bottom one.

Redrawing is cheaper if we do not need to recompute. If we keep the various icons, frames, and interiors as separate windows, we need more memory, but we save on computing time. A blank terminal screen is best represented as **stdscr** because this window can logically be considered to be underneath all other windows.

The *View* Structure

```
typedef struct view View;
    struct view {
            WINDOW * v_icon;        /* icon */
            WINDOW * v_frame;       /* frame() */
            WINDOW ** v_sub;        /* [NSUB] interiors */
            WINDOW * v_view;        /* current: icon or sub[v_now] */
            int v_pid;              /* secondary process */
            unsigned v_top;         /* counts top calls */
            short v_seq;            /* used to sort by top calls */
            unsigned char v_now;    /* current interior */
            char * v_user;          /* user's extension */
    };
```

At this point, most components of **View** have evolved. There is not yet any need to store a process number in **.v_pid**. Exchanging interiors like pictures in a frame is also not yet required, i.e., the component **.v_now** would be invented later, and **.v_sub** is most likely a pointer and not the start address of a vector. Still, we will continue our presentation with the final data structure to avoid rehashing trivial changes in Chapter 5.

How do we keep track of the sequence in which views are brought to the top? If we do not, we can only refresh views according to their names, i.e., their position in some vector. One way to keep track is to reorder the vector of views whenever a view is brought to the top, but then we would have to store the name of a view inside **View** and referencing a view by name would involve a search. Another technique is to stamp a view with a new, higher number whenever the view is brought to the top. If we redraw the terminal screen or select a previous view, we need to sort views according to these numbers. Views may be too large to move, so we use an index vector with elements stored as part of each **View**. We will call the numbers **.v_top** and the vector elements **.v_seq**.

Finally, we need to know the current state of a view: is it an icon or a frame, and if it is a frame, which picture is in it? While the picture is (later) identified by **.v_now**, the difference between icon and frame state could be encoded as a flag. When we refresh the screen, however, we will have to refresh at least one window per view for either state. It saves some code if we encode the state as a pointer **.v_view** to the current window, i.e., the icon or the interior. The application will only be confronted with open views and **.v_view** is a convenient way to pass the window onto which the application is supposed to draw.

In the next section we will see that our application also maintains some view-specific data items. To keep the view manager totally independent of the application, we only support a pointer **.v_user** in **View**. The application can attach a convenient data structure at this pointer and access it using a suitable cast.

Access Macros

Integrity of the **View** data structure is crucial to view management. We will certainly separate application programming from managing the views, but some components of **View** must be accessible by both. A secure way to hide information is to grant access to **View** only through functions in the view management module. A less restrictive but more efficient version of this idea is to encapsulate components as *access macros* defined in the same header file as **View**. If only access macros are used in application programming, we have a single place where they are bound to **View**. Here are the published components of **View**:

```
#define vframe(vp) ((WINDOW *) (vp) -> v_frame) /* frame window */
#define view(vp)   ((WINDOW *) (vp) -> v_view)  /* current (sub)window */
#define vnow(vp)   ((vp) -> v_now)               /* current interior */
#define vpid(vp)   ((vp) -> v_pid)               /* secondary process */
```

If we need to, we can easily replace an access macro by a function and thus control or trace its use. The casts cause no additional code to be generated, but they do prohibit using a macro call as target of an assignment.

Module Structure

View management is separate from application programming. The common information is in a header file *view.h*. How do we design the interface between the view manager *vm.c* and an application such as *wish*?

Judging by our desk calculator in Section 3.4, the application expects to be called with a window pointer, or perhaps a **View**, in which it can conduct its business. The application will release control because of some input such as end of file, or because of an interrupt. Some applications might provide control statements to invoke view management explicitly.

This analysis suggests embedding an application into view management as the main program. Then the view manager can initialize screen processing, intercept signals to catch an interrupt, and call the application as a subroutine. Additionally, the view manager must offer a function to be called for explicit view manipulations.

Either **main()** is now part of the view manager and the application starts with a standard name like **application()**, or we reserve **main()** for the application and insist that the view manager be called for initialization. The latter approach has advantages. The application can first process command arguments and then pass initialization options to the view manager.

Where is the main loop? The interface is a lot simpler if the view manager runs the application, rather than the application having to issue standard calls to the view manager as part of the main loop. Consequently, the application calls the view manager for initialization and passes the actual application processor as a function parameter to the initialization routine, which then executes the main loop.

This follows the standard pattern for filters and other UNIX utilities. **main()** analyzes the command line, extracts options, and calls a processor function for each file argument. Here, the application's main program can extract options before it lets the view manager call the application's processor function. The view manager is simply a layer within the driving mechanism of the program, and this layer has the job of turning a single terminal into multiple and perhaps independent views.

If the application wants to run different tasks in different views, it needs to dispatch work in the processor function passed to the view manager. We shall elaborate on this technique in the remaining chapters.

4.2 A View Calculator

Before we turn to implementing the view manager, let us look at a version of the desk calculator which uses views. **main( )** can be simple enough:

```
#include <signal.h>

main()
{
        vcatch(SIGFPE);
        vcatch(SIGSYS);
        vmain(command, ... );
        return 0;
}
```

The desk calculator provides access to library functions and system calls, and we have to anticipate some strange signals. Either we tie all signals to **response( )**, or we use a view manager function **vcatch( )** to arrange for screen processing to terminate gracefully before our process is aborted by a strange signal.

Our main program from Section 3.6 is turned into a function **command( )** to be called by the view manager's main loop **vmain( )**. At this point, it is not clear if we need more parameters and how they might be passed. We will present a general solution for this problem in Section 4.6.

What about the other functions? **_reply( )**, **reply( )**, **response( )**, and **yyerror( )** are application specific and remain with the calculator in *wish.c*. **_reply( )** now uses a current view **vcur** which is posted by **command( )**. Functions such as **crt_off( )**, **exit( )**, and **fatal( )** are general services provided by the view manager and are moved to *vm.c*. Before it runs the calculator dialog, **command( )** is responsible for setting the terminal state:

```
static View * vcur;              /* current view */
static jmp_buf on_response;      /* restart command */
static int nscroll;              /* count down to more */

static command(vp)               /* run command language */
        View * vp;
{       register WINDOW * cur;
        char buf[CLEN], * bp;

        echo(), nocbreak();
        vcur = vp;
        cur = view(vcur);
        wmove(cur, cury(cur), 0), wclrtoeol(cur);
```

```
            setjmp(on_response);
            for (;;)
            {       scrollok(cur, TRUE);
                    do
                    {       wgetstr(cur, buf), bp = trim(buf);
                            if (*bp == ('D' & 31))
                                    return;
                    } while (! *bp);

                    if (strcmp(bp, "!!"))
                            strcpy(vhistory(vp), bp);
                    else
                            strcpy(bp = buf, vhistory(vp)),
                            mvwaddstr(cur, cury(cur)-1, 0, buf),
                            waddch(cur, '\n'),
                            wrefresh(cur);

                    nscroll = maxy(cur);
                    lexi_buf(bp), yyparse();
            }
    }
```

command( ) posts the current view as **vcur** and accesses the current window **cur** with the access macro **view( )**. It turns out later that **command( )** should clear the current line in **cur**: if **_reply( )** is interrupted while asking for **more?**, the view manager may call **command( )** again, but not with the cursor at the left margin of a blank line.

```
    static char * trim(bp)                   /* clip leading/trailing blanks */
            register char * bp;
    {       register char * tp = bp + strlen(bp);

            while (isspace(*bp))
                    ++ bp;
            while (tp -- > bp && isspace(*tp))
                    *tp = '\0';
            return bp;
    }
```

trim( ) is a convenience for our user: after reading an input buffer, we clip its leading and trailing white space. If the input line is empty, we can immediately read another one.

We have taken a cue from *cdc* and installed the simple history mechanism. For each view, the most recent non-empty input line is kept in a buffer **vhistory(vp)** and recalled through **!!**. The access macro **vhistory(vp)** references an application-specific part of the view data structure. We have provided a pointer component **.v_user** in **View** to attach another structure, and **vmain( )** will have to be persuaded to allocate memory. Our own structure **User** is defined in *wish.h* thus far as follows:

```
#define CLEN     256                /* command buffer (unchecked) */


typedef struct user User;
        struct user {
                char u_history[CLEN];
                };


#define _vu(vp)        ((User *) (vp) -> v_user)
#define vhistory(vp)   (_vu(vp) -> u_history)  /* last input */
```

The proper component selector is a bit tricky and we hide it behind an access macro.

View Management Options

This is all it takes to run our calculator in several views. We have merely skipped the details of the call to **vmain( )**:

```
vmain(command,

                V_LUSER, sizeof(User),
                V_INFO, info,
                V_SIG, SIGINT,
                0);
```

vmain( ) has a very large number of options to tailor view management to the needs of an application. Rather than insisting on a fixed order for a huge argument list, or employing a concealed argument structure, we will implement a variable length, variable order argument list. The user function to be run by **vmain( )** is the mandatory first argument. Other arguments are introduced by an identifying value such as **V_LUSER** to pass the length of the buffer to be attached to each **.v_user**. The identifier is usually followed by another argument such as the length value or a signal number, etc. The argument list is terminated if the identifying value is zero. Clearly, the identifiers are defined in *view.h*.

   User contains the history buffer and we need to pass its length. We also need to pass a signal number so that the view manager supports an interrupt to enter view management. Finally, the appearance of the frame surrounding an open view is controlled by the application. The view manager will only write the view name in the top left corner. We pass an information function which the view manager will call when a view is topped:

```
static info(vp)                          /* identify current view */
        register View * vp;
{       register WINDOW * wp = vframe(vp);

        wframe2(wp, 0, 0, 0, 0);
}
```

Commands for View Management

Because our calculator provides access to library functions, we can use the macro processor to add new commands:

```
def quit kill(getpid(), SIGTERM)        # quit wish
def vm   kill(getpid(), SIGINT)         # manage views
```

SIGTERM is caught and reissued by the view manager to put the terminal back into a normal state before termination. Since we did not make different arrangements, **SIGTERM** will terminate our process, and we tie the signal to a simple command word through the macro.

SIGINT was set up as the signal to enter view management. The macro **vm** demonstrates that we could use almost arbitrary signals for this purpose. (Yes, there are some reasons for supporting the C library, constants, and system calls in the desk calculator!)

We can, however, add more interesting commands to the calculator language. The view manager supports a function **vm( )** which is intended for entering view management from an application. The function could be added to our desk calculator, or specific calls can be hidden behind new commands. Since **vm( )** restarts the main loop in **vmain( )** and does not return, we add the new commands at the input buffer level of our grammar:

```
buffer  : stmts
        | CW ie                 { vm(0, $2); /* range?? */ }
        | DW                    { vm('d'); }
        | FW                    { vm('f'); }
```

cw changes to a new view† specified as a number or character constant. **dw** sets the default view, **fw** sets the full screen as the view. The difference between these commands and the macro based on **kill( )** is that **vm( )** can pass an argument. After a signal we still need to read a character to select the desired operation.

4.3 A View Manager: *vm.c*

A few pieces of the view manager can be taken from previous calculator releases: **crt_off( )**, **exit( )**, and **fatal( )** have been developed in Chapter 3; **crt_on( )** can be taken from *cdc* in Section 3.7. Building **vcatch( )** is a trivial exercise:

---

† *change window* is probably the better mnemonic for the user of *wish*. **cv** and *vish* would sound rather fishy to the German author.

```
#include <signal.h>

static int (* oldsig[SIGTERM - SIGHUP + 1])();   /* intercepted signal state */

static quit(sig)                              /* terminated by signal */
        register int sig;
{
        crt_off();
        signal(sig, oldsig[sig - SIGHUP]);
        kill(getpid(), sig);
}

vcatch(sig)                                   /* soft signal() */
        register int sig;
{
        assert(sig >= SIGHUP && sig <= SIGTERM);
        if ((oldsig[sig - SIGHUP] = signal(sig, SIG_IGN)) != SIG_IGN)
                signal(sig, quit);
}
```

If we publish only **vcatch( )** but not **quit( )**, we can be sure that only those signals arrive in **quit( )** which have been properly connected in **vcatch( )**. Signal names are portable, but the numerical values are not. **assert( )** is a safeguard against dubious conventions.

The Main Loop: *vmain( )*

As environment for a *curses* program **vmain( )** takes its cues from Section 3.2. The actual application is passed as a function parameter, and for the moment we can assume that this is the only one:

```
static View * views, * cur;          /* all and current view */
static WINDOW * noicon;              /* current icon cover */
static int vsig;                     /* signal to get to vm() */
static jmp_buf on_vm;                /* vm()'s exit to vmain() */

int vmain(command)
        int (* command)();
{       int i, (* oldvsig)();
        unsigned luser = 0;

        import();

        vcatch(SIGHUP);
        vcatch(SIGINT);
        vcatch(SIGQUIT);
        vcatch(SIGTERM);
```

```
if (vsig)
        oldvsig = signal(vsig, SIG_IGN);

initscr(), on_screen = 1;
nonl();

if (vsig)
        prompt();
refresh();

for (i = 0; i < NVIEW; ++ i)
        make(i, luser);
if (! (noicon = newwin(ILINE, ICOL, 0, 0)))
        fatal("no room");
```

So far, we import the environment for the desk calculator, intercept typical signals, and set up for screen processing. **nonl**() improves output performance in *curses* because *newline* is no longer followed by *return* on output. On input, however, we will receive *return* as **\r** and not as **\n**.

If the view manager is connected to a signal, the signal number must be in **vsig** and we display the available options with **prompt**(). We clear the terminal screen with **refresh**() since allocating all the necessary windows will take some time.

Calling **import**() technically makes the view manager application dependent. This call could just as well be moved to precede the call to **vmain**() in the application. However, suspending view management on the screen and executing a shell is a standard service that our view manager should always provide. Before we can use **exec**(2) to start another process, conventions in our desk calculator require us to call **export**(). Either we include code to call a shell with each application, or we let the view manager access **export**() as well.†

We are ready for the main loop of *wish*. We still need to set up an exit for the view management function **vm**(), and if required we connect **vsig**, but then...

```
if (i = setjmp(on_vm))
        i -= VIEW0;
if (vsig)
        signal(vsig, vmsig);
while (i >= 0)
{       vopen(cur = views + i), doupdate();
        (* command)(cur);
        vclose(cur);
        i = select();
}
if (vsig)
        signal(vsig, oldvsig);
doupdate(), crt_off();
return 0;
}
```

† Die-hard purists can use the technique shown in Section 4.6 to pass both functions as optional arguments of **vmain**().

Initially, **setjmp**(3) returns zero. Later, the return value is set as argument to **longjmp**() and we decode it as a view number relative to the first view name **VIEW0**. Unless the resulting value is negative, it is an index in the array **views**[ ] of **View** data structures, and we let **cur** point to the view about to be managed.

vopen() and **vclose**() are central functions of the view manager. **vopen**() is responsible for opening a view and bringing it to the top of the screen. **vclose**() will close the view, i.e., return it to icon state. **select**() returns the index of the view which was most recently brought to the top of the screen.

A view is closed if the user's function (***command**)() returns. If **select**() cannot find another open view, it returns -1 and the main loop ends. If set, we reset the view management signal **vsig**, before we terminate screen processing with a call to **crt_off**() and return from **vmain**().

doupdate() is called to output whatever changes **vclose**() may have made. Normally, **vclose**() is followed by **vopen**(), and to avoid partial refresh operations we produce all output with calls to **wnoutrefresh**() and call **doupdate**() only once a new arrangement of views is completely set up.

We have silently omitted parameter passing and the associated declarations. This part can be safely postponed until Section 4.6. We have also assumed a few new functions: **prompt**() needs to display a menu of view management options available following an interrupt. **make**() must allocate all required windows and the user buffers; **luser** will later be passed as a parameter. **noicon** is a blank window which will be used to cover the icon of the current view. For the moment, **ILINE** and **ICOL** could be defined constants. **vopen**() and **vclose**() each manipulate a view. Finally, **vmsig**() is entered in response to the view management signal **vsig**. This function needs to set up a call to the view management function **vm**() which will return to the top of the main loop with **longjmp**().

Management Menu

An interesting **prompt**() is an exercise in attributes. Options are selected by single characters, which are the initials of words describing each option. If possible, we should highlight the initial:

```
static prompt1(s, a)              /* show one option */
        register char * s;        /* option */
        register int a;           /* highlight */
{
        addch(' '), addch(*s | a), addstr(s+1);
}
```

Open views or icons are not allowed to cover the prompt. Therefore, we store it permanently on **stdscr**. Attributes can be passed together with a character to **addch**(). Highlighting, however, may cause a gap on certain terminals. We let **prompt**() check the *terminfo* description to avoid stuttering:

```
#include <term.h>

static prompt()                          /* show interrupt options */
{        register int a = magic_cookie_glitch > 0 ? 0 : A_STANDOUT;

#define length  ( sizeof "interrupt to" - 1 \
                + sizeof " close" - 1 \
                + sizeof " default" - 1 \
                + sizeof " full" - 1 \
                + sizeof " move" - 1 \
                + sizeof " quit" - 1 \
                + sizeof " size" - 1 \
                + sizeof " ! shell" - 1 \
                + sizeof " 0-9 select" - 1 \
                )

        if (COLS <= length)
                fatal("screen too small");
```

magic_cookie_glitch should indicate if there is a problem. If not, **A_STANDOUT** is supposed to be an attribute denoting the terminal's best highlighting mode − and our user certainly deserves nothing less!

We would like to center the prompt on the terminal screen. Rather than counting ourselves, we let C perform the chore. **length** is introduced to make the text easier to maintain. While we cannot prevent text duplication entirely, we can at least make it convenient to change things:

```
        move(PLINE, (COLS - length)/2);
        a && standout(), addstr("interrupt"), standend();
        addstr(" to");
        prompt1("close", a);
        prompt1("default", a);
        prompt1("full", a);
        prompt1("move", a);
        prompt1("quit", a);
        prompt1("size", a);
        prompt1("! shell", a);
        addch(' '), addch(VIEW0 | a);
        addch('-'), addch((VIEW0 + NVIEW - 1) | a);
        addstr(" select");

#undef  length
}
```

PLINE, the prompt line on the terminal screen, and **NVIEW**, the number of managed views, can be additional defined constants.

Allocating Views

make( ) has the job of creating all dynamic data structures for a single view. Each view needs a vector of picture pointers, **.v_sub**. For our desk calculator we can assume the number of interiors of a view **NSUB** to be one. Later, it might be a parameter. Next, a view might have a user buffer attached to it. If we cannot allocate either one, we are in real trouble:

```
static make(i, luser)                      /* allocate views[i] */
        int i, luser;
{       register View * vp = views + i;
        register WINDOW * wp;
        int j;
        char * calloc();

        if (! (vp -> v_sub = (WINDOW **) calloc(NSUB, sizeof(WINDOW *)))
            || luser > 0 && ! (vp -> v_user = calloc(1, luser)))
                fatal("no room");
```

Next, a view gets a frame window and the first interior as a subwindow. The default size and position of the frame could again be defined constants:

```
        if (! (wp = vp -> v_frame = newwin(FLINE, FCOL, FY(i), FX(i)))
            || ! (vp -> v_sub[0] = subwin(wp, maxy(wp)-2, maxx(wp)-2,
                                              begy(wp)+1, begx(wp)+1)))
                fatal("no room");
```

Further interiors cannot be subwindows. They are allocated as new windows with the same size and position as the first interior:

```
        for (j = 1; j < NSUB; ++ j)
            if (! (vp -> v_sub[j] = newwin(maxy(wp)-2, maxx(wp)-2,
                                             begy(wp)+1, begx(wp)+1)))
                    fatal("no room");
```

Finally, the icon is allocated, surrounded by a frame, and marked with the view name. Defined constants can supply icon size and position. Most views are initially in icon state, therefore, we arrange for the icon to be displayed:

```
        if (wp = vp -> v_icon = newwin(ILINE, ICOL, IY(i), IX(i)))
        {       wframe(wp, 0, 0, 0, 0);
                mvwaddch(wp, ILINE/2, ICOL/2, VIEWO + i);
                wnoutrefresh(wp);
        }
        else
                fatal("no room");

        vp -> v_view = vp -> v_icon;
}
```

make( ) sets **.v_view** to indicate icon state for the new view.

Changing View States: *vopen( )* and *vclose( )*

make( ) allocates a new view in icon state. The next function in the life of a view is **vopen( )**. The view manager can call this function with a new view pointer and thus really access a view in icon state. The application only knows a current view pointer and can use **vopen( )** to redisplay the current open view with a new interior. Thus it is safe to publish **vopen( )**.

```
vopen(vp)                     /* display current view */
        register View * vp;
{       static unsigned call;

        mvwin(noicon, begy(vp -> v_icon), begx(vp -> v_icon));
        if (vp -> v_view == vp -> v_icon)
                touchwin(noicon), wnoutrefresh(noicon);
        vp -> v_view = vp -> v_sub[vp -> v_now];

        if (vinfo)
                (* vinfo)(vp);

        mvwaddch(vp -> v_frame, 0, 0, VIEW0 + (vp - views));
        touchwin(vp -> v_frame), wnoutrefresh(vp -> v_frame);

        touchwin(vp -> v_view), wnoutrefresh(vp -> v_view);

        vp -> v_top = call ++;         /* record topping sequence */
}
```

   vopen( ) always moves the icon cover **noicon** to the view's icon position. The icon cover is blank, refreshing it will effectively conceal the view's icon on the terminal screen. Of course, we need to call **touchwin( )** to persuade *curses* to add all those blanks to the next output.
   vopen( ) makes any open view the top one on the terminal screen. Since the application is allowed to change **.v_now**, i.e., to insert a new picture into the frame prior to calling **vopen( )**, we correct the pointer **.v_view** to the current interior in **vopen( )**.
   With the current interior set up, we call an information function **vinfo** so that the application can scribble on the new top frame. Finally, we add the view name to the frame and make sure that the frame and the entire current interior are sent to the terminal.
   vclose( ), unfortunately, needs to redraw the terminal screen if we really close an open view. We redraw **stdscr** to erase all icons and open views. Then, we redraw the frames of all open views and **.v_view**, i.e., icon window or current interior, for all views. Without *curses*, this would cause considerable flicker on the terminal screen, but we delegate computing the actual output to **doupdate( )** to keep the flicker to a minimum:

```
static vclose(vp)                   /* erase current view, display icon */
        register View * vp;
{       register int i;

        if (vp -> v_view != vp -> v_icon)
        {       vp -> v_view = vp -> v_icon;
                touchwin(stdscr), wnoutrefresh(stdscr);
                topsort();
                for (i = 0; i < NVIEW; ++ i)
                {       vp = views + views[i].v_seq;
                        if (vp -> v_view != vp -> v_icon)
                                touchwin(vp -> v_frame),
                                wnoutrefresh(vp -> v_frame);
                        touchwin(vp -> v_view), wnoutrefresh(vp -> v_view);
                }
        }
}
```

Another little complication is that the order in which views were brought to the top should be preserved. **vopen( )** has stamped a sequence number into each open view. Before we redraw, we sort the views according to these sequence numbers. Rather than moving views, we move index components within each view. **qsort**(3) only sorts a contiguous array and thus cannot be used for this purpose; therefore, we borrow Shell's sort from Kernighan and Ritchie (1988):

```
static topsort()                    /* Shell-sort v_seq by topping sequence */
{       int gap, i, j;
        short temp;

        for (i = 0; i < NVIEW; ++ i)
                views[i].v_seq = i;
        for (gap = NVIEW/2; gap > 0; gap /= 2)
                for (i = gap; i < NVIEW; ++ i)
                        for (j = i - gap; j >= 0
                                && views[views[j].v_seq].v_top
                                        > views[views[j+gap].v_seq].v_top;
                                j -= gap)
                        {       temp = views[j].v_seq;
                                views[j].v_seq = views[j+gap].v_seq;
                                views[j+gap].v_seq = temp;
                        }
}
```

Yes, the code definitely reminds one of a once-famous television commercial.†

---

† It's ugly, but it gets you there! (An add for the Volkswagen 'Beetle' showing the lunar excursion module.)

Selecting Views

We are almost off and running. **select()**, of course, sorts the views just like **vclose()** did, but it then searches from last to first to find the most recently topped view not in icon state:

```
static int select()                     /* find open view */
{       register int i = NVIEW;
        register View * vp;

        topsort();
        while (i --)
        {       vp = views + views[i].v_seq;
                if (vp -> v_view != vp -> v_icon)
                        return vp - views;
        }
        return -1;
}
```

A first release of the view manager is completed, but without a view management signal and the view management function **vm()** we cannot really get to a new view. **vm()** returns to the top of the main loop where the view management signal is set up again and the application's processor is restarted. This function is required to set the terminal state. Therefore, **vmsig()** can be rather brutal about getting an input character:

```
static vmsig(sig)                       /* manipulate view -- signal entry */
        register int sig;
{
        signal(sig, SIG_IGN);           /* reset in vmain() */
        noecho(), cbreak();             /* reset by application */
        wmove(noicon, ILINE/2, ICOL/2), wrefresh(noicon);
        vm(wgetch(noicon), 0);
}
```

The icon cover **noicon** is over the icon position of the current view. If we read a character through the center of **noicon**, we really place the terminal cursor at the icon position of the current view as a quiet reminder to our user. **vm()** is now required to sort the options out:

```
vm(ch, code)                            /* manipulate view */
        register int ch;                /* command */
        register int code;
{       int ncur = cur - views, next = VIEW0 + ncur;

        switch (ch) {
        case 0:                         /* select by code */
                ch = code < ' ' ? VIEW0 + code : code;
        default:                        /* select by letter */
                if (ch >= VIEW0 && ch < VIEW0 + NVIEW)
                        next = ch;
                break;
```

```
case 'c':                       /* close */
        vclose(cur), doupdate();
        next = VIEW0 + select();
        break;
case 'D' & 31:                  /* end of file */
case 'q':                       /* quit */
        exit(code);
}
longjmp(on_vm, next);
}
```

prompt( ) indicated that there are more cases to the **switch**, but for a first release this is quite sufficient. **case 0** is for the benefit of the application, which can pass a view name in **code** as a small number or as a printable character. **default** will catch illegal choices and existing view names alike; an illegal choice will simply restart the application processor in the current view. *control*-D is for the benefit of average UNIX users, who expect that character to terminate a program.

4.4 Excursion to the Shell

vm( ) offers an option ! to suspend view management, return the terminal to a normal state, and execute a shell. The whole feature is typical for interactive UNIX programs, but it requires special care in the context of our view manager. We could just call the function **System**( ) used in *cdc*, but **System**( ) uses **system**(3) and it would call a shell just to execute another shell. Therefore, we program our own expedition:

```
vm(ch, code)                    /* manipulate view */
{       ...

        switch (ch) {
        case '!':               /* shell */
                shell();
                break;
        ...
```

shell( ) must call a shell from a dialog program. Kernighan and Pike (1984) have discussed a number of possible complications. One does not apply: applications of our view manager will always use *curses*, so we can be relatively sure that standard input and output are connected to a terminal. Another complication is real: we need to protect the view manager, and thus the application, from terminal signals while the shell is running. If we do not, the shell survives, but the suspended view manager process could be terminated and then its caller competes with the shell for the terminal.

```
static shell()
{       register int pid;
        register char * shell;
```

```
    char * getenv();
    char * prompt = "Press return to continue";
    int (* sigint)(), (* sigquit)();

    if (! (shell = getenv("SHELL")))
            shell = SHELL;

    crt_off();
    fprintf(stderr, "%s:\n", shell);

    switch (pid = fork()) {
    case -1:
            perror(shell);
            break;
    case 0:
            export(), execl(shell, "-sh", (char *) 0);
            perror(shell);
            _exit(127);
    default:
            sigint = signal(SIGINT, SIG_IGN);
            sigquit = signal(SIGQUIT, SIG_IGN);
            while (vwait((int *) 0) != pid)
                    ;
            signal(SIGINT, sigint);
            signal(SIGQUIT, sigquit);
            prompt = (char *) 0;
    }

    crt_on(prompt);
}
```

As a special touch, we check the environment variable **SHELL** for the path name to call. This way we can set up a private shell, or even editors like *vi* or *ed*, as hosts of the excursion.

One would normally search the environment just once, and remember **shell** as a **static** pointer. Our own version of **getenv()** from Section 2.5 will definitely return a dynamic string which we cannot preserve through a simple pointer. Even the library function **getenv**(3) does not necessarily return a permanent result because the library function **putenv**(3) can be used to substitute a new pointer!

Process Management: *vwait( )*

The system call **wait**(2) is used to wait for termination of a process created with **fork**(2). We will later control different processes from different views. Therefore, a simple **wait**() might well return a different process number while we are waiting for our shell to run to completion. Throwing an unexpected process number away is not advisable because sooner or later the responsible view will be looking for it. Prematurely perhaps, but nevertheless, we introduce **vwait**() to post process numbers with views:

```
int vwait(sp)                           /* record completion */
        int * sp;                       /* return status here */
(       register int pid;
        register View * vp = views + NVIEW;
        int (* oldvsig)();

        if ((pid = wait(sp)) != -1)
        (       if (vsig)
                        oldvsig = signal(vsig, SIG_IGN);
                while (vp -- > views)
                        if (vp -> v_pid == pid)
                                vp -> v_pid = 0;
                if (vsig)
                        signal(vsig, oldvsig);
        )
        return pid;
)
```

Applications must cooperate. If they start a process in a view, they must post the process number in **vpid(vp)**. If a view wants to look for its process, it should call **vwait**( ) only if **vpid(vp)** is not zero. In a parallel processing situation the return value can be ignored since it has been posted. If **vpid(vp)** is now zero, the view's own process has terminated.

The model is sufficient for a single process per view. We can even use the view management signal **vsig** to interrupt the wait mechanism. There is a small possibility that we loose a process number if a signal arrives before we can post the process number, but the gap is fairly small.

4.5 Changing Windows

Windows can be moved or their size can be changed. A move will not change window contents, as long as we do not permit a window to be moved off the terminal screen. Resizing, however, requires some rearranging of the content. Either operation starts as an option in **vm**( ):

```
vm(ch, code)                            /* manipulate view */
(       ...

        switch (ch) (
        case 'm':                       /* move */
                shift(cur);
                break;
        case 's':                       /* size */
                size(cur);
                break;
        ...
```

The moving function **shift( )** and the resizing function **size( )** both follow the same pattern. The terminal cursor is set to a significant position, arrow keys may be used to place it to a reasonable new position, and the resulting position is used as parameter for the operation. To move a view, we move the top left corner; to resize a view, we move the bottom right corner. In both cases we must restrict possible cursor positions to something less than the full screen:

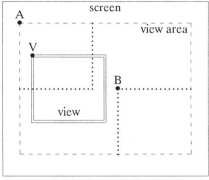
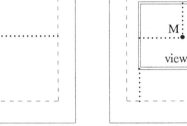

shift( ): V between A and B   **size( ):** W between M and C

Clearly, we package pointing the cursor as a separate function **point( )** with a window argument to restrict the cursor's freedom. **point( )** expects the cursor to start out at the current position within the window and returns the new position as current position in the window. The only problem is to start out with the proper window in the first place.

    shift( ) is the easier situation. The possible window is limited by the points A and B in the diagram. If the top left position of the view area is defined as **AY, AX** and the size as **ALINE, ACOL**, the window has the same origin and is just small enough to accommodate the current view at the bottom right:

```
static shift(vp)                    /* move top left of frame */
        register View * vp;
{       register WINDOW * wp;        /* range for cursor */
        int i, y, x;

        if ((y = ALINE+1 - maxy(vp -> v_frame)) <= 1
            || (x = ACOL+1 - maxx(vp -> v_frame)) <= 1
            || ! (wp = subwin(stdscr, y, x, AY, AX)))
                return;

        y = begy(vp -> v_frame) - begy(wp);
        x = begx(vp -> v_frame) - begx(wp);
        wmove(wp, y, x);                /* point cursor */
```

```
        if (! setjmp(on_point))
        {       if (vsig)
                        signal(vsig, pointed);

                point(wp);
                y = begy(wp) + cury(wp), x = begx(wp) + curx(wp);

                remake(vp, maxy(vp -> v_frame), maxx(vp -> v_frame), y, x);

                if (vsig)
                        signal(vsig, SIG_IGN);
        }
        delwin(wp);
}
```

Note that we need to compute the initial cursor position as the top left of the current frame, but relative to the new window. The result needs to be translated back in a similar fashion.

If the current view already occupies the entire area available to views, or if pointing is interrupted by the view management signal **vsig**, we simply return from **shift( )**. Otherwise we let a new function **remake( )**, a close relative of **make( )**, worry about view movement.

size( ) is a similar exercise in analytic geometry. This time pointing starts out at W and is restricted by the bottom right corner C of the viewing area and some minimum required view size at M. If we assume the minimum size as some constants **MLINE, MCOL**, we can reduce resizing also to calls on **point( )** and **remake( )**:

```
    static size(vp)                         /* move bottom right of frame */
            register View * vp;
    {       register WINDOW * wp;           /* range for cursor */
            int i, y0, x0, y, x;

            getbegyx(vp -> v_frame, y0, x0);

            if ((y = y0 + MLINE - 1) >= AY + ALINE - 1
                || (x = x0 + MCOL - 1) >= AX + ACOL - 1
                || ! (wp = subwin(stdscr, AY + ALINE - y, AX + ACOL - x, y, x)))
                    return;

            y = y0 + maxy(vp -> v_frame) - 1 - y;
            x = x0 + maxx(vp -> v_frame) - 1 - x;
            wmove(wp, y, x);                 /* point cursor */

            if (! setjmp(on_point))
            {       if (vsig)
                            signal(vsig, pointed);

                    point(wp);
                    y = cury(wp) + MLINE, x = curx(wp) + MCOL;
```

```
                    remake(vp, y, x, y0, x0);

                    if (vsig)
                            signal(vsig, SIG_IGN);
            }
            delwin(wp);
    }
```

Once again, if the view already occupies the entire available area, or if we cannot allocate the cursor window for **point( )**, or if pointing is interrupted, we silently return and **vm( )** will start the main loop over.

Pointing the Cursor

doodle in Section 3.3 is a simple introduction to cursor tracking. **point( )** is very similar, except that we move within a window and provide a better technique of function key mapping:

```
    static jmp_buf on_point;             /* point()'s exit */

    static pointed()                     /* point signal exit */
    {
            signal(vsig, SIG_IGN);
            longjmp(on_point, 1);
    }

    static point(wp)                     /* point cursor */
            WINDOW * wp;
    {       int ch, y, y0, oy, x, x0, ox;

            getyx(wp, y0, x0);           /* entry point (legal assumed) */
            getyx(wp, y, x);             /* proposed next point */

            for (;;)
            {       switch (ch = mvwgetkey(wp, oy = y, ox = x)) {
                    backspace:
                    case '\b':
                    case 'h':
                    case KEY_LEFT:   -- x; break;
                    case ' ':
                    case 'l':
                    case KEY_RIGHT: ++ x; break;
                    case '\t':       x += 8, x &= ~7; break;
                    case 'k':
                    case KEY_UP:     -- y; break;
                    case 'j':
                    case KEY_DOWN:  ++ y; break;
```

```
                        case KEY_A1:    -- x, -- y; break;
                        case KEY_A3:    ++ x, -- y; break;
                        case KEY_C1:    -- x, ++ y; break;
                        case KEY_C3:    ++ x, ++ y; break;
                        first:
                        case KEY_B2:    x = x0, y = y0; break;
                        case KEY_LL:    x = 0, y = maxy(wp) - 1; break;
                        case KEY_HOME:  x = y = 0; break;
                        case '\r':
                        case '\n':      return;
                        default:        if (ch == erasechar()) goto backspace;
                                        if (ch == killchar()) goto first;
                        }
                        if (x < 0 || x >= maxx(wp) || y < 0 || y >= maxy(wp))
                                x = ox, y = oy;
                }
        }
```

mvwgetkey( ) reads a key press from the keyboard, much like **mvwgetch( )**, but it decodes function keys and we support a sensible approach to mapping keys before they are returned by **mvwgetkey( )**. The details are presented in Section 4.7.

Remaking Windows

Is **remake( )** hard? Why do we use the same function for moving and resizing a view? If neither view position nor size are changed, we do not have to do anything. If only the position changes, a number of calls to **mvwin( )** do the job. If the size changes, we allocate new windows, use **copywin( )** to transfer as much of the contents as possible, and remove the old windows with **delwin( )**. If we decide to support a combined move and resize operation, we can still let **remake( )** handle the actual work because it will minimize the effort.

```
        static remake(vp, rows, cols, y0, x0)    /* reallocate and copy */
                register View * vp;
                int rows, cols, y0, x0;          /* new frame */
        {       register int i;

                if (rows != maxy(vp -> v_frame) || cols != maxx(vp -> v_frame))
                {       register WINDOW * wp, * swp;

                        vclose(vp);

                        if (! (wp = newwin(rows, cols, y0, x0))
                            || ! (swp = subwin(wp, rows-2, cols-2, y0+1, x0+1)))
                                fatal("no room");
                        remake1(vp -> v_sub[0], swp);
                        delwin(vp -> v_sub[0]), vp -> v_sub[0] = swp;
                        delwin(vp -> v_frame), vp -> v_frame = wp;
```

```
                        for (i = 1; i < NSUB; ++ i)
                        {       if (! (swp = newwin(rows-2, cols-2, y0+1, x0+1)))
                                        fatal("no room");
                                remake1(vp -> v_sub[i], swp);
                                delwin(vp -> v_sub[i]), vp -> v_sub[i] = swp;
                        }
                }
                else if (y0 != begy(vp -> v_frame) || x0 != begx(vp -> v_frame))
                {       vclose(vp);
                        mvwin(vp -> v_frame, y0, x0);
                        for (i = 0; i < NSUB; ++ i)
                                mvwin(vp -> v_sub[i], y0+1, x0+1);
                }
        }
```

If anything changes we call **vclose**() to redraw the screen. **remake**() always applies to the current view which **vopen**() will later redraw on the top.

The order of the **mvwin**() operations is not critical, but copying and deleting must be done in an orderly fashion. The frames need not be copied, since **remake**() will return to **vm**(). From there, the main loop is restarted and **vopen**() will take care of the frame information.†
The first interior must once again become a subwindow, and it needs to be copied. The old subwindow must be deleted before its enclosing frame. The remaining interiors are independent windows and can be copied in any order.

Copying, however, is a bit difficult. If a window gets larger, we copy the old contents to the top left of the new window and position the cursor just below. If a window gets smaller, we copy as much as possible from just above the old cursor to the new window and place the cursor at the bottom left of the new window. This is done often enough to merit another function **remake1**():

```
        static remake1(old, new)                /* copy one window */
                register WINDOW * old, * new;
        {       int y, x;

                getyx(old, y, x);
                copywin(old, new,
                                y >= maxy(new) ? y+1 - maxy(new) : 0, 0,
                                0, 0, maxy(new) - 1, maxx(new) - 1, FALSE);
                if (wmove(new, y, x) == ERR)
                        wmove(new, maxy(new) - 1, 0);
        }
```

We let *curses* determine where the cursor should go. At least if we try to move beyond the bottom or right edge of a window, the move functions will return **ERR**.

remake() is flexible enough to implement quickly two more view management options:

---

† The application may decide to center a title on a frame. There is no way for us to do this correctly here.

```
vm(ch, code)                              /* manipulate view */
{      ...


    switch (ch) {
    case 'd':                             /* default shape */
            remake(cur, FLINE, FCOL, FY(ncur), FX(ncur));
            break;
    case 'f':                             /* full shape */
            remake(cur, ALINE, ACOL, AY, AX);
            break;
```

d will return a view to its default position and size; **f** will turn the entire view area over to a single view. We made **remake( )** general enough to handle both cases efficiently.

4.6 A Variable Parameter List

vmain( ) has a bewildering variety of values to initialize. We have already seen that the application should pass the length **luser** of the buffer to be attached to **View** structures during allocation. It can also set the view management signal number **vsig** and the information function to be called by **vopen( )**.

Certainly, our view manager becomes more flexible if the number of views **NVIEW** and the number of interiors **NSUB** can be chosen by the application. The number of views influences icon size **ILINE, ICOL**. If there are more than about ten views, icons can no longer be five columns wide and still appear unobscured at the top of the terminal. The number of views also influences the default size for frames **FLINE, FCOL**. We would like to arrange them diagonally across the terminal screen and not completely overlapping.

Icon size and icon position determine the area available for views. We have assumed that the origin is at **AY, AX** and that the size is **ALINE, ACOL**. If the icons are at the top of the screen, the view area origin is at **ILINE, 0** and the size is **LINES – ILINE, COLS** because then the view area is the rest of the terminal screen below the icons. A prompt line might have to be subtracted. If we write the prompt at the bottom of the screen, we prevent a view from touching the terminal's 'funny bone'.

Since we have used symbolic references such as **IY( ), IX( )** and **FY( ), FX( )** throughout *vm.c*, we can still decide what they should mean. View management is perhaps more appealing, if the screen layout can be selected as well. Icons must be at least one line high, and should really be more than three columns wide and with some space between them if at all possible. A few icons look good across the top or bottom of the screen, but a larger number of icons might look better at the left or right edge.

Most of the values described above can just as well be selected by the user through command arguments. Some people are organized enough to be comfortable with a *wish* with twenty views.

Well, how do we pass all this to **vmain( )**? We could introduce an enormous parameter list, but setting defaults gets a bit tricky in this case. We could collect the parameter list as a structure and provide short initialization macros, but that just camouflages the situation. We could agree on very many global variables, but if they are changed while **vmain( )** is running, view management might turn into chaos.

What we need is a variable length parameter list for **vmain( )**, and a way to specify just those parameters where the default should not apply. Of course, we want to specify the parameters in any order.

We have already seen a portable way of programming a variable length parameter list: functions like **fatal( )** or **reply( )** use the header file *varargs.h*. The new idea is to announce parameter groups by identifying values, and to dispatch parsing the groups based on the identifier:

```
#include <varargs.h>

typedef int (* Function)();         /* varargs needs type names */
static int vsig;                    /* signal to get to vm() */
static Function vinfo;              /* user's info function */

static int NSUB = 1;                /* interiors */
static Vmain layout = V_TOP;        /* layout type */
static int ILINE = 3, ICOL = 5, IDIST;  /* icon shape */
static int FLINE =10, FCOL =30, FDIST;  /* frame shape */
static int ALINE, ACOL, AY, AX;     /* playground */

int vmain(va_alist)                 /* command, V_?, ..., 0 */
        va_dcl
{       int i, (* oldvsig)();
        register va_list ap;
        Vmain v;
        Function command;
        unsigned luser = 0;

        import();

        va_start(ap);
        command = va_arg(ap, Function);
        while (v = va_arg(ap, Vmain))
                switch (v) {
                case V_ARG:
                        ... see below ...
                case V_BOT:
                case V_LEFT:
                case V_RIGHT:
                case V_TOP:
                        layout = v;
                        break;
                case V_FRAME:
                        FLINE = va_arg(ap, int), FCOL = va_arg(ap, int);
                        break;
                case V_ICON:
                        ILINE = va_arg(ap, int), ICOL = va_arg(ap, int);
                        break;
```

```
                    case V_INFO:
                            vinfo = va_arg(ap, Function);
                            break;
                    case V_LUSER:
                            luser = va_arg(ap, unsigned);
                            break;
                    case V_NSUB:
                            NSUB = va_arg(ap, int);
                            break;
                    case V_NVIEW:
                            NVIEW = va_arg(ap, int);
                            break;
                    case V_SIG:
                            vsig = va_arg(ap, int);
                            break;
                    }
            va_end(ap);
```

command is the only required parameter, and it must be specified first. After all, we need to know what application function to run. It is interesting to note that *varargs.h* can only handle type names or simple type specifications with pointers as mode arguments to **va_arg( )**. **Function** demonstrates how we can circumvent the syntactic obstacles.

The **while** loop is the interesting part. **Vmain** is an **enum** type defining all the parameter group identifiers like **V_ARG**, etc. We fetch the next identifier from the parameter list, and if it is not zero, further decoding will depend on it. Illegal numbers are silently skipped because we trust our application to some degree.

Once all parameters are in, an initialization function can check them, set up the vector **views[ ]**, and compute constants such as the area available to views:

```
static init()                           /* fill in layout */
{       char * calloc();

        if (NVIEW <= 0 || NVIEW >= 27)
                fatal("illegal number of views");
        VIEW0 = NVIEW > 10 ? 'A' : '0';

        if (NSUB <= 0)
                fatal("illegal number of interiors");

        switch (layout) {
        case V_TOP:
        case V_BOT:
                IDIST = 2, FDIST = 1 + 40 / NVIEW;
                ALINE = LINES - ILINE - 1, ACOL = COLS;
                AX = 0;
                AY = layout == V_TOP ? ILINE : 0;
                break;
```

```
                default:
                        IDIST = 0, FDIST = 1 + 20 / NVIEW;
                        ALINE = LINES - 1, ACOL = COLS - ICOL;
                        AX = layout == V_LEFT ? ICOL : 0;
                        AY = 0;
                }

                if (ILINE < 1 || ICOL < 1 || IX(0) < 0 || IY(0) < 0
                    || FLINE < MLINE || FCOL < MCOL || FX(0) < AX || FY(0) < AY)
                        fatal("impossible layout");

                if (! (views = (View *) calloc(NVIEW, sizeof(View))))
                        fatal("no room");
        }
```

NVIEW and VIEW0 need to be available to the application in case the information function decides to display them. These variables and the parameter identifiers are defined in the header file *view.h*:

```
#ifdef  GLOBAL
#define INIT(x) = x
#else
#define GLOBAL  extern
#define INIT(x)
#endif


#define MLINE   4                       /* min # lines in frame */
#define MCOL    20                      /* min # columns in frame */


#define PLINE   (LINES-1)               /* prompt's line position */


GLOBAL int NVIEW INIT(10), VIEW0;       /* # views, low name */


typedef enum {                          /* vmain()'s arguments */
        /* 0 */         /* end of list */
        V_ARG = 1,      /* , (int) argc, (char **) argv, (char *) opt */
        V_ICON,         /* , (int) ILINE, (int) ICOL */
        V_INFO,         /* , (int (*)()) vinfo */
        V_FRAME,        /* , (int) FLINE, (int) FCOL */
        V_LUSER,        /* , (int) sizeof (* v_user) */
        V_NSUB,         /* , (int) NSUB */
        V_NVIEW,        /* , (int) NVIEW */
        V_SIG,          /* , (int) vsig */
        V_BOT, V_LEFT, V_RIGHT, V_TOP   /* layouts */
        } Vmain;
```

With initialization accomplished, positioning icons and default views is easy. Icon positions depend on the desired **layout** and are best implemented as functions, while default view positions depend on the view area and can be defined as macros:

```
static int IY(i)                              /* icon's position */
        register int i;
{
        switch (layout) {
        case V_TOP:     return 0;
        case V_BOT:     return LINES - ILINE - 1;
        }
        return (LINES - NVIEW * ILINE - (NVIEW-1) * IDIST)/2
                + (i) * (ILINE + IDIST);
}

static int IX(i)
        register int i;
{
        switch (layout) {
        case V_LEFT:    return 0;
        case V_RIGHT:   return COLS - ICOL;
        }
        return (COLS - NVIEW * ICOL - (NVIEW-1) * IDIST)/2
                + (i) * (ICOL + IDIST);
}

#define FY(i)   (AY + (ALINE - FLINE - (NVIEW-1))/2 + (i))
#define FX(i)   (AX + (ACOL - FCOL - (NVIEW-1) * FDIST)/2 + (i) * FDIST)
```

Sharing Command Arguments

One parameter group is particularly interesting to implement. View manager applications could support command arguments to select screen layout, number of views, etc. It is probably a good idea if these values are always introduced with the same option letters. Applications are more likely to comply, if they do not even contain this part of the code. Therefore, **vmain**( ) accepts command arguments with the identifier **V_ARG** and parses them using **getopt**(3). The option descriptor must also be passed with **V_ARG**. Unrecognized options are silently ignored. This way, **main**( ) and **vmain**( ) can conveniently share an argument list.

```
int argc; char aflag = 0, ** argv, * opt;
extern char * optarg;
extern int optind;

        switch (v) {
        case V_ARG:
                argc = va_arg(ap, int), argv = va_arg(ap, char **);
                opt = va_arg(ap, char *);
                optind = 1;
                while ((i = getopt(argc, argv, opt)) != EOF)
                        switch (i) {
                        case 'a':
                                aflag = 1;
                                break;
                        case 'b':
                                layout = V_BOT;
                                break;
                        case 'f':
                                if (sscanf(optarg, "%d,%d",
                                                &FLINE, &FCOL) != 2)
                                        return -1;
                                break;
                        case 'i':
                                if (sscanf(optarg, "%d,%d",
                                                &ILINE, &ICOL) != 2)
                                        return -1;
                                break;
                        case 'l':
                                layout = V_LEFT;
                                break;
                        case 'n':
                                NVIEW = atoi(optarg);
                                break;
                        case 'q':
                                vsig = SIGQUIT;
                                break;
                        case 'r':
                                layout = V_RIGHT;
                                break;
                        case 't':
                                layout = V_TOP;
                        }
                break;
```

If an option such as −f requires two values as a parameter, we parse them using **sscanf**(3). If we cannot find suitable values, **vmain**() returns -1 to the application. Here is a typical call to **vmain**() where the application verifies the argument list before passing it:

```
main(argc, argv)
        int argc; char ** argv;
{       int i;
        char * opt = "bf:i:lrt";
        extern int optind;

        optind = 1;
        while ((i = getopt(argc, argv, opt)) != EOF)
                if (i == '?')
                        exit(1);
        if (optind < argc
           || vmain(command,
                        V_INFO,   info,
                        V_LUSER,  (unsigned) sizeof(User),
                        V_NSUB,   2,
                        V_SIG,    SIGINT,
                        V_ARG,    argc, argv, opt,
                        0))
                fatal("bad command argument");
        return 0;
}
```

Clearly, more elaborate error messages can be added and private arguments extracted.

4.7 Key Mapping: *mvwgetkey( )*, *loadmap( )*, and *keymap( )*

point( ) demonstrates a typical problem. The function reacts to a large number of single key presses. The various reactions are designed to correspond to special key names on 'standard' terminals. Arrows move the cursor around, *home* or *lower left* make the cursor jump to the indicated places on the screen, etc. *doodle* in Section 3.3 recognized even more special keys: *insert line*, *delete character* and many others are quite meaningful for an editor and should reduce the learning effort for such a program.

Unfortunately, most terminals are not 'standard'. *terminfo* (7) and *curses.h* define many more special key names than any single terminal has. Even if a terminal has special keys, chances are that its entry in the *terminfo* database does not mention them, or that it connects a key such as *end* on an IBM PC enhanced keyboard or *do* on a DEC keyboard to some strange name in *curses.h*.

Letting *curses* decode a special key is simple. The following function solves the typical problem: we want to receive a single key press at a particular screen position in some window.

```
        static int (* getkeymap)();              /* set by keymap(), loadmap() */

        int mvwgetkey(wp, y, x)                           /* get (mapped) key */
                WINDOW * wp;                      /* in this window */
                int y, x;                         /* at this position */
        {       register int key;


                wmove(wp, y, x), wrefresh(wp);

                keypad(wp, TRUE);
                key = wgetch(wp);
                keypad(wp, FALSE);
                return getkeymap ? (* getkeymap)(key) : key;

        }
```

wmove( ) and **wrefresh**( ) make sure that the physical cursor is in the right spot. Setting **keypad**( ) to **TRUE** will implicitly disable input echo, turn single key input (**cbreak**) on, and arrange for special keys to be mapped to the key names in *curses.h*. If we set **keypad**( ) back to **FALSE**, we re-enable the original terminal state.

mvwgetkey( ) implements a trick, however. If **getkeymap** is set, it points to a function which can replace any key value, special key name or ASCII character, by an arbitrary code to be returned by **mvwgetkey**( ). For execution speed, the map function is based on two vectors. One applies to ASCII characters from null byte to *delete*, the other vector deals with the key names defined in *curses.h*:

```
        static short ascii[128];              /* could change dimension */
        static short special[HI_KEY - LOW_KEY + 1];

        static int map(key)                   /* perform the map */
                register int key;
        {
                if (key >= 0 && key < DIM(ascii) && ascii[key])
                        key = ascii[key];
                else if (key >= LOW_KEY && key <= HI_KEY && special[key - LOW_KEY])
                        key = special[key - LOW_KEY];
                return key;

        }
```

All we need to do now is to fill the translation tables in a sensible fashion. In our desk calculator, or in the command language of an editor, etc., we can support access to a function **keymap**( ) which adds or deletes a single transformation from the tables:

```
int keymap(from, to)                               /* add to map */
      int from, to;
{     int result = -1;                    /* error */

      if (from >= 0 && from < DIM(ascii))
              result = ascii[from],
              ascii[from] = to;
      else if (from >= LOW_KEY && from <= HI_KEY)
              result = special[from - LOW_KEY],
              special[from - LOW_KEY] = to;
      else
              return result;
      getkeymap = map;
      return result;

}
```

If **from** is within range, **to** is the value to be returned if **from** is read from the keyboard. If **to** is zero, **map**( ) will return **from** rather than zero itself, i.e., we can erase a translation table entry. The drawback is that we cannot map a code to zero.

If an application is confronted with a particularly intelligent terminal or an average *terminfo* entry, it can now call **keymap**( ) often enough to create a reasonable supply of special keys represented, for example, by control characters.

This solution is still rather awkward, but it is preferable to some alternatives. Before calling **initscr**( ) we could point the environment variable **TERMINFO** to a private directory and store our own database, but maintenance of the database is rather difficult. Instead, we could code many more cases into the **switch** in **point**( ): *control*-B, **KEY_LEFT**, '\b', **erasechar**( ), 'h', and '**4**' are all about equally reasonable for moving the cursor to the left. Of course, we need to document them all, and we are out of luck if *terminfo* specifies **KEY_BACKSPACE**, or if we invent more cursor reactions than we can reasonably mimic in the union of all possible terminal quirks.

keymap( ) is a layer of abstraction between decoding special keys according to the whims of *terminfo* and using a problem-oriented selection of special keys to simplify the application. However, we should take a cue from *terminfo* and store the information for **keymap**( ) in files. The files are application and terminal specific, but they are easily changed by a user. We can still distribute binary versions of our programs, and they can be locally adapted to strange environments.

Loading a Key Map File

loadmap( ) is a small parser for a text file with **keymap**( ) information. The file name can be passed as an argument, or it can be constructed from **TERM** and some standard path:

```
#ifndef MAPFILE
#define MAPFILE "/usr/lib/keymap/%s"     /* default location of map file */
#endif

#define NONE    -1                        /* have seen nothing */
#define ASCII   0                         /* have seen ascii */
#define KEYPAD  (DIM(ascii)+1)            /* have seen keypad; no value */
```

```
int loadmap(term)                      /* load map from file */
      char * term;                     /* explicit file name */
{     int result = -1;                 /* syntax error */
      FILE * fp;
      char buf[BUFSIZ], ** np, * getenv();
      int ch, val, mode = NONE;
      long strtol();

      if (term)
      {     if (! (fp = fopen(term, "r")))
                  return -2;           /* cannot open */
      }
      else if (! (term = getenv("TERM")))
            return -3;                 /* no TERM */
      else
      {     sprintf(buf, MAPFILE, term);
            if (! (fp = fopen(buf, "r")))
                  return -2;           /* cannot open */
      }
```

The file contains the two tables. The keyword **ascii** is followed by a sequence of codes which are entered into the vector **ascii**[ ] in order, i.e., the codes are returned for the ASCII values beginning at null. This arrangement appears reasonable because control characters are likely to be mapped, while other characters are not.

The keyword **keypad** is followed by pairs of codes, which act as **from** and **to** in a call to **keymap**( ), i.e., the first code will be mapped into the second one. The sequence of key values in *curses.h* is rather random and it would be unreasonable to require the key map file to specify these codes in order.

So far, **loadmap**( ) is a small finite state machine. The keyword **ascii** sets the state counter **mode** to the first index in **ascii**[ ], i.e., to zero. Each code from the file is then written into the vector and the mode counter is advanced. The keyword **keypad** sets the state counter to a special value, the next code is remembered as a state and index to **special**[ ], the following code is entered into the vector, and the state counter is reset.

```
while (fscanf(fp, "%s", buf) == 1)
{     switch (* buf) {
      default:
            if (strcmp(buf, "ascii") == 0)
            {     if (mode != NONE && mode != KEYPAD)
                        goto exit;
                  mode = ASCII;
                  continue;
            }
            if (strcmp(buf, "keypad") == 0)
            {     if (mode == KEYPAD || mode >= LOW_KEY)
                        goto exit;
```

```
                                mode = KEYPAD;
                                continue;
                        }
                }
                if (mode >= 0 && mode < DIM(ascii))
                        ascii[mode++] = val;
                else if (mode == KEYPAD)
                {       if (val < LOW_KEY || val > HI_KEY)
                                goto exit;
                        mode = val;
                }
                else if (mode >= LOW_KEY && mode <= HI_KEY)
                        special[mode - LOW_KEY] = val, mode = KEYPAD;
                else
                        goto exit;
        }
        if (! ferror(fp) && feof(fp))
                getkeymap = map, result = 0;            /* loaded ok */
        else
                result = -4;                            /* i/o error */

exit:   fclose(fp);
        return result;
}
```

We make **loadmap**( ) convenient to use by supporting a flexible input format and providing many ways to specify codes:

```
^D                 # control characters
'x'                # characters
1 02 0x3           # integer constants
home left          # curses key names
f(10)              # function key names
```

White space is ignored and comments can follow # to the end of a line. Thanks to library functions like **scanf**(3) and **strtol**(3) the parser remains very compact:

```
static char * names[] = {
                                        /* low: LOW_KEY */
        "break", "down", "up", "left",
        "right", "home", "backspace", "f0",
                                        /* gap: KEY_F(1..63) */
        "dl", "il", "dc", "ic",
        "eic", "clear", "eos", "eol",
        "sf", "sr", "npage", "ppage",
        "stab", "ctab", "catab", "enter",
        "sreset", "reset", "print", "ll",
        "a1", "a3", "b2", "c1",
        "c3" };
```

```
        while (fscanf(fp, "%s", buf) == 1)
        {       switch (* buf) {
                case '#':                       /* # .. \n ignored */
                        while ((ch = getc(fp)) != '\n' && ch != EOF)
                                ;
                        if (ch == EOF)
                                goto exit;
                        continue;
                case '^':                       /* ^x: control-x */
                        val = buf[1] & 31;
                        break;
                case '\'':                      /* 'x: character x */
                        val = buf[1];
                        break;
                case 'f':                       /* f(n: KEY_F(n) */
                        if (buf[1] == '(' && isdigit(buf[2])
                            && (val = atoi(buf+2)) < 64)
                        {       val += KEY_F0;
                                break;
                        }
                default:
                        if (isdigit(*buf))      /* 1 01 0x1 0X number */
                        {       val = strtol(buf, (char **) 0, 0);
                                break;
                        }
                        if (strcmp(buf, "ascii") == 0)
                        ...
                        val = 0;
                        for (np = names; np < names + DIM(names); ++ np)
                                if (strcmp(buf, *np) == 0)
                                {       val = (np - names) + LOW_KEY;
                                        if (val > KEY_F0)
                                                val += 63;
                                        break;
                                }
                        if (! val)
                                goto exit;
```

loadmap( ) is very quiet about input errors. We can assume that production key maps are correct and a missing file need not be a problem. Every library function should have a test driver. The test driver *getkey* has an option −**v** to produce output as a key map is read; it displays a map symbolically, and it displays the effects of arbitrary key presses, with or without key mapping. *getkey* is very useful for debugging a key map description, and it helps in unveiling the mysteries of yet another emulation of the all too popular VT100 terminal. The code is straightforward, and it is part of the software package accompanying this book.

4.8 Conclusion

Once a program like our desk calculator runs in a single *curses* window, it is easily connected to our view manager to be run in many views. A program that believes in line-oriented input and scrolled output may lose output speed, but it does gain a lot of advantages. Several views can help in separating thoughts, keeping more information accessible than one screen can hold, and hiding information behind icons until it is needed again.

The view manager is much more than an exercise in using *curses* functions. It takes care of a number of awkward chores that no screen application can do without: moving windows, changing their size, making them appear on top, and hiding them somewhere. **vm( )** also provides access to a shell, which any interactive UNIX program should have, and which is tricky to support when *curses* own the screen.

The view manager was very carefully designed to be independent of a particular application.† We have seen how we can tie user information to a data structure owned and operated by a separate module. View management is a complex service, but **vmain( )**, **vm( )**, and perhaps **vopen( )** and **vcatch( )** provide a small, comprehensible interface. The usability of a service depends less on its functionality and more on the elegance of its interface. **vmain( )** illustrates a very useful technique to provide almost arbitrary options and still keep the parameter list short.

The view manager does not support multiple concurrent processes sharing the same physical screen and using separate views. By synchronizing processes prior to a refresh operation, and by implementing an interruptible input function, we can for example run a digital clock concurrently with our desk calculator. The terminal, however, has only one physical cursor, and there is no portable way to restore it from one process for another one.

The view manager does support different work in different views, and the work can well be carried out in cooperation with other processes. The remaining chapters will elaborate on suitable techniques.

---

† **import( )** and **export( )** remain as slight blemishes.

## CHAPTER FIVE

A Viewer
file.c

5.1 Architecture

Chapter 1 indicated that we can do more than run a calculator inside each of our views. With view management out of the way, we will now turn to application programming and the particular complications in systems programming encountered along the way. This chapter deals with various aspects of looking at files and pipes.

No matter what options we provide inside a view, we must pass a single function which **vmain**( ) will call whenever it selects a view. If we support more than the desk calculator, the basic architecture of **command**( ) seems to be the following:

```
static command(vp)
        register View * vp;
{
        ... post current view ...

        setjmp(on_response);
        for (;;)
        {       ... read command line ...
                if (...file viewing requested...)
                {       ... connect to file ...
                        ... display ...
                        ... disconnect ...
                }
                ...
                else
                        ... execute calculator line ...
        }
}
```

If it is impossible to **connect to file**, the customary call to **response**( ) gets us back on the regular track.

File viewing could be made a service of the calculator at the statement or even at the function level. Macros could then be used to request file access. Unless we support a new input token class, however, a file name would have to be specified as a string. This makes file viewing sufficiently unpleasant to design a solution outside the calculator. Single prefix or postfix characters are easier to recognize and dispatch than words, and they interfere much less with the calculator. As long as we select memorable special characters, the prefix notation should be easy to use.

File viewing may not be a frequent job for *wish*. However, any file display mechanism should be able to handle pipe input as well. We are then ready to run other programs concurrently and look at their output in a view. This service could be popular enough that there should be a way to circumvent the prefix notation. Similarly, a help mechanism might be useful enough for our user to want to dedicate a view to it. This is why we interpret a prefix without a command as a request to change the mode for input lines.

View States

Our design thus far has a fundamental flaw, however. Looking at a file undoubtedly will take time, and it is more than likely a view will be deselected, moved, or enlarged while involved in a display operation. The view manager returns control to the view by calling our application function again. As we have sketched so far, **command( )** will begin by reading another input line and interpreting it as a command line, even if the view was deselected while displaying a file and is really expecting a request to move forward or backward.

We need to store a view state and a view prefix. The default view state requires **command( )** to read an input line. The view prefix applies in the absence of an explicit prefix in the input. The default view prefix arranges for the command line to be interpreted by the desk calculator. The application-specific part of the **View** data structure is extended as follows:

```
typedef struct user User;
      struct user {
              char u_prefix;
              char u_history[CLEN];
              Function u_exec, u_info;
              union {
                      ... state specific part ...
                      } u_;
              };

#define _vu(vp)         ((User *) (vp) -> v_user)

#define vprefix(vp)     (_vu(vp) -> u_prefix)   /* current implicit prefix */
#define vhistory(vp)    (_vu(vp) -> u_history)  /* last input */
#define vexec(vp)       (_vu(vp) -> u_exec)     /* command processor */
#define vinfo(vp)       (_vu(vp) -> u_info)     /* information function */
```

Storing a state as a function pointer may seem strange, but we will see that it makes the overall design much more flexible. Different view states are characterized on the terminal screen by different frame styles, and state-specific information is written onto the frame. It makes sense to let different information functions handle the situation.

Dispatching View States

Simply storing the state is not sufficient. We need to rearrange **command( )** so that input is only
read if the view state is ready for it. Basically, if **vexec(vp)** is not a null pointer, it should point
to the function which handles the current view state:

```
static command(vp)                              /* run command language */
        View * vp;
{       register WINDOW * cur;
        char buf[CLEN], * bp, * tp;
        register Function func = vexec(vp);

        echo(), nocbreak();
        vcur = vp;
        if (! setjmp(on_response))
                while (func)
                        func = (* (Function (*)()) func)(vp);
```

Most file viewing programs have three phases: *open*, *display*, and *close*. There may even be
more phases if we are going to wait for a process to complete before we look at the output in a
temporary file. Different viewing cycles, however, may well share some phases. This is why we
use a C variety of *threaded code* to drive the view states. We return to this topic below.

    command( ) sets the terminal state, posts the current view for the benefit of **_reply( )**,
and sets a return point for **response( )**. If **vexec(vp)** is set, the appropriate function is executed
until the view state reverts to reading another command line. Now we are ready to proceed just
as in Chapter 4 before we invented view states:

```
cur = view(vcur);
wmove(cur, cury(cur), 0), wclrtoeol(cur);

setjmp(on_response);
for (;;)
{       ... read input ...
        ... handle history ...
        bp = ...begin of command...
        tp = bp + strlen(bp) - 1;           /* end of command */

        if (func = select(*bp))
        {       if (bp[1] == '\0')
                {       vprefix(vp) = *bp != '=' ? *bp : 0;
                        vopen(vp);
                        continue;
                }
                bp = trim(bp + 1);
        }
}
```

select( ) uses a table to convert a prefix character to a view state function pointer that might be
stored in **vexec(vp)**. For an unknown prefix **select( )** will return a null pointer.

If **select( )** recognizes a prefix, and if the command line contains only the prefix, we store it as the view's default **vprefix(vp)** and top the view so that the information function will display the new prefix on the frame. = is the default prefix value and is therefore converted to a null byte.

If the prefix preceded an argument, we use **trim( )** from Section 4.2 to move past white space following the prefix. **func** points to the function to be executed for the prefix on the argument.

If **select( )** did not recognize the first command character, there are other ways to get to a processing function:

```
else if (func = select(*tp | 0x80))
        *tp = '\0';
else if (vprefix(vp))
        func = select(vprefix(vp));
else
        func = (Function) calculator;
```

Either **select( )** recognizes the trailing character of the command, which is marked by the high bit set in the selection table, or we might have a default prefix for the view which **select( )** can definitely convert. If all else fails, we will call the desk calculator.

func is set and we are ready to execute the chosen function. Up to now we have not set **vexec(vp)**, i.e., if we are interrupted by view management, **command( )** is reselected later and will directly proceed to reading new input. If we move into file display, the first function call will happen as shown below, and we can pass the current input buffer directly without having to reparse **vhistory(vp)**:

```
while (func = (* (Function (*)()) func)(vp, bp))
        ;
        }
}
```

It is up to the chosen function to set **vexec(vp)** and **vinfo(vp)** and to arrange for further functions to be called in sequence. The desk calculator is remarkably primitive since it remains strictly one-shot:

```
static Function calculator(vp, bp)        /* run calculator */
        register View * vp;
        register char * bp;
{
        nscroll = maxy(view(vp));
        lexi_buf(bp), yyparse();
        return (Function) 0;
}
```

Later functions in a sequence cannot rely on the buffer pointer **bp** being set. As soon as **vexec(vp)** has been set, a function may be called without a current buffer.

Selecting View State Functions

select( ) is based on a table which can be extended easily. Since the table is searched several times per input line, we keep the source sorted by prefix characters and use **bsearch**(3) to perform a binary search in the table.

```
static int tcmp(a, b)
        register unsigned char ** a, ** b;
{
        return *a - *b;
}

static Function select(ch)              /* convert prefix to Function */
        unsigned char ch;
{       register struct table * tp;
        char * bsearch();

        if (tp = (struct table *)
                        bsearch(& ch, table, DIM(table), sizeof *tp, tcmp))
                return tp -> func;
        return (Function) 0;
}
```

We cheat ever so slightly. **bsearch( )** calls the comparison function once per level and always passes the search key as left argument. If we define the prefix as the first component of table entries, we can avoid initializing a dummy entry for the benefit of **bsearch( )**. The arguments to **select( )** and **tcmp( )** must be **unsigned char** to accommodate our markup with **0x80** for trailing characters. Here is a typical selection table:

```
Function bgopen();
Function fileopen();
Function helpopen();
Function pipeopen();

static struct table {                   /* function table */
        unsigned char prefix;           /* MUST be first */
        Function func;
} table[] = {                           /* sorted by prefix */
                                        /* 0x80 denotes postfix use */
                { '!',          (Function) pipeopen },
                { '&',          (Function) bgopen },
                { '<',          (Function) fileopen },
                { '=',          (Function) calculator },
                { '?',          (Function) helpopen },
                { '|',          (Function) pipeopen },
                {0x80|'&',      (Function) bgopen },
                {0x80|'|',      (Function) pipeopen },
};
```

If we format the table as shown, we can sort the source by executing *sort*(1) on an editor buffer. 0 follows space in the ASCII collating sequence just as characters with **0x80** set are larger **unsigned** values than other characters.

Threaded Code

Threaded code is a popular technique for interpreters and compiler implementation on small systems.† A program is represented as a vector of pointers and the threaded code program counter is an index into this vector. The pointer at the index must designate a function. The index is incremented and the function is called. The function could retrieve constant arguments at the index, as long as the index points to another function upon return. The process repeats as the index is incremented and the next function called.

The functions can be viewed as higher level machine instructions, and the vector of pointers contains the execution thread of a program to be executed on this machine; thus the name threaded code.

We could implement **command**( ) using threaded code as described above. **select**( ) would return an index into some function vector, **vexec(vp)** stores the index rather than a pointer, and the function calls in **command**( ) would use indirection through the function vector at the appropriate index. Code sharing is then a bit more difficult and a static initialization of the function vector requires a certain amount of bookkeeping to get the indices right.

We chose to store function pointers directly and require a threaded code function to return a pointer to the next function to be called. Once a threaded code function returns a null pointer, a sequence of threaded code stops, i.e., command input is resumed.

Dreaded Cast

Implementing this idea, however, requires some insight into the darker aspects of type specifications in C. Here is the definition of a simple function and of a pointer to it:

```
int fun(i) int i; { return i+1; }
int (* p)() = fun;
```

The correct definition of a function returning a pointer to a function is perhaps more of a challenge. It is advisable to use a type definition:

```
typedef int (* Function)();     /* pointer to function */
Function fun(f) Function f; { return f; }
```

Here is a pointer to this second **fun**( ):

```
Function (* p)() = fun;
```

---

† Kernighan and Pike (1984) implement their calculator using threaded code.

Do not despair if you feel as though you have seen this before; the feeling is wholly intentional! **Function** in the second example is the equivalent of **int** in the first. The first example, however, should be familiar:

```
int fun(i) int i; { return i+1; }
int (* p)() = fun;
int j = (* p)(10);
```

If we call through **p** we get an **int** value back, which clearly cannot be assigned back into **p**.

A function cannot be declared so that it can return a pointer to itself as a result. We lose one reference along the way. Without casts there is no uniform design of our view state interpreter. Here is a sketch of how we must declare:

```
struct { ... Function func; ... } table[];

Function select() { ... return table[x].func; }

command(vp)
        struct { ... Function u_exec; ... } * vp;
{       Function func;

        func = vp -> u_exec;            /* view state function */
        func = select( ... );           /* selection by prefix */

        while (func)                    /* null pointer?? */
                func = (* (Function (*)()) func)(vp);
}
```

The last cast is probably unexpected. The following call might appear much more logical:

```
func = (Function) (* func)(vp); /* FALSE */
```

Here, the function pointed to by **func** is called and the result is cast into a function pointer. Since **Function** was declared as a pointer to a function returning **int**, the result of the function call is assumed to be **int** and is cast to pointer. Even if the function actually returned a pointer, C implementations will clobber the result if **int** cannot contain a pointer!

The correct solution shown above casts **func** as a pointer to a function returning **Function**. Now the return value is understood to be **Function** and can be assigned back to **func** unchanged. The cast is not critical because it only corrects the interpretation of the return value of the function, not the interpretation of the pointer **func** itself.

Continuing in our sketch, we need to look at a more complicated threaded code sequence than **calculator()**:

```
Function fileopen(vp, bp)               /* connect to file */
{       Function file();

        ... return vp -> u_exec = (Function) file;
}
```

```
static Function file(vp)                /* view a file */
{       Function fileclose();


        ... return vp -> u_exec = (Function) fileclose;
}

static Function fileclose(vp)           /* disconnect */
{
        ... return vp -> u_exec = (Function) 0;
}
```

Yes, the casts are required. As a reference, the name of a function represents a constant pointer value, i.e., in the assignment in the **return** statement, **file** has the type 'pointer to function returning **Function**'. However, **u_exec** and the result value of **fileclose** must be **Function**, i.e., 'pointer to function returning **int**'. Hence the cast. The same kind of cast is required for the initialization of the selection table:

```
Function fileopen();

struct { ... Function func; ... } table[] = {
        { '<', (Function) fileopen }, ... };
```

The casts are a bit ugly, but the mechanism as such has its merits. The table for **select**( ) is very easy to extend, and prefix character conventions are only stored there. There is a clear design for the participating functions, and the structure fits perfectly into our view management, where execution sequences may be interrupted and resumed or aborted at a later stage.

We could have passed more than one function to **vmain**( ), rather than insisting on a common application driver. As our example shows, however, we need a common driver to implement a common interface for reading application commands. If we want to run each view independently through its own function, we would probably still share a common command language routine, and the interface to **vmain**( ) would definitely be more complicated.

5.2 Viewing Files

_reply( ) outputs one line at a time, suppresses autowrap, scrolls the output window, and paginates output if it exceeds one window. Essentially, these are the basic services which a text file viewer must provide. **_reply**( ), however, keeps the bottom line of the output window free for dialog input, and it shifts the output over by one tab position. Text file viewing can thus be patterned after **_reply**( ), but it will require a display mechanism of its own.

Display Primitives

Let us look at text file display bottom up. First we need a function **put( )** to output one text line to a particular line in a window. Unlike **_reply( )**, which keeps the bottom line of a window free, we need to design **put( )** to use the entire window. Writing into an empty bottom line needs to be distinguished from writing into a full bottom line. In the latter case, **put( )** must scroll the window up and add the new line to the bottom. Therefore, we pass the position of the line preceding the line to be output as parameter:

```
static put(wp, y, buf)                    /* output line */
        register WINDOW * wp;
        register int y;                   /* prior line */
        char * buf;
{
        if (y < maxy(wp) - 1)
                ++ y;
        else
                scrollok(wp, TRUE), scroll(wp);

        scrollok(wp, FALSE);
        mvwaddstr(wp, y, 0, buf);
        if (cury(wp) > y)
                wmove(wp, y+1, 0), wclrtobot(wp);
        wmove(wp, y, 0);
}
```

put( ) is a very close relative of **_reply( )**. This time, however, the cursor is left on top of the output line.

With the actual output function in place, we can build a function **next( )** to output just one more line from a stream to a view. The stream is represented as a **FILE** pointer **vfp(vp)** in the application and view state specific part of the **View** structure. **next( )** receives the output position required by **put( )** as a parameter. This should normally be **cury(view(vp))**, i.e., the current row in the current interior.

```
static int next(vp, y)                    /* show next line */
        View * vp;
        int y;                            /* prior line */
{       register FILE * fp = vfp(vp);
        register WINDOW * wp = view(vp);
        char buf[BUFSIZ];

        if (! fgets(buf, sizeof buf, fp))
                return EOF;

        put(wp, y, buf);
        return 0;
}
```

next( ) is responsible for reading the line to be output. Therefore, **next( )** will return zero if a line was available and **EOF** if not.

Given **next( )** and its ability to output to specific lines in a view, we can build **screen( )** to fill the entire view with lines from a stream. If we let **next( )** handle the actual reading, we have only one place in the program where the buffer size for reading is specified.

```
static int screen(vp)                      /* show next screen */
        View * vp;
{       register WINDOW * wp = view(vp);
        register int y;
        FILE * fp = vfp(vp);

        ungetc(getc(fp), fp);              /* set EOF flag */
        if (feof(fp))
                return EOF;

        for (werase(wp), y = -1; y < maxy(wp) - 1; ++ y)
                if (next(vp, y) == EOF)
                        break;
        return 0;
}
```

There is no need to erase the view if there is no more output. This could be used to stop at the end of a stream without wiping out the last page.

A text paginator should be able to go backwards in a stream. A flexible solution requires remembering line positions in the stream so that backing up can be measured in lines. A cheap solution would back up a number of characters based on the size of the view and scan forward to a line separator before resuming the display. We opt for even less:

```
static prev(vp)                            /* reposition */
        register View * vp;
{
        rewind(vfp(vp));
}
```

rewind(3) will simply return to the beginning of a file. Of course, **prev( )** cannot be used on pipes.

Connections: *fileopen( )* and *fileclose( )*

We have all the functions to handle file viewing. There are three primitives: for displaying another screen, for advancing one line, and for backing up. We also need to store the file pointer in the **View** structure:

```
        typedef struct user User;
                struct user {
                        ... common part ...
                        union {
                                struct {
                                        FILE * f_p;
                                        int (* f_screen)(), (* f_next)(), (* f_prev)();
                                        int f_pos;
                                        } u__f;
                                } u_;
                };

        #define _vu(vp)          ((User *) (vp) -> v_user)

        #define _vuf(vp)         _vu(vp) -> u_.u__f      /* file viewing */

        #define vfp(vp)          (_vuf(vp).f_p)          /* input file */
        #define vfscreen(vp)     (_vuf(vp).f_screen)     /* advance one screen */
        #define vfnext(vp)       (_vuf(vp).f_next)       /* advance one line */
        #define vfprev(vp)       (_vuf(vp).f_prev)       /* backup */
        #define vfpos(vp)        (_vuf(vp).f_pos)        /* help: next position */
```

vfpos( ) will be needed in Section 5.4 when we view the usage database.

If a stream connection can be established, **setup( )** initializes the file display mechanism and displays the first screen. While there may be different pieces to assemble for different stream display operations, keeping the actions together in a single function makes it harder to forget part of the initialization:

```
        static setup(vp, screen, next, prev, error)     /* change state */
                register View * vp;
                Function screen, next, prev;
                register char * error;
        {       static Function fileclose();

                vfscreen(vp) = screen, vfnext(vp) = next, vfprev(vp) = prev;
                vinfo(vp) = (Function) info, vnow(vp) = N_FILE, vopen(vp);
                if ((* screen)(vp) == EOF)
                        fileclose(vp), response(error);
        }
```

We store the required function pointers, set up our own information function, select a different interior for file display,† call **vopen( )** to redraw the frame, and try to display the first screen. If there is none, **fileclose( )** must know how to clean everything up, and we complain and return by way of **response( )**. Based on **setup( )**, it is easy to write **fileclose( )**. We simply need to reverse most assignments made in **setup( )**, close the stream if any, and return a null pointer in case the function is called as part of a sequence:

---

† ...which must be requested when **vmain( )** is called!

```
static Function fileclose(vp)                           /* end cycle */
       register View * vp;
{
       vexec(vp) =
       vinfo(vp) = (Function) 0, vnow(vp) = N_CMD, vopen(vp);
       if (vfp(vp))
               fclose(vfp(vp)), vfp(vp) = (FILE *) 0;
       return (Function) 0;
}
```

Note that **vopen( )** does not execute **doupdate( )**. If nothing can be displayed, **fileclose( )** will revert to the original frame, and only **response( )** will update the terminal screen. *curses* is expensive in terms of computer time, but by minimizing output to the terminal it also protects the user from visual noise when nothing really needs to be changed.

Keeping Files Private

fileopen( ) must establish a file connection, invoke **setup( )** with suitable parameters, and arrange for a driver to be called later to run the dialog controlling the actual display.

```
#include <fcntl.h>

#define private(fd)     fcntl(fd, F_SETFD, 1)          /* close on exec */

Function fileopen(vp, bp)                      /* start cycle */
       register View * vp;
       register char * bp;
{
       if (! (vfp(vp) = fopen(bp, "r")))
               response("?cannot open");
       private(fileno(vfp(vp)));

       setup(vp, screen, next, prev, "?end of file");

       return vexec(vp) = (Function) file;
}
```

private( ) is an interesting complication and rather typical for a program like *wish* that can handle several operations more or less concurrently. If a view has a file connection and we use **fork( )** to create a new process, the process inherits the file connection. Unless we set the *close on exec* flag for the file connection, it will also remain if the new process changes to a different program using **exec**(2). Many views compete inside *wish* for file connections, but there is no reason to bother descendant processes as well. Additionally, a stray seek operation in an unreliable descendant can cause rather obscure effects in a totally unrelated display operation.

Therefore, a program like *wish* should be very careful to arrange for all its file connections to be closed on **exec**. As the definition shows, this can be accomplished with a simple **fcntl**(2) call following each **open**(2).

Display Dialog: *file( )*

file( ) is the function managing a file display dialog. It must prompt the user, read a command, and change the display accordingly. **file**( ) should be patterned after commands like *pg*(1), but following Kernighan and Pike (1984) we will let a basic version only do what is minimally useful.† Single key presses should move forward by screens or lines, and if there is a no way to back up, the customary key press should be quietly ignored. When we reach the end of the stream, or when the user demands it, we arrange for the dialog to terminate by setting **fileclose**( ) as the next function.

```
static Function file(vp)                  /* display from FILE pointer */
        register View * vp;
{       register WINDOW * wp = view(vp);
        int ch;
        static Function fileclose();

        for (;;)
        {       switch (ch = mvwgetkey(wp, cury(wp), curx(wp))) {
                default:                        /* default: one line */
                        if (ch == erasechar())  /* \b */
                                ;
                        else if (ch < VIEW0 || ch >= VIEW0 + NVIEW)
                        {       if ((* vfnext(vp))(vp, cury(wp)) == EOF)
                                        break;
                                continue;
                        }
                        else                    /* VIEW0... select */
                case 'c':                       /* close window */
                case 'd':                       /* default window */
                case 'f':                       /* full window */
                case 'm':                       /* move */
                case 's':                       /* size */
                case '!':                       /* shell */
                        vm(ch);
                        /* not reached */
                case '\b':                      /* \b: rewind */
                case '-':
                        if (! vfprev(vp))
                                continue;
                        (* vfprev(vp))(vp);
                case '\n':                      /* \n: next screen */
                case '\r':
                case '+':
                        if ((* vfscreen(vp))(vp) != EOF)
                                continue;
```

---

† Regrettably, that does exclude a pattern search based on **regexp**(3).

```
        case 'q':                              /* q: quit viewing */
        case 'D' & 31:
                break;
        }
        return vexec(vp) = (Function) fileclose;
    }
}
```

The **switch** is perhaps a bit convoluted, but a **switch** is the best selector for key presses, and many inputs happen to require the same reaction in the code. It turns out to be convenient if we can switch from controlling the file display directly to view management. **vm**( ) was carefully engineered to support just that.

Section 4.7 introduced **mvwgetkey**( ). This function combines all operations needed in **file**( ): the cursor is positioned, the window refreshed, and a key press is read, decoded, and returned. Since the results of **mvwgetkey**( ) can be mapped through **keymap**( ) in the desk calculator, users of an intelligent terminal could even bind keys like *next page* or *scroll* to our pagination mechanism. Alternatively, we could consent to a few more cases in the **switch**...

5.3 Viewing Another Process

fopen(3) connects to a file; **popen**(3) connects to another process. Both functions return a FILE pointer. **fseek**(3) cannot be applied to the pointer returned by **popen**( ), but this is the only difference. All other input and output functions from the *stdio* library can be used on file connections or on pipes alike. Therefore, we should be able to view output from another process simply by replacing **fopen**( ) in **fileopen**( ) by **popen**( ) and by not supplying access to **rewind**( ).

Fine Print in *popen( )*

Unfortunately, things are not quite that simple in the context of multiple views. If **popen**( ) is used to establish a preprocessor, the new process will share standard input with its caller. In our case, if the preprocessor decided to read standard input, a very confusing situation would result at the terminal keyboard.

popen( ) only connects standard output of a preprocessor to the returned FILE pointer. Diagnostic output is shared with the caller. In our case, if the preprocessor decided to write to diagnostic output, view management and error messages would be cheerfully mixed on the terminal screen.

Finally, **popen**( ) does not change signal settings. We usually dedicate a terminal signal as **vsig** to enter the view manager. The view manager connects **vsig** with an internal function. Following **exec**(2) in the new process created by **popen**( ), the signal **vsig** will revert to default state because the code of the internal function is gone.

A terminal signal, however, is sent to all processes with the same controlling terminal, and the controlling terminal is inherited by descendant processes like those created by **popen**( ). Once we cause **vsig** at the terminal to enter view management in *wish*, we are likely to destroy the new process at the same time.

Clearly, we need to build our own version of **popen( )**. We only need the preprocessor side, but we should connect standard and diagnostic output of the preprocessor to our FILE pointer in *wish*. We should assign the null device as standard input for the preprocessor, and we must arrange for **vsig** to be ignored:

```
#define nulldev()       open("/dev/null", O_RDWR)

static load(bp, fd)                     /* load image */
        register char * bp;             /* from this file */
        register int fd;                /* to this output */
{
        sigdefault();
        if ((close(0), nulldev() == 0)
            && (close(1), dup(fd) == 1)
            && (close(2), dup(1) == 2))
                export(),
                execl(SHELL, "sh", "-c", bp, (char *) 0);
        _exit(127);
}
```

load( ) must be executed in the new process, i.e., following **fork( )** within our version of **popen( )**.

sigdefault( ) is responsible for a reasonable signal state. If we plan to use our file and process viewing package as part of other applications, we may have various signal conventions. Therefore, **sigdefault( )** is application specific and should be placed near that point of the code where **vmain( )** and **vcatch( )** are called, i.e., in *wish.c*:

```
sigdefault()                            /* undo our damage */
{
        signal(SIGINT, SIG_IGN);
}
```

What about the excursion to the shell from the view manager discussed in Section 4.4? Why did we not call **sigdefault( )** there? If we had to, we would make the view manager more application dependent. But that excursion to the shell is under control of the view manager and the parent process ignores the terminal signals **SIGINT** and **SIGQUIT** while the descendant is running. All other signals may as well follow normal UNIX conventions there. They cannot be caused by the terminal for the parent, and the descendant should inherit their state from the parent as usual.

An excursion to the shell is patterned after **system**(3). This mechanism suspends the parent and turns execution and terminal control over to the descendant. **popen( )** and our variation does not suspend the parent, because we really want concurrency and communication through a pipe. Here we need to protect the descendant from a terminal signal that is deliberately supported to control the parent.

Viewing Output from a Command: *pipeopen( )*

With special effects delegated to **load**(), we are ready to connect a view to the output of a concurrent process. **pipeopen**() sets up a pipe, builds a **FILE** pointer for viewing at one end, and creates the new process at the other so that **load**() can be called there:

```
Function pipeopen(vp, bp)                    /* display output of command */
        register View * vp;
        register char * bp;
{       FILE * fp;
        int fds[2];

        if (pipe(fds))
                response("?cannot make pipe");
        private(fds[0]), private(fds[1]);

        if (! (fp = fdopen(fds[0], "r")))
        {       close(fds[0]), close(fds[1]);
                response("?cannot connect");
        }

        switch (vpid(vp) = fork()) {
        case -1:
                fclose(fp), close(fds[1]);
                response("?cannot create process");
        case 0:
                load(bp, fds[1]);
        }

        close(fds[1]);

        vfp(vp) = fp;
        setup(vp, screen, next, (Function) 0, "?no output");
        return vexec(vp) = (Function) file;
}
```

Of course, the new file descriptors must be private. *close on exec* is a property of the file descriptor, not of the file connection it represents. If we duplicate a file descriptor, the copy does not inherit *close on exec*. This is why we can safely call **private**() in **pipeopen**() and need not fear that our pipe is disconnected as soon as the new program is loaded by **exec** in **load**().

Throughout **pipeopen**() we must be very careful that we do not lose resources if we run into error conditions, and that we do not end up with copies of *wish* competing for the terminal if loading the new program fails.

load() is executed in a new process. If anything goes wrong, **load**() must not return. It should also not flush any *stdio* buffers, since they belong to the old process. Therefore, **load**() must be terminated with _**exit**(). If we called **exit**(), we would actually end up in our own function in the view manager, terminate screen processing, and reset the terminal state!

Back in *wish*, if we can create a pipe in **pipeopen( )**, but if we cannot convert it to a FILE pointer with **fdopen**(3), or if we cannot create a new process with **fork( )**, we have to free whatever resources we have acquired at this point.

It is also quite easy to overlook some of the four file descriptors resulting from the combination of **pipe( )** and **fork( )**. None is closed explicitly in **load( )**, but the *close on exec* state takes care of closing the two file descriptors in the new process. One file descriptor in the old process is wrapped into a FILE pointer, stored in **View**, used during file viewing, and finally closed in **fileclose( )**. The final file descriptor is closed just before **setup( )**.

Closing a Pipe

How does our concurrent process end? If we keep viewing its output from the pipe, the process should eventually complete its work, and we will receive an end of file condition. However, **pipeopen( )** has set up **file( )** as dialog control function, and **file( )** will call **fileclose( )** once we decide to quit viewing.

If the last process reading a pipe terminates, a process writing the pipe receives SIG-PIPE, but only when it performs a write operation. If the concurrent process uses *stdio*, output will be buffered and it takes a while before it is actually written. If the concurrent process is grinding away without writing, it does not receive the signal. Processes, or more precisely, process descriptions in the vector of all processes kept by the UNIX kernel, are a scarce resource for *wish*, and we should not leave a more or less discarded process occupying a precious process table slot. Consequently, if our view controls a process, we arrange for **fileopen( )** to send it an explicit SIGPIPE signal. The following lines are added:

```
if (vpid(vp) > 0)                /* pipe and no output?? */
        kill(vpid(vp), SIGPIPE), vpid(vp) = 0;
```

Signals are a bit brutal as means of process communication. If a process is coded to only expect SIGPIPE during a write operation on standard output, it may be caught by surprise. The advantage of conserving resources, however, outweighs the potential drawback of clobbering a very tightly coded program.

Viewing the Log of a Command: *bgopen( )* and *bgwait( )*

We cannot back up in a pipe. When running a compiler, for example, it might be better to catch the output in a temporary file so that we can move back and forth in reviewing the results.

It turns out that a small modification of **pipeopen( )** is sufficient to provide this service implicitly. Basically, we connect the output from the concurrent process to a temporary file created with **tmpfile**(3) and arrange for the view responsible to wait until process completion:

```
Function bgopen(vp, bp)                              /* start cycle */
        register View * vp;
        register char * bp;
{       static Function bgwait();

        if (! (vfp(vp) = tmpfile()))
                response("?cannot make log");
        private(fileno(vfp(vp)));

        switch (vpid(vp) = fork()) {
        case -1:
                fclose(vfp(vp)), vfp(vp) = (FILE *) 0;
                response("?cannot create process");
        case 0:                                     /* child process */
                load(bp, fileno(vfp(vp)));
        }

        vinfo(vp) = (Function) bginfo, vopen(vp), doupdate();
        return vexec(vp) = (Function) bgwait;
}
```

Waiting will probably take a while. Therefore, we set up a special information function **bginfo**( ) to change the appearance of the view on the terminal screen, and we introduce a separate view state function **bgwait**( ) to be called by the view manager if our view is reselected while we are waiting.

```
static Function bgwait(vp)                           /* join file cycle */
        register View * vp;
{
        while (vpid(vp) > 0)
                vwait((int *) 0);

        prev(vp);

        setup(vp, screen, next, prev, "?no output");
        return vexec(vp) = (Function) file;
}
```

bgwait( ) completes the preparations for **file**( ). Once the concurrent process is done, the temporary file is rewound. Now we are at the beginning of a file that can be viewed as if it had been accessed by **fileopen**( ).

    bgwait( ) is the beneficiary of the **vwait**( ) mechanism. Clearly, if we require a view to wait for process completion, we must not lose track of the process. **wait**(2) is not process specific, i.e., we cannot postpone hearing about process completion even if we would temporarily like to. This is why we added a wait mechanism to the view manager that receives the information from **wait**( ) and informs the responsible view.

    If **command**( ) calls **bgwait**( ), we will execute **vwait**( ) repeatedly until our own process terminates and the view manager informs us by resetting **vpid(vp)**. Our user might get bored and issue a view management signal to switch to another view. The signal will interrupt **wait( )** within **vwait( )**, and the current view is then deselected. Once it is selected again, waiting continues unless *wish* has waited somewhere else, our process has completed, and **vwait( )** has already reset our **vpid(vp)**.

It should be clear now why we had to call **vwait( )** during the excursion to the shell from the view manager in Section 4.4. Processes connected to views might complete there. The **vwait( )** mechanism will only work if it is used throughout the application.

5.4 Help

UNIX systems keep manual pages online to serve as quick reference. Unfortunately, there are very many pages, and on most systems they need to be formatted before they can be looked at. More often than not, the SYNOPSIS is all we really need at the terminal. Schreiner (1987) suggests building a 'usage' database, for example by extracting the SYNOPSIS sections from the manual pages, and delivering the information with a new command *use* in place of *man*(1). Tests show that the usage database can be kept online even on small systems. *use* requires on the order of one second real time and negligible amounts of CPU time where *man* takes 5 seconds of CPU time in 18 seconds of real time.

use outperforms *man* because it avoids directory searches and formatting. The usage database is kept as a single text file with the information ready to be displayed. A sorted index, which *use* can load with three **read**(2) operations, aids in quickly locating the information within the database. The index is built with a program *mkuse* from Schreiner (1987). This program can also be used to extract parts of an existing database, add new information, and rebuild the index.

The usage database is a very convenient way to add online information to a program such as *wish*. In this section we will briefly review the design of the database and show how easily viewing the database can be integrated with our text display mechanism. The sources of *use* and *mkuse* are enclosed with the software for this book available from the publisher.

The Usage Database

The usage database was developed with the following criteria in mind: the database is a single file to avoid the directory searches which account for a large amount of the real time overhead of *man*; the database is a text file to simplify processing; the amount of information per search key in the database is not limited; there is an index which can be loaded with very few **read( )** operations and provides quick access to information for the various search keys; several search keys can refer to the same information; contents of the database do not change very often; building and rebuilding the database is a stream operation performed in a single pass by a separate program.

The database can be built in a single pass if the index is at the end of the file. The index can be loaded quickly if its beginning and size are known. If there is no predefined limit on the information in the database, index size and position must be written into the database. This information can be written at the very end of the file and with a standard format of known length. Here is a very small database describing *cdc* and *use*:

```
# use.1 help ?
use [-e] [-n] [-u database] [-v] [term...]
# cdc.1 curses
cdc [-c cmdlines] [-o out] [-v] [file...]
##
?        15
cdc.1    73
curses   73
help     15
use.1    15
plen=0003 nlen=0011 num=0005
```

The database consists of groups of information lines preceded by key lines. A key line starts with the flag character which is at the same time the first character in the database file. The rest of the key line is optional. If the database is used as input to the database rebuilder *mkuse*, the key line must contain one or more keys separated by white space.

A key line starting with two flag characters separates the information part of the database from the index. The index consists of index lines with fixed lengths sorted by keys. The index is followed by the position information: **plen** is the length of the position field in each index line and is large enough to accommodate every position in the database file; **nlen** is the length of an entire index line and accommodates **plen**, the longest key and a newline; **num** is the number of index entries. Keys are blank padded.

Clearly, the position information can be obtained with a single **lseek**(2) and **read**(2) system call. Given this information, one more **lseek**() and **read**() will retrieve the index. The index is suitable for **bsearch**(3) as long as we use a modification of **strcmp**(3) that allows white space to terminate a key.† If we code carefully, **bsearch**() can even be used to locate the first one in a sequence of keys selected by a prefix. Given an index entry, one more **lseek**() operation makes the information accessible. The details, as well as building the index and extracting a database from online manual pages, are discussed in Schreiner (1987).

Accessing a Usage Database

Access to a usage database can be packaged as a few simple functions. *use* can even be implemented as a test driver for the functions.

```
int loaduse(fnm, db) char * fnm, * db;
int finduse(s) char * s;
FILE * seekuse(n) int n;
```

loaduse() is called to initiate access to a database. A specific pathname can be passed as **fnm**. If **fnm** is a null pointer, **db** specifies a filename in a standard directory. The directory may be overridden with the environment variable **USE**. If the database index can be loaded, **loaduse**() returns the flag character. **EOF** indicates an error. **loaduse**() may be called again to access a different database.

---

† With white space, the database file is easier to handle with editors and other standard tools.

        finduse( ) is called to find an index entry matching the key or prefix **s**. If the result is zero, no matching key could be found. A positive result indicates an exact match, a negative result specifies the first of possibly several keys matching the prefix. If **s** is a minus sign, **finduse( )** will return -1 to provide access to all keys.

        seekuse( ) is called with the result of **finduse( )** and will return the database file pointer, correctly positioned to the beginning of the information. **seekuse( )** will return a null pointer if the argument is invalid or if the file connection cannot be positioned correctly. If the database is no longer needed, it could even be disconnected by applying **fclose( )** to the result of **seekuse( )**.

Viewing a Usage Database

Given the access functions for a usage database, we can easily display the information in a view. We assume that one database entry fits in a view and we use the **vfprev(vp)** and **vfnext(vp)** functions to move back and forth among neighboring entries. **helpopen( )** must connect us to the database:

```
static int helpflag = EOF;              /* usage database delimeter */

Function helpopen(vp, bp)               /* start cycle */
        register View * vp;
        char * bp;
{       register int n;

        if (helpflag == EOF || *bp == '?')
        {       FILE * fp, * seekuse();
                char * db;

                if (*bp != '?' || ! *(db = bp+1 + strspn(bp+1, " \t")))
                        db = USEDB;

                if ((helpflag = loaduse((char *) 0, db)) == EOF
                    || ! (fp = seekuse(1)))
                {       helpflag = EOF;
                        response("?cannot open database");
                }
                private(fileno(fp));

                if (*bp == '?')
                        return (Function) 0;
        }

        if (! (n = finduse(bp)))
                response("?%s", bp);
        vfpos(vp) = n > 0 ? n : - n;

        vfp(vp) = (FILE *) 0;
        setup(vp, nexthelp, nexthelp, prevhelp, "?i/o problem");
        return vexec(vp) = (Function) file;
}
```

If we do not know a flag character yet, or if the user requests access to a specific database using **??**,† we try to access the database using **loaduse()**. If successful, we obtain the file pointer by pretending an interest in the first entry with **seekuse(1)** and make it **private()**.

If the user passed a database name, we are done. Otherwise, **finduse()** must be able to find a matching key. Because we want to be able to move back and forth in the database, we need to store the current index as part of the information in our **View**. Displaying help thus necessitates another component **vfpos(vp)**.

Clearly, the database index does not need to be reloaded for every query, even from another view, and the file pointer should belong to the *use* module. We store a null pointer as **vfp(vp)** and **fileclose()** has been coded carefully to leave well enough alone. Therefore, we can join the normal display cycle in **file()** with our own moving functions **nexthelp()** and **prevhelp()**.

```
        static int nexthelp(vp)                /* show next entry */
                register View * vp;
        {       register int y;
                WINDOW * wp = view(vp);
                FILE * fp, * seekuse();
                char buf[BUFSIZ];

                if (! (fp = seekuse(vfpos(vp) ++)))
                        return EOF;

                for (werase(wp), y = -1; y < maxy(wp) - 1; ++ y)
                {       fgets(buf, sizeof buf, fp);
                        if (*buf == helpflag)
                                break;
                        put(wp, y, buf);
                }
                return 0;
        }
```

nexthelp() positions to the current entry with **seekuse()** and advances the entry number for the next call. The actual display is patterned after **screen()** and based on **put()** from Section 5.2. A flag character indicates the end of the current entry, and if **seekuse()** cannot position properly we are probably at the end of the database.

```
        static prevhelp(vp)                    /* backup one entry */
                register View * vp;
        {
                vfpos(vp) -= 2;                /* is at next */
        }
```

prevhelp() must be coded carefully. Following **nexthelp()**, the position component **vfpos(vp)** already designates the next entry. Consequently, we must back up two positions. This can get us at most back to zero, i.e., **seekuse()** will return a null pointer when it is subsequently called from **nexthelp()**.

---

† The first **?** is removed by prefix extraction in **command()**, but we will receive the second one.

5.5 Information Functions

We have skipped the issue of information functions thus far. A single function can be passed to **vmain( )** with the parameter identifier **V_INFO** to be called whenever **vopen( )** is called for a view. We have seen a very simple information function in Section 4.2.

With our different view states and default prefixes we need to provide more visual clues to the user. If a view expects command input, we let the default information function surround it by a double frame. If there is a default prefix, we display it in the center of the top edge of the frame:

```
static info(vp)                         /* dispatch information */
        register View * vp;
{
        if (vinfo(vp))
                (* vinfo(vp))(vp);
        else
        {       register WINDOW * wp = vframe(vp);

                wframe2(wp, 0, 0, 0, 0);
                if (vprefix(vp))
                        mvwprinta(wp, 0, 0, maxx(wp), "CC %c ", vprefix(vp));
        }
}
```

This function is passed to **vmain( )**. We will discuss **mvwprinta( )** below.

For other states, where a view is not expecting command input, we extend the idea of view state functions to local information functions as well. The application-specific part of the **View** structure has a component **vinfo(vp)** and, if it is set, **info( )** will call this function rather than drawing the double frame. The file display module normally uses the following function:

```
static info(vp)                           /* mark frame */
        register View * vp;
{       register WINDOW * wp = vframe(vp);

        wframe(wp, 0, 0, 0, 0);
        if (vprefix(vp))
                mvwprinta(wp, 0, 2, maxx(wp)-4, "CC %c %s ",
                        vprefix(vp), vhistory(vp));
        else
                mvwprinta(wp, 0, 2, maxx(wp)-4, "CC %s ", vhistory(vp));

        if (vfprev(vp))
                mvwprinta(wp, maxy(wp)-1, 2, maxx(wp)-4,
                        "RL \\n \\b cdfmqs! %c-%c ", VIEW0, VIEW0 + NVIEW - 1);
        else
                mvwprinta(wp, maxy(wp)-1, 2, maxx(wp)-4,
                        "RL \\n cdfmqs! %c-%c ", VIEW0, VIEW0 + NVIEW - 1);
}
```

info( ) is local to *file.c* since it is only posted by way of **vinfo(vp)**. It draws a single frame and writes the command that initiated the display operation in the center of the top edge. This command is the last input buffer and is stored in **vhistory(vp)**. If there is a default prefix set in **vprefix(vp)** it is also displayed, since it may have influenced command execution.

    info( ) prompts with the key presses for file viewing on the bottom edge of the frame. **\b** is only permitted if there is a way to back up, i.e., if **vfprev(vp)** is set. The prompt conflicts less with the text display if it is shown at the right end on the bottom edge of the frame.

    No input is permitted while a view is waiting for a process to complete so that its output can be displayed from a temporary file. Therefore, **bgopen( )** posts its own information function **bginfo( )** which is replaced by **info( )** once the process is done and text is shown:

```
static bginfo(vp)                        /* "waiting" */
        register View * vp;
{       register WINDOW * wp = vframe(vp);

        wframe(wp, 0, 0, 0, 0);
        if (vprefix(vp))
                mvwprinta(wp, 0, 2, maxx(wp)-4, "CC %c ", vprefix(vp));
        mvwprinta(wp, maxy(wp)-1, 2, maxx(wp)-4, "RL waiting ");
}
```

This display is very similar to the default. It is a single frame with **vprefix(vp)** on the top and the word **waiting** on the bottom edge. Note that **bgopen( )** sets up this information function, calls **vopen( )** to issue the call back to **bginfo( )**, and then calls **doupdate( )** to make sure the new frame is really sent to the terminal.

Aligned Output: *mvwprinta( )*

The information functions are often faced with the problem of arranging formatted output in a 'pretty' position on the screen. The *curses* function **printw( )** will do the job if there is enough room and if we want to control the starting position, i.e., if the output is to be left aligned. Aligning the right end or centering text is also not too hard. However, if the desired output is too long, we have another three possibilities: we can show the beginning, the end, or the center part of the output within the available space.

    mvwprinta( ) is a private library function to solve all of these problems. It takes almost the same arguments as **mvwprintw( )**, and it interprets the first two characters of the format as alignment control.

```
int mvwprinta(wp, y, x, wid, fmt, ...)
        WINDOW * wp;                     /* output window */
        int y, x, wid;                   /* position and width */
        char * fmt;                      /* output format */
```

The output is formatted by **sprintf**(3) and tab characters are replaced by blanks to avoid surprises in the output window. If the output fits in **wid** columns, the first character of **fmt** controls alignment: **C** centers the result, **R** produces right aligned output, any other character arranges for left alignment. If the output does not fit in **wid** columns, the second character of

fmt selects the part of the output to be shown: **C** selects the center, **R** selects the right end, any other character selects the left end. Both alignment control characters are not passed to **sprintf( )**.

5.6 Conclusion

In this chapter we have significantly enhanced our window shell, and we have built some simple file viewers that are perhaps more useful than the calculator discussed in the previous chapters. *wish*, however, is more a vehicle to study implementation issues in the context of *curses* than an end or tool in its own right. Let us review a few of the lessons learned.

Chapter 3 discussed scrolling. The technique developed there to keep the bottom line free adapts equally well to a situation where an entire window is to be filled. We could just as easily go back to automatic wraparound at the right margin, as long as we do not scroll the window up by outputting too much at the bottom. The only difficult problem in this context would be to reconnect autowrapped lines automatically once a view is made bigger.

Chapter 4 introduced the view manager for a single application. Section 5.1 has shown a general technique to run almost arbitrary applications in individual views. Section 5.5 demonstrated, that each application can even have its own information function to mark up the view frame.

Writing a single application to run under control of the view manager and a dispatching function like **command( )** is nearly as easy as writing a stream-oriented application. We just need to make sure that the current view state function posted in **vexec(vp)** may be restarted from the top if our view is reselected by the view manager. An application does not concern itself at all with other applications that may have been linked to the same view manager and dispatching function. In this way, applications exhibit a lot of the properties of concurrent sequential processes.

Viewing files, and even a usage database, are applications requiring very little code. However, we have seen that a few conventions have to be carefully observed even for such simple applications.

- We need to keep our open files **private( )** to avoid interference between otherwise unrelated applications.
- We need to monitor carefully and post all process completions if we expect to wait for a specific process to complete. In this respect, applications cannot be coded as if they were entirely independent.
- We need to guard even more carefully than usual against loss of resources such as file descriptors and process table slots. Multiple views are intended for multiple amounts of work, and they are likely to consume more resources than a single thread program.
- Finally, we must keep our signal management straight. If we use a terminal signal for view management, we must protect descendant processes from it. Starting a descendant process in its own process group would also protect it, but if the descendant opens another terminal, it might unexpectedly get it as a new control terminal.

All things considered, view programming is not much harder than using *stdio*, and the results are certainly more versatile. However, we must observe a few extra restrictions as described above. The last chapter deals with the problem of two-way conversations between a view and another process.

## CHAPTER SIX

An Editor
edit.c

6.1 Windows and Pads

Windows are limited to the size of the terminal screen. **newwin( )** will create a window only if
the requested size is small enough, and **subwin( )** can at most extract the entire enclosing window. In return, **wrefresh( )** is a fairly obvious operation which is even performed implicitly during echoed input or scrolled output as we have seen in Chapter 3.

Sometimes there is a need for much bigger windows which can still be changed with
functions like **waddch( )** or **winsertln( )**, but only a small part of which is displayed on the
terminal screen. The new objects are called *pads*. They are still described by
WINDOW structures but are manipulated with a few new functions:

```
WINDOW * newpad(rows, cols)              /* create */
delwin(pp) WINDOW * pp;                  /* delete */

prefresh(pp, yp,xp, y0s,x0s, y1s,x1s)    /* refresh and update */
pnoutrefresh(pp, yp,xp, y0s,x0s, y1s,x1s)  /* refresh */
        WINDOW * pp;
```

newpad( ) creates a pad but does not assign a screen position to it. **delwin( )** removes
the dynamic memory allocated by **newpad( )**. Once the pad is allocated, normal window functions can be used.†

curses need more information about refreshing a pad than about refreshing a window.
wrefresh( ) must not be called for a pad. Instead, **prefresh( )** takes a top left corner in the pad
and a rectangle on the terminal screen, and sends the rectangle from the pad to the screen.
pnoutrefresh( ) defers sending the output to a subsequent update operation as usual. Error
checking appears to be rudimentary – it is best if the rectangle does not exceed either the terminal screen or the pad.

Why use pads? Pads are useful if we have more information than we can show in a window. The editor in this chapter was designed to demonstrate things that can easily be done with
pads. Using **prefresh( )**, a display rectangle can easily be scrolled horizontally and vertically
over a pad. Scrolling and inserting and deleting lines and characters in a pad are fairly efficient
because the **WINDOW** structure supports this type of operation.

---

† Experiments on XENIX with *cdc* from Section 3.7 reveal a number of peculiarities. At present, it is probably wise to
stick to output functions and to use **scroll( )** explicitly.

As another example, our view manager could have been designed with pads rather than windows. If we identify our idea of a current interior with the bottom left part of a pad, we can get more pleasing results when we change the size of a view. The solution is hardly more costly, since we could use a single pad as large as the terminal screen for each interior, which would then never need to be reallocated.

However, managing pads for views is more complicated. For a pad, we need to remember which part is currently mapped to the terminal screen. Most likely, we would provide a way to review currently hidden parts of the pad from the view, which would further complicate the command language interface of view management. For example, if we type a character at a view, where should it go if the view is not at the bottom left of its pad?

The border between usability of a screen interface and functionality of the view manager is easily crossed in the wrong direction. Window systems on bitmap screens like ATARI, BLIT, or SUN, provide scroll bars and sliders to visualize what part of a 'pad' is currently mapped to the window. When using a mouse, and moving the hand away from the keyboard, sliders are an inviting interface. However, they are hardly practical in our alphanumerical situation.

6.2 Editing with a Pad

As a simple application using pads, let us look at a full screen editor for small files. Following the pattern established by file viewing, the editor consists of three view state functions: **editopen**( ) allocates a pad and loads the file to be edited, **edit**( ) manages the editing dialog, **editclose**( ) writes the pad into the file if requested.

edit( ) is an extension of the cursor control mechanisms that we have seen for *doodle* in Section 3.3 and for changing views in Section 4.5. From the view manager we take the idea of key mapping as encapsulated by the function **mvwgetkey**( ). From *doodle* we borrow the idea of depositing visible characters in the window and using function keys to indicate insertions and deletions. Here is the structure of the main loop:

```
static Function edit(vp)
        register View * vp;
{       register WINDOW * wp = view(vp);
        int ch, y, x, new;
        static Function editclose();

        getyx(vepad(vp), y, x);          /* unchanged by vm */
        new = 1;

        for (;;)
        {       ... force y,x into used part of pad ...
                if (new)
                        ... copy visible part of pad to wp ...

                wmove(vepad(vp), y, x);
                ch = mvwgetkey(wp, y - vetop(vp), x - veleft(vp));
```

```
switch (ch) {
case 'D' & 31:                    /* control D */
            if (x == 0 && y == 0)
                        return (Function) editclose;
            x = y = 0;
            continue;
case 'X' & 31:                    /* control X */
zap:        if (x == 0 && y == 0)
            {       delwin(vepad(vp)),
                    vepad(vp)  = (WINDOW *) 0;
                    return (Function) editclose;
            }
            x = y = 0;
            continue;
backspace:
case '\b':
case KEY_BACKSPACE:
case KEY_LEFT:  -- x; continue;
        ... cursor control applies to y,x ...
case KEY_HOME:  x = veleft(vp);
                y = vetop(vp);
                continue;
        ... jumps are within visible part ...
case '\t':      do
                        waddch(vepad(vp), ' '), ++ x;
                while (x < maxx(vepad(vp)) && (x & 7));
                new = 1;
                continue;
default:        if (ch == erasechar()) goto backspace;
               if (ch == killchar()) goto zap;
               if (isascii(ch) && isprint(ch))
                        waddch(wp, ch),
                        waddch(vepad(vp), ch), ++ x;
               continue;
    }
  }
}
```

The pad is stored as **vepad(vp)** in the application-specific part of **View**. We let **y** and **x** denote the current position in the pad. At the beginning of **edit( )**, the coordinates are initialized from the pad because the view manager does not know it exists.

Cursor moves are simply applied to **y** and **x** and the initial part of the loop will make sure that the move is legal and that the text cursor lies within the view. If not, the cursor may have to be corrected, and **new** is set if the current window must be redrawn from the pad. This is certainly the case when we are just starting.

We need to remember how many lines of the pad contain text and which part of the pad is mapped to the current view. **veuse(vp)** is the current number of text lines, **vetop(vp)** and **veleft(vp)** are the pad coordinates of the top left of the view. This is also application-specific information in **View**:

```
typedef struct user User;
        struct user {
                ... common part ...
                union {
                        ... state specific part ...
                        struct {
                                FILE * e_p;
                                WINDOW * e_pad;
                                char * e_fnm;
                                int e_top, e_left, e_use;
                                } u__e;
                        } u_;
                };

#define _vu(vp)          ((User *) (vp) -> v_user)

#define _vue(vp)         _vu(vp) -> u_.u__e      /* file editing */

#define vep(vp)          (_vue(vp).e_p)          /* edit i/o file */
#define vepad(vp)        (_vue(vp).e_pad)        /* edit pad */
#define vefnm(vp)        (_vue(vp).e_fnm)        /* edit file name */
#define vetop(vp)        (_vue(vp).e_top)        /* top line in window */
#define veleft(vp)       (_vue(vp).e_left)       /* left column in window */
#define veuse(vp)        (_vue(vp).e_use)        /* lines in use */
```

vep(vp) and **vefnm(vp)** describe the file being edited. They are used by **editclose( )** to rewrite the file or remove it if it was created by mistake. The selection **zap** shows that we use **vepad(vp)** as hidden parameter for **editclose( )**: if that pointer is a null pointer, the file cannot be rewritten.

As the preceding code shows, moving the cursor and adding characters is simple. *curses* are powerful enough to handle even complicated operations such as adding or deleting lines and characters. Either we keep the view window and the pad synchronized or we set **new** to redraw the window:

```
case KEY_DL:     if (-- veuse(vp) < 1)
                         veuse(vp) = 1;
                 while (y >= veuse(vp))
                         -- y;
                 wdeleteln(vepad(vp)), new = 1;
                 continue;
case KEY_IL:     if (veuse(vp) >= maxy(vepad(vp)))
                         repad(vp);
                 ++ veuse(vp);
                 winsertln(wp), winsertln(vepad(vp));
                 continue;
case KEY_DC:     wdelch(vepad(vp)), new = 1;
                 continue;
case KEY_IC:     winsch(wp, ' '), winsch(vepad(vp), ' ');
                 continue;
```

Inserting a blank line or a blank character does not change the cursor position, i.e., we can avoid setting **new**. Deleting a line or a character requires some redrawing. Deleting the entire file, or from the cursor to the end of the file, is dangerous enough to call for some safeguarding. We only execute these operations if the cursor is at the beginning of the file or a line. If not, we move it there:

```
case KEY_CLEAR: if (x == 0 && y == 0)
                        werase(vepad(vp)),
                        veuse(vp) = 1, new = 1;
                else
                        x = y = 0;
                continue;
case KEY_EOS:   if (x == 0)
                        veuse(vp) = y <= 1 ? 1 : y,
                        wclrtobot(vepad(vp)), new = 1;
                else
                        x = 0;
                continue;
```

veuse(vp) is not permitted to drop below one. We use the same design as $vi(1)$ and assume even an empty file to contain one blank line. This decision greatly simplifies dealing with an empty file.

If a *newline* or *return* is pressed, we erase the rest of the current line and move to a new line. A similar effect can be achieved with **KEY_EOL**:

```
case '\n':
case '\r':      if (++ y >= veuse(vp))
                {       if (veuse(vp) >= maxy(vepad(vp)))
                                repad(vp);
                        ++ veuse(vp), new = 1;
                }
                x = 0;
case KEY_EOL:   wclrtoeol(wp), wclrtoeol(vepad(vp));
                continue;
```

If we receive *newline* or *return* at the end of the used part of the pad, our user probably wants to add a line to the text. Eventually the pad will overflow and we propose to let a new function **repad()** take care of the problem. **repad()** already sneaked in when a blank line was inserted at **KEY_IL** above.

curses are not horribly fast in decoding function keys. Our editor is more comfortable to use if we support a few keys for moving forward and backward by pages and for moving the view up and down in the text by a line while preserving the text cursor position. It turns out that all four operations can be handled by a single function:

```
case KEY_SF:    vetop(vp) = shift(& y, vetop(vp),
                        1,
                        maxy(wp), veuse(vp), & new);
                continue;
```

```
       case KEY_SR:      vetop(vp) = shift(& y, vetop(vp),
                             -1,
                             maxy(wp), veuse(vp), & new);
                         continue;
       case KEY_NPAGE: vetop(vp) = shift(& y, vetop(vp),
                             maxy(wp) - 1,
                             maxy(wp), veuse(vp), & new);
                         continue;
       case KEY_PPAGE: vetop(vp) = shift(& y, vetop(vp),
                             - (maxy(wp) - 1),
                             maxy(wp), veuse(vp), & new);
                         continue;
```

This already concludes the development of a moderately comfortable screen editor for small files. *curses* do most of the character handling work and keep the screen quiet.

Service Functions

shift( ) moves the mapped part of the pad by an amount **delta**. It needs to know the **size** of the view window, the line number **map** of the top window line in the pad, and **lim**, the number of used lines in the pad. **shift( )** returns the line number of the pad which is the new top of the window, and it sets **new** if the window must be redrawn. **shift( )** is useful because it handles four complicated vertical moves and it copes with a number of special cases:

```
   static int shift(posp, map, delta, size, lim, remap)
       int * posp;                  /* -> current position */
       int map;                     /* current low end */
       int delta;                   /* proposed shift */
       int size;                    /* mapped range */
       int lim;                     /* high value */
       int * remap;                 /* set if shift ok */
   {
       if (map + delta >= 0 && map + delta < lim)
               map += delta, *remap = 1;
       else if (delta < 0 && map > 0)
               map = 0, *remap = 1;
       else if (delta > 0 && map < lim - delta)
               map = lim - delta, *remap = 1;
       if (*posp < map)
               *posp = map;
       else if (*posp >= map + size)
               *posp = map + size - 1;
       return map;
   }
```

Depending on the move direction, if we cannot move **delta** lines, we position the top or bottom line of the view near the top or bottom of the used part of the pad. Similarly, the proposed cursor line ***posp** is corrected if it is not within the mapped range.

repad() must increment the space available for text. An efficient solution would only extend the line vectors _y[ ], _firstch[ ], and _lastch[ ], but we opt for more portability and use copywin(). Thus, repad() is very similar to remake1() in Section 4.5:

```
static repad(vp)
        register View * vp;
{       register WINDOW * p;
        int y, x;
        static Function editclose();

        if (p = newpad(maxy(vepad(vp)) + LINES, COLS - 2))
        {       getyx(vepad(vp), y, x);
                copywin(vepad(vp), p, 0, 0,
                        0, 0, maxy(vepad(vp))-1, maxx(vepad(vp))-1, FALSE);
                delwin(vepad(vp)), vepad(vp) = p;
                wmove(p, y, x);
        }
        else
        {       delwin(vepad(vp)), vepad(vp) = (WINDOW *) 0;
                editclose(vp);
                response("?too big");
        }
}
```

This editor is meant for small files so we extend the pad by one terminal screen at a time. If we run out of memory, we let editclose() arrange things to leave the old file intact and return to command mode by way of response(). The view state function bgwait() in Section 5.3 already required that response() can be called from a view state that is not the first in a cycle.

Finally, how do we let the view follow the text cursor and redraw the current view if necessary? shift() hints that we can move by a set amount and take view and cursor with us without really knowing if the computation is concerned with a vertical or a horizontal move. Therefore, we solve the positioning check with a function clip() that takes a proposed position and returns the permitted one:

```
static int clip(pos, map, size, lim, remap)
        int pos;                        /* proposed position */
        int * map;                      /* -> low end */
        int size;                       /* mapped range */
        int lim;                        /* high value */
        int * remap;                    /* set if *map changes */
{
        if (pos < 0)
                pos = 0;
        else if (pos >= lim)
                pos = lim - 1;
        if (*map >= lim)
                *map = lim - size, *remap = 1;
        if (*map < 0)
                *map = 0, *remap = 1;
```

```
                    if (pos < *map || pos >= *map + size)
                    {      if ((*map = pos - size/2) < 0)
                                  *map = 0;
                           *remap = 1;
                    }
                    return pos;
            }
```

If the proposed position is not within limits, we set it to the low or high end. If the mapped range is not within the permitted limit, we correct it. Finally, if the corrected position is outside the corrected mapped range, we change the mapped range once again to center the corrected position as well as possible.

All of these operations have influenced **new**. Here is how we replot the view if necessary:

```
        static Function edit(vp)
                ...
                for (;;)
                {      y = clip(y, & vetop(vp), maxy(wp), veuse(vp), & new);
                       x = clip(x, & veleft(vp), maxx(wp), COLS - 2, & new);

                       if (new)
                       {      werase(wp);
                              for (new = 0; new < maxy(wp); ++ new)
                                     mvwaddch(wp, new, 0, '~');
                              if ((new = veuse(vp) - vetop(vp)) > maxy(wp))
                                     new = maxy(wp);
                              copywin(vepad(vp), wp, vetop(vp), veleft(vp),
                                     0, 0, new - 1, maxx(wp) - 1, FALSE);
                              new = 0;
                       }

                       wmove(vepad(vp), y, x);
                       ch = mvwgetkey(wp, y - vetop(vp), x - veleft(vp));
                       ...
```

We cannot use **prefresh()**! View management permits interruptions. When **edit()** is started again, only the current window is redrawn without flickering. If we call **prefresh()** rather than copying the mapped part of the pad to **view(vp)**, and if we interrupt editing and overlay the view, on return a blank view would be drawn and immediately refilled with the text.

It is also interesting that the ˜ to mark empty lines cannot be in the unused part of the pad. On the one hand they would have to be maintained when lines are deleted from the pad. On the other hand they would not be visible when the view is horizontally scrolled away from the edge of the pad. It is simpler to write ˜ and overwrite it during **copywin()** than to piece the view together from special cases. Once again, *curses* waste some CPU time to minimize output and protect the observer from 'visual noise'.

6.3 Loading a File

editopen( ) must create a pad and load a text file into it. The pad will in fact be our edit buffer and must accommodate new lines. Therefore, we count the number of lines in the text file before we allocate a slightly bigger pad. Since our editor is intended for small files, this is reasonably efficient. For larger files we could resort to executing **fstat**(2) and computing the expected number of lines based on the file size and an average line length.

```
static int lc(fp)                            /* count lines */
        register FILE * fp;
{       register int ch, lc = 0;

        while ((ch = getc(fp)) != EOF)
                if (ch == '\n')
                        ++ lc;
        return lc;
}


Function editopen(vp, bp)
        register View * vp;
        char * bp;
{       register int ch, y, x;
        static Function edit(), editclose();
        char * strsave();

        vefnm(vp) = strsave(bp);

        if (vep(vp) = fopen(bp, "r+"))
                veuse(vp) = lc(vep(vp)), rewind(vep(vp));
        else if (vep(vp) = fopen(bp, "w"))
                veuse(vp) = 0;
        else
                response("%s: cannot create", bp);
        private(fileno(vep(vp)));

        if (veuse(vp) < 1)
                veuse(vp) = 1;

        if (! (vepad(vp) = newpad(veuse(vp) + LINES, COLS-2)))
        {       editclose(vp);
                response("?too big");
        }
```

We shall see in the next section why we have to save the file name with the other view information. We have explained in the previous section that even an empty file should contain one blank line. Reserving only one terminal screen full of extra lines is naive – but we really want to edit only small files.

We could now read the file in big chunks and rely on **waddstr( )** to add the chunks to the pad. However, we do not want to cope with invisible characters. We shall see in the next chapter that editing tabs is quite complicated. Therefore, we rely on *stdio* buffering, read single characters from the file, add only visible characters to the pad and expand tabs as blanks.

```
        y = x = 0;
        while ((ch = getc(vep(vp))) != EOF)
                switch (ch) {
                case '\b':
                        if (x > 0)
                                -- x;
                        continue;
                case '\n':
                        ++ y, x = 0;
                        continue;
                case '\r':
                        x = 0;
                        continue;
                case '\t':
                        x += 8, x &= ~7;
                        continue;
                default:
                        if (isascii(ch) && isgraph(ch))
                                mvwaddch(vepad(vp), y, x, ch);
                        ++ x;
                }
        rewind(vep(vp));

        vinfo(vp) = (Function) info, vnow(vp) = N_FILE, vopen(vp);
        werase(view(vp));
        wmove(vepad(vp), 0, 0), vetop(vp) = veleft(vp) = 0;
        return vexec(vp) = (Function) edit;
}
```

Once we are all set, we change the appearance of the frame, clear the old interior of the view, and map the top left corner of the pad, before we switch to **edit( )** as the new view state.

info( ) is almost the function described in Section 5.5. All it lacks is the prompt information at the bottom. A private information function is much easier to maintain than if we added another special case to the function in module *file.c*.

6.4 Saving a Window

editclose( ) is called to wrap things up. In fact, things might be a bit sticky. If editing was aborted, or if it never got going, we should neither clobber an old file nor leave an empty new one behind.

Of course, we could wait to create a new file until we really need it. However, our user might then find out after a lengthy editing session that the new file cannot be written. If we do not implement more editing commands, we can at that point just throw the edit buffer away in despair.

In **editopen( )** we have accessed an existing file in update mode by specifying "r+" as mode for **fopen**(3). A new, empty file was created using "w" to make sure that we can write the edit buffer if desired.

If **editclose( )** finds a null pointer at **vepad(vp)**, editing was aborted. An existing file must now be left alone, a newly created file should be removed. We cannot check if the file is empty: even an empty file should not be removed if editing is aborted and the file existed prior to editing.

We could add yet another flag to our view information, but it turns out that the file itself reveals its old state. **fcntl**(2) can be used to retrieve the flags specified when the file was opened. An existing file is opened with **O_RDWR**, a new file with **O_WRONLY**. This gives us a safe decision to **unlink**(2) a newly created file if editing is aborted. **vefnm(vp)** was saved because it can differ from **vhistory(vp)** and it is needed for removing the file.

```
static Function editclose(vp)
        register View * vp;
{       register int y;

        vexec(vp) =
        vinfo(vp) = (Function) 0, vnow(vp) = N_CMD, vopen(vp);
        if (! vepad(vp))
        {       if (fcntl(fileno(vep(vp)), F_GETFL, 0) == O_WRONLY)
                        unlink(vefnm(vp));
                reply("unchanged");
        }
        else
        {       for (y = 0; y < veuse(vp); ++ y)
                        writeln(vep(vp), vepad(vp), y);
                delwin(vepad(vp)), vepad(vp) = (WINDOW *) 0;
                reply("%d line(s) written", veuse(vp));
        }
        free(vefnm(vp));
        fclose(vep(vp));
        return (Function) 0;
}
```

We have already seen that view state functions can call **response( )**, as long as the current interior of the view is **N_CMD**, i.e., command input. **response( )** does not return, it only calls **_reply( )** to arrange for the output. If we desire a return, we may call **reply( )**. Here we use it to report the result of editing to the user. **editclose( )** must return, otherwise we cannot call it for cleanup from functions like **editopen( )** or **repad( )**, which want to terminate by issuing their own error messages through **response( )**.

writeln( ) is a local function to write a line from a window or pad into a text file. There is no marker in the window line which can be used as a newline indication. Therefore, we first determine the rightmost column in the window after which there is only white space.

```
static writeln(fp, wp, r)
        FILE * fp;
        WINDOW * wp;
        int r;
{       register int ch, c, i = maxx(wp) - 1;

        do
                ch = mvwinch(wp, r, i),
                ch = toascii(ch);
        while (! isgraph(ch) && -- i >= 0);
        for (c = 0; c <= i; ++ c)
        {       ch = mvwinch(wp, r, c);
                ch = toascii(ch);
                if (! isgraph(ch)) ch = ' ';
                putc(ch, fp);
        }
        putc('\n', fp);
}
```

mvwinch() returns the attributed character in a specific position of a window. We take the ASCII value and consider invisible characters to be white space. Once we know the end of the line to write, we output the ASCII values of all characters and replace invisible characters by blanks. This is where tabs should be inserted before the output is written.

Race Conditions

Cleaning up is best confined to a single function. This makes it harder to forget something in a special case. However, the order of cleaning up in functions like **editopen**() does matter. We should certainly not write a pad to a file twice, or worse yet, free a filename twice.

As long as we have a single cleanup function, we have only one place where things can get out of control. Writing the pad into the file might take a while. If the user interrupts us between terminating editing and receiving the confirmation, at least the signal was intentional. The output, however, gets truncated.†

Real trouble would start if, by way of view management, **editclose**() were run twice. This is why we clear **vexec(vp)** before we do anything else. The view manager reselects a view through the view state dispatcher described in Chapter 5. The dispatcher runs the function posted as **vexec(vp)**. As long as we do not provide a way back, **editclose**() might get interrupted and thus pre-empted, but it cannot be run twice in the same edit cycle.

Once signals are used for intentional process control, race conditions cannot be completely eliminated under the signal implementation in System V. Interlocks like our use of **vexec(vp)** must be employed to make a program reasonably secure.

---

† This could be avoided by ignoring the view management signal while we read or write the file.

6.5 Conclusion

Simple is beautiful, and from this point of view our little editor might even be appealing. Still, a more serious editor must handle tabs and longer lines, and it needs a bit more comfort in accessing files. The editing pad should not be reallocated and copied, and reserving fixed length line buffers is a horrible idea for larger files.

The editor was included in *wish* as an example for pads. The code demonstrates that even more sophisticated *curses* output functions like **winsertln( )**, **wdelch( )**, or **wclrtobot( )** can be applied to pads.

A striking effect becomes apparent when the size of an editor view is changed. **edit( )** is then rerun from the top, i.e., **new** is set and the pad is copied to the new interior. If this interior is larger, the old text remains unchanged on the terminal screen, and additional text from the pad appears and continues the old text up to the new edges of the view. Such an effect may be very desirable for file viewers.

The editor also exhibits a principal problem with *curses*: decoding of function keys is quite slow. Experienced users of *vi* know only too well that **hjkl** are often preferable to arrow keys because the letters move the cursor much faster on a busy system. Our editor demonstrates this effect even on a dedicated PC.

While we can still improve our code, we will get an acceptable solution only by changing the decoding of function keys. *curses* are too general. For example, the left arrow key is decoded if it returns a lengthy escape sequence or if it returns a backspace. If *escape* is entered slowly enough, it is decoded as a single character even if it starts all function key sequences. If we really require the full generality, we have to live with sluggish decoding on a busy system. On the other hand, if *escape* is dedicated to only and always start a function key sequence, a much better decoder can be constructed which can still be dynamically configured for various terminals; consult Rochkind (1988) for details and the code.

## CHAPTER SEVEN

Dialog with a Command
talk.c

7.1 Connection Architecture

In Section 5.3 we have seen how to connect a view in order to listen to the output of another process. In this chapter we will attack a similar problem: a view is to host a dialog with another process, i.e., we would like to pass input from the keyboard to a concurrent process, and show input echo and standard and diagnostic output from the other process intermixed in a view. We will call the concurrent process the *client*.

It should really not be too hard to do. Our function **load( )** in Section 5.3 already connects standard and diagnostic output of a client to a pipe constructed in *wish*.

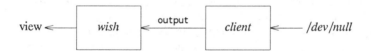

If we introduce another pipe, we can channel input from *wish* to the client as well:

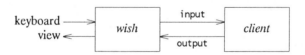

It may come as a surprise that we need two independent pipes – **input** and **output**. However, if *wish* and the client used a single pipe for input and output, either process might read its own output back in.

Given appropriate file descriptors, the basic algorithm for the dialog view state function **talk( )** should be something like the following:

```
while (1)
{       wgetstr(view(vp), buf);
        write(input, buf, strlen(buf));
        n = read(output, buf, sizeof buf);
        buf[n] = '\0';
        waddstr(view(vp), buf), wrefresh(view(vp));
}
```

We use the system calls **read**(2) and **write**(2) to avoid any problems which buffering in *stdio* might cause.

Unfortunately, this simple algorithm has a few problems. **wgetstr**( ) will block until a full line has been entered at the keyboard. **write**( ) will block until the buffer has been written into the pipe. If the client decides not to read standard input, the pipe will eventually fill to capacity and **write**( ) will block forever. **read**( ) will block until the client writes something into the pipe, and if the client does not produce standard or diagnostic output, this will also be forever. There is even a possibility for *deadlock* if the client fills **output** to capacity while *wish* is waiting for the client to read **input**. Only **waddstr**( ) should proceed without major obstacles.

Clearly, we need to ensure that reading the keyboard and communicating with the pipes does not block progress around the loop for long periods of time. **fstat**(2) can be used to check if there is data in a pipe, and we can devise a scheme by which we do not overflow **input** and avoid blocking on read when **output** is empty. However, according to the System V Interface Definition (1986), we cannot find out with **fstat**(2) if there are data waiting to be read from the keyboard.

There is a better technique. **fcntl**(2) can be used to set the **O_NDELAY** flag for a file descriptor. Reading or writing a pipe will not block the calling process if this flag is set. Instead, zero is returned if the operation is not successful, i.e., if a write would overflow or if there are no data waiting to be read.†

curses support a function **nodelay**( ) which sets **O_NDELAY** for the keyboard and keeps **wgetch**( ) from blocking until a key is pressed. Unfortunately, **nodelay**( ) has a few problems. The function has a window argument and should apply to one window at a time, but it appears to be part of the terminal state instead. **endwin**( ) does not reset this condition, usually much to the surprise of the caller of a *curses* program using **nodelay**( ). Finally, the line-oriented *curses* input functions like **getstr**( ) or even **scanw**( ) are unable to cope with **nodelay**( ).

nodelay( ) for the keyboard is not such a good idea anyway. If we make our entire loop non-blocking, *wish* will keep the CPU very busy but without tangible results. Therefore, we read the keyboard but arrange for a timeout using **alarm**(2). Experiments show that **alarm**( ) does not break through **getch**( ). Therefore, we will implement our own line input function **winput**( ) in Section 7.2.

Our basic algorithm can now be adjusted to incorporate non-blocking pipe i/o. **winput**( ) is used to introduce a small timeout interval where the CPU can devote some attention to other processes:

```
sense(sig)
        int sig;
{
        signal(sig, sense);
}

talk(vp)
...
        fcntl(input, F_SETFL, O_NDELAY);
        fcntl(output, F_SETFL, O_NDELAY);
        sense(SIGALRM);
```

† This looks just like end of file. The System V Interface Definition (1986) states that eventually **read**( ) will return -1 and set **EAGAIN** as **errno**.

```
            while (1)
            {       if (winput(view(vp), buf, ... timeout 1 second ...))
                            write(input, buf, strlen(buf));
                    if (n = read(output, buf, sizeof buf))
                    {       buf[n] = '\0';
                            waddstr(view(vp), buf), wrefresh(view(vp));
                    }
            }
```

A few details still need to be cleaned up. If **write**( ) does not succeed, we need to skip calls to **winput**( ) until we can pass on accumulated keyboard input. In this case, the loop will no longer contain a timeout, but we cannot remove the **O_NDELAY** flag from **input** because a deadlock might result.

If our client process terminates, **read**( ) will receive an end of file indication, but this is indistinguishable from an unsuccessful **read**( ) with **O_NDELAY** set. **write**( ) would cause **SIG-PIPE** to be sent back to *wish*, but **write**( ) is not executed until there is more input from the keyboard.

Even if we expect **SIGPIPE**, it may come at the wrong moment. We are better off ignoring the signal altogether. If **write**( ) returns an error, we can check **errno** for **EPIPE** and continue accordingly.

Unfortunately, neither end of file on **read**( ), which we cannot find out anyway, nor **EPIPE** on **write**( ) is a secure indication that our client has passed away. Our loop should really be run until either both pipes are disconnected or the client has terminated. It turns out that **kill**(2) can be used to check if a particular process exists. This condition can be used in **while** to terminate the loop.

7.2 Impatient Input: *winput( )*

We need a function for keyboard input which does not block forever. The basic idea is to set a timeout interval using **alarm**(2), start reading, and sort things out once either a character or **SIGALRM** arrives. **wgetch**( ) does not get broken by the signal,† therefore, we must use **getchar**( ) to read characters and we must inform *curses* by way of **waddch**( ) and **wrefresh**( ).

```
    #ifndef echochar                        /* prior to sysV.3 */
    #define wechochar(wp, ch)       waddch(wp, ch), wrefresh(wp)
    #endif

    int winput(wp, buf, col, p, lim, timeout)
        WINDOW * wp;
        char buf[];                         /* buffer */
        unsigned char col[];                /* window positions */
        char ** p;                          /* next buffer position */
        int lim;                            /* DIM(buf) */
        unsigned timeout;                   /* for alarm() */
    {       register int ch;
```

---

† At least in **keypad**( ) state it must do its own timeout processing.

```
        -- lim;                         /* room for \0 */
    do
    {       getyx(wp, ch, col[*p - buf]);   /* note position */

        if (! timeout)
                ch = getchar();
        else
        {       alarm(timeout);
                if ((ch = getchar()) == EOF)
                        return 0;       /* timed out */
                alarm(0);
        }
```

Volume 3 of the System V Interface Definition (1986), i.e., release 3 of System V, promises an optimized function **wechochar( )** for immediately displaying a single character. Until then we need to supply a suitably conditionalized definition.

winput( ) could be done right here: a single character or a timeout arrives and is returned. However, most of the time we will need an edited line or an indication that a complete line is not yet ready. Line editing in a scrolling window is not exactly simple. Therefore, it makes sense to package it into **winput( )** once and for all.

```
        switch (ch) {
        case '\b':
                backspace(wp, buf, col, p);
                break;
        case 'D' & 31:              /* ^D */
                if (*p == buf)
                        return EOF;
                goto endline;
        case '\r':
                ch = '\n';
        case '\n':
                wechochar(wp, ch);
                *(*p)++ = ch;
        endline:
                **p = '\0';
                return *p - buf;
        case '\t':
                tab(wp, buf, p);
                break;
        default:
                if (ch == erasechar())
                {       backspace(wp, buf, col, p);
                        break;
                }
```

```
                              if (ch == killchar())
                              {       while (*p > buf)
                                              backspace(wp, buf, col, p);
                                      break;
                              }
                              if (isascii(ch) && isprint(ch))
                              {       wechochar(wp, ch);
                                      *(*p)++ = ch, **p = '\0';
                              }
                      }
                      if (*p >= buf + lim)
                              return lim;
              } while (! timeout);
              return 0;
      }
```

Deferring finer points like **backspace**( ) for the moment, there are three possible outcomes: end of file, i.e., *control*-D at the beginning of a new input, an incomplete line, or a complete one. We can indicate the outcomes by the results **EOF**, zero, and a positive line length.

If the result is zero, **winput**( ) might well be called again to continue the operation following some actions related to timing out. This is where we not only need the line buffer **buf[ ]** as an argument, but also the next input position in the buffer ***p**. This position is moved along the buffer, i.e., it must be passed as the address of the actual pointer so that **winput**( ) can change it.

winput( ) might be used by various views to collect simultaneously several input lines. This is why all information, even the current buffer position, must be maintained in parameters and cannot be local to the function.

As the code above shows, collecting a line is not too difficult. There are only two complications: tab characters and backspaces. Tab characters may move us forward beyond the edge of a window and it is best to let *curses* decide when to quit:

```
      static tab(wp, buf, p)
              WINDOW * wp;
              char buf[], ** p;
      {       register int y, x, n = 0;

              *(*p)++ = '\t', **p = '\0';
              do
              {       wechochar(wp, ' ');
                      getyx(wp, y, x);
              } while ((x & 7) && ++ n < 8);
      }
```

We enter a true tab into the line buffer, but we add up to eight blanks to the window until we reach a tab position. This solution works correctly even if scrolling is disabled in a very small window.

Having just moved to a tab stop, we are ready for a request to backspace. Actually, we are not. If we hit the bottom right corner of a window with scrolling disabled, input must continue while there is no more echo. This is just how **wgetstr( )** or normal terminal input on a dumb terminal works. As a result, there is no simple relationship between a character in the line buffer and its position in the window.

If we knew where input originally started we would have a chance. Alas, even if we remember the current window column when the buffer pointer ***p** is at the beginning of the buffer **buf[ ]**, we can still not reconstruct character positions because output may be intermixed with our input.

There is an elegant solution, but it requires a second buffer as long as the line buffer. We simply note the column position of each input character as it is stored. There is no need to store the row: if the column position of the preceding character is larger than the the column position of the current character, we need to move up one row in backspacing.

```
static backspace(wp, buf, col, p)
        WINDOW * wp;
        char buf[];
        unsigned char col[];
        char ** p;
{       int y, x, lastx;

        if (*p <= buf)
                return;
        * -- *p = '\0';

        getyx(wp, y, x);
        lastx = col[*p - buf];

        if (lastx > x && y > 0)              /* BUG at top of window */
                -- y;
        x = lastx;
        mvwaddch(wp, y, x, ' '), wmove(wp, y, x), wrefresh(wp);
}
```

Tabs cannot interfere with moving up one row, since there is a minimum window width enforced in the view manager. We are only out of luck at the top of the window because we cannot scroll text back down.

7.3 Talking to Another Process

winput( ) was deliberately built to be line oriented. Our model client process should believe that it is talking directly to a terminal. Normally, a read operation will return one edited input line. If we passed a single character at a time into the input pipe, we could not perform line editing and the client would receive its input a character at a time, i.e., more or less in 'raw' mode.

We are ready to implement the dialog algorithm designed in Section 7.1. **View** is extended once more with application-specific components:

```
#define TLEN     128              /* dialog buffer */

typedef struct user User;
        struct user {
                ... common part ...
                union {
                        ... state specific part ...
                        struct {
                                char t_alk[TLEN], * t_p;
                                unsigned char t_col[TLEN];
                                int t_fds[2], t_len;
                                } u__t;
                        } u_;
                };

#define _vu(vp)        ((User *) (vp) -> v_user)

#define _vut(vp)       _vu(vp) -> u_.u__t        /* talking to process */

#define vtout(vp)      (_vut(vp).t_fds[0])       /* output from client */
#define vtin(vp)       (_vut(vp).t_fds[1])       /* input to client */
#define vtlen(vp)      (_vut(vp).t_len)          /* full in vtalk */
#define vtalk(vp)      (_vut(vp).t_alk)          /* dialog buffer */
#define vtp(vp)        (_vut(vp).t_p)            /* next position in vtalk */
#define vtcol(vp)      (_vut(vp).t_col)          /* column positions */
```

Unfortunately, we need two buffers as part of **View** to keep **winput**() happy. However, input lines should be short and we can use a separate dimension for the buffers. **winput**() will monitor the buffer limit. (An extreme test is to put two views into dialog state and switch views between key presses to accumulate two independent input lines simultaneously. Even that works.)

talkopen() must construct the pipes and the client process. This is a variation on the theme introduced by **load**() in Section 5.3:

```
Function talkopen(vp, cmd)
        register View * vp;
        char * cmd;
{       register int fd;
        int status;
        static int _fds[] = { -1, -1, -1, -1 };
        static Function talk();

#define input(x)        _fds[0 + (x)]    /* from us to command */
#define output(x)       _fds[2 + (x)]    /* from command to us */
#define closeall()                                      \
        for (fd = 0; fd < DIM(_fds); ++ fd)             \
                if (_fds[fd] >= 0)                       \
                        close(_fds[fd]), _fds[fd] = -1;

        closeall();
```

```
if (pipe(& input(0)) == -1
    || pipe(& output(0)) == -1
    || fcntl(input(1), F_SETFL, O_NDELAY) == -1
    || fcntl(output(0), F_SETFL, O_NDELAY) == -1)
{       closeall();
        response("?pipes");
}

for (fd = 0; fd < DIM(_fds); ++ fd)
        private(_fds[fd]);
```

We need two pipes and a total of four file descriptors. This is a large amount of a very scarce resource. We use initialized **static** storage and first reclaim any unused file descriptors left over from an interrupted previous call.

It is easy to get confused when we connect four file descriptors in two processes in two directions. To make things more transparent, we introduce the names **input( )** and **output( )** for the two pipes and connect according to the following diagram:

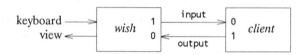

Here is the corresponding code:

```
switch (vpid(vp) = fork()) {
        char * getenv();
case -1:
        response("?fork");
case 0:
        sigdefault();

        if ((close(0), dup(input(0)) == 0)
            && (close(1), dup(output(1)) == 1)
            && (close(2), dup(1) == 2))
        {       export();
                if (cmd)
                        execl(SHELL, "sh", "-c", cmd, (char *) 0);
                else
                {       if (! (cmd = getenv("SHELL")))
                                cmd = SHELL;
                        execl(cmd, "sh", "-i", (char *) 0);
                }
        }
        _exit(127);
}
```

The rest is mostly copied from **load**( ) in Section 5.3. Since a dialog may often only involve a shell as the client, we implement this as a special case: if the argument **cmd** of **talkopen**( ) is a null pointer, we connect to a shell selected by the environment variable **SHELL** or to the regular shell by default. By convention, the argument **−i** makes this shell interactive, i.e., it will prompt and ignore terminal signals. If **cmd** was specified, we pass it as a string value for option **−c** to the regular shell just like **system**(3) would.

```
        vtout(vp) = output(0), output(0) = -1;
        vtin(vp) = input(1), input(1) = -1;
        closeall();

        vinfo(vp) = (Function) info, vnow(vp) = N_FILE, vopen(vp);
        scrollok(view(vp), TRUE);
        werase(view(vp)), wrefresh(view(vp));
        vtp(vp) = vtalk(vp), vtlen(vp) = 0;
        return vexec(vp) = (Function) talk;

#undef   input
#undef   output
#undef   closeall
}
```

Once the client is set up, we post a new information function, switch the current interior and redisplay the frame. The interior must be erased and shown because it may take a while before **winput**( ) refreshes the screen.

info( ) is yet another slight variation on the usual theme. This time we show the process number of the client on the top right corner of the frame, i.e., if **vpid(vp)** is not null, it is displayed by **info**( ). This simplifies eliminating an obstinate client from another view because we already know its process number.

main( ) and **sigdefault**( ) in the module *wish.c* must be changed a bit. We must **sense**( ) the signal **SIGALRM** as shown in Section 7.1, and we must ignore **SIGPIPE** within *wish*. While **SIGALRM** automatically reverts to default state in the client following **exec**(2), an ignored signal such as **SIGPIPE** must be explicitly reset before the client is started.

The view management signal is a slight complication for **talk**( ): it is likely that **winput**( ) will be interrupted when our user enters view management by way of a signal to change to another view. In this case, a timeout may not yet have expired. Just like the view manager offers **vcatch**( ) to intercept signals and clean up the terminal state before the signal is reissued, **talk**( ) needs to intercept the view management signal, reset a timeout interval, and reissue the view management signal:

```
static int (* sigvm)();            /* saved signal state */

static wrapup()                    /* restore environment */
{
        alarm(0);
        signal(SIGVM, sigvm);
}
```

```
static intercept()                            /* intercept SIGVM */
{
        signal(SIGVM, SIG_IGN);
        wrapup();
        kill(getpid(), SIGVM);
        fatal("intercept bug");
}
```

talk( ) works just about as promised in Section 7.1. We arrange to intercept the view management signal and set the proper terminal state for **winput( )**. If our client has not been found terminated by some other view† and if **kill( )** believes that the process number is legal, we are ready to move the dialog.

```
static Function talk(vp)
        register View * vp;
{       static Function talkclose();

        sigvm = signal(SIGVM, intercept);
        noecho(), cbreak();

        while (vpid(vp) && kill(vpid(vp), 0) == 0)
        {       if (vtin(vp) >= 0 && copyout(vp) == EOF)
                {       close(vtin(vp)), vtin(vp) = -1;
                        fcntl(vtout(vp), F_SETFL, 0);
                }
                if (! copyin(vp) && vtin(vp) == -1)
                        break;
        }
        wrapup();
        vexec(vp) = (Function) talkclose;
        vpid(vp) = 0, vopen(vp), doupdate();
        wgetch(view(vp));                          /* pause for last screen */
        return vexec(vp);
}
```

Once the dialog is over we would normally move on to **talkclose( )** as the next view state. However, our user might like to see the final dialog view even after the client is gone. Therefore, we remove the process number from the view frame but wait for an arbitrary key press with **wgetch( )** before changing the view state. Signals are already restored to normal and **talkclose( )** is set in **vexec(vp)**; if view management is entered in this situation, **talkclose( )** is called once our view is reselected.

copyout( ) is concerned with moving data from the keyboard to the client. It normally returns the result of **winput( )**:

---

† ...which would have cleared our **vpid(vp)** through **vwait( )**, see Sections 4.4 and 5.3.

```
static int copyout(vp)                    /* keyboard to client */
        register View * vp;
{       register WINDOW * wp = view(vp);

        if (! vtlen(vp))
                vtlen(vp) = winput(wp, vtalk(vp), vtcol(vp),
                                   & vtp(vp), sizeof vtalk(vp), 1);
        if (vtlen(vp) && vtlen(vp) != EOF)
                switch (write(vtin(vp), vtalk(vp), vtlen(vp))) {
                case 0:
                        break;
                case -1:
                        if (errno != EPIPE)
                                fatal("dialog write i/o error");
                        vtlen(vp) = EOF;
                        break;
                default:
                        vtp(vp) = vtalk(vp), vtlen(vp) = 0;
                }
        return vtlen(vp);
}
```

talkopen() initialized the current buffer length **vtlen(vp)** to zero. Later, if our input buffer is still full, **vtlen(vp)** is set and we skip reading. Otherwise, **winput()** will let us know if we have a complete line. The line is written to the client's input pipe. If the client has closed the pipe, we receive **EPIPE** and return **EOF** to **talk()** since we should no longer read the keyboard.

To avoid busy waiting, **talk()** clears the **O_NDELAY** flag on the client's output pipe in this case so that further input operations will block. We also close the client's input pipe and set **vtin(vp)** to -1 to prevent further transfers to the client.

copyin() must move data from the client to our view. We cannot run into **EPIPE**, but if **read()** is a blocking call and receives end of file, we are no longer talking or listening to the client. Therefore, **copyin()** returns the result of **read()** so that **talk()** may break the dialog loop.

```
static int copyin(vp)                     /* client to view */
        register View * vp;
{       register WINDOW * wp = view(vp);
        int n;
        char buf[BUFSIZ];

        switch (n = read(vtout(vp), buf, sizeof buf - 1)) {
        case 0:
                break;
        case -1:
                fatal("dialog read i/o error");
        default:
                buf[n] = '\0';
                waddstr(wp, buf), wrefresh(wp);
        }
        return n;
}
```

That is all. Once we reach **talkclose( )** we free the remaining resources and send **SIG-PIPE** to the client just in case:

```
static Function talkclose(vp)
        register View * vp;
{
        vexec(vp) =
        vinfo(vp) = (Function) 0, vnow(vp) = N_CMD, vopen(vp);
        close(vtout(vp));
        if (vtin(vp) >= 0)
                close(vtin(vp));
        if (vpid(vp) > 0)
                kill(vpid(vp), SIGPIPE), vpid(vp) = 0;
        vm(-1);                          /* fix echo, etc. */
}
```

talkclose( ) must restore the proper terminal state. While we happen to know that command language input is next, and that command language input requires **echo( )** and **nocbreak( )**, we should not hardwire it into **talkclose( )**. If a function in a view state cycle influences the terminal state, the last function in the cycle can let the view manager reselect the current view and thus restore the terminal state in a more consistent fashion.

7.4 Killing a Zombie

In high hopes that our dialog works we issue the following command:

```
$ sleep 5
```

The view changes to dialog state, and nothing happens. Five seconds pass but the process number on the top right edge of the frame does not disappear. **winput( )** returns once per second, and the **while** loop in **talk( )** uses **kill( )** to check if the client still exists. *sleep* has terminated, but until *wish* as parent process calls **wait(2)** the *sleep* process is a 'zombie'. They are quite appropriately named: we can **kill( )** a zombie as often as we like, without an error indication!

In our example, if we press *return*, **winput( )** completes a line and the transfer attempt in **copyout( )** fails with **EPIPE**. Now **talk( )** believes the end of file result of **copyin( )** and breaks the loop. The process number disappears from the frame, we are still in **talk( )** at the final call to **wgetch( )**, and another key press will return us to command language input.

There is a way to kill zombies. Or rather, we arrange for somebody else to wait for our client's demise and run it through the zombie state without our intervention. If a parent process terminates before its descendants, they are inherited by the *init* process which is just about always waiting for processes to terminate. If we arrange for our client to be waited upon by *init*, it will not remain a zombie for very long and our *sleep* experiment will come to a less tiresome, and confusing, conclusion.

wish must create a setup process which in turn creates the client and terminates. This way the client's immediate parent process does not exist anymore and the client is turned over to *init*. We still need to know the client's process number and our setup process must pass it back by way of yet another pipe. Here is the revised arrangement:

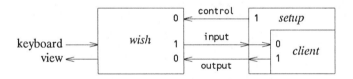

The changes are entirely confined to **talkopen**() and they are not even very complicated, given the picture above:

```
Function talkopen(vp, cmd)
        ...
        static int _fds[] = { -1, -1, -1, -1, -1, -1 };

#define control(x)      _fds[4 + (x)]    /* from setup to us */

        if (pipe(& input(0)) == -1
            || pipe(& output(0)) == -1
            || pipe(& control(0)) == -1
                ...

        switch (vpid(vp) = fork()) {
                int pid;
        case -1:
                response("?fork");
        case 0:
                sigdefault();

                if ((close(0), dup(input(0)) != 0)
                    || (close(1), dup(output(1)) != 1)
                    || (close(2), dup(1) != 2))
                        _exit(2);        /* dup trouble */

                switch (pid = fork()) { /* client */
                        char * getenv();
                case 0:
                        export();
                        if (cmd)
                                execl(SHELL, "sh", "-c", cmd, (char *) 0);
                        else
                        {       if (! (cmd = getenv("SHELL")))
                                        cmd = SHELL;
                                execl(cmd, "sh", "-i", (char *) 0);
                        }
```

```
                       case -1:
                               _exit(127);        /* reported to init */
                       }
                       _exit(write(control(1), & pid, sizeof pid) != sizeof vpid(vp));
               }

               do
                       vwait(& status);
               while (vpid(vp));

               if (status
                   || read(control(0), & vpid(vp), sizeof vpid(vp)) != sizeof vpid(vp))
               {      closeall();
                      response("?fork");
               }
               ...
       #undef control
```

Most of the code is as before. We simply use **fork()** to create the setup process as descendant of *wish* and wait for it to complete using **vwait()**. The setup process creates the client just like *wish* did earlier, and writes the process number into the **control()** pipe before terminating. *wish* reads the process number into **vpid(vp)** and closes the pipe. Now we have the same invariants as before.

    vwait() may take a while. When viewing a completed process in Section 5.3, we turned this phase into a separate view state. Here we chose not to do this: our user is likely to wait briefly for the frame appearance to change after a command is issued. The *setup* process should terminate very quickly compared with a background process started with **&**.

Restrictions

The client process may believe it is connected to a terminal, but it is not. For example, *ps*(1) needs to know its controlling terminal in order to display the right selection of process table entries. Run by any of the mechanisms discussed in this chapter and in Chapter 5, *ps* will fail. Unfortunately, it tries to determine the controlling terminal from file descriptor 2 which we must connect back to our view.†

    Other restrictions are much less subtle. *vi* will never run in a view, and not only because *terminfo* cannot be persuaded to work away from the top left corner of the physical screen. We can simulate either line input from the keyboard or character input, but there is no way for the client to request one or the other as it would with **ioctl**(2) from the terminal driver. It makes more sense to opt for line input, and it is less costly in terms of CPU time.

    Finally, there is only a single end of file. While we could ignore *control*-D at the keyboard, or **EOF** as a result of **winput()**, and keep on reading, we cannot send end of file across the pipe to the client and continue to keep the pipe open. End of file must be sent by closing the pipe, which is then gone for all processes using it as input. If we run a shell as client, and if we start, for example, *sort*(1) from the shell and type input at it, we will receive output back in

---

† A terminal can be passed explicitly with option −**t**, see *ps*(1).

our view once we send end of file to *sort*, i.e., once we close the client's input pipe. Output will arrive as predicted, but the end of file also reaches the client shell and it terminates together with *sort*.

Appendix

This appendix contains the manual pages for all commands and functions which are implemented in this book and one-line descriptions of the functions built into *cdc* and *wish*. It does not contain the manual pages for the desk calculator, *cdc*, and *wish*, because Chapter 1 describes these programs in more detail. All manual pages are distributed with the sources to this book.

1 Commands

getkey: test function keys and key mapping

> getkey [−m] [−v] [file]

getkey loads the standard key map or the indicated *file*, displays the key map, and arranges to test the keyboard. The command must be terminated by a signal. If −m is specified, no map is loaded. In this way, an unknown keyboard can be tested. If −v is specified, the loading process is annotated for debugging, and the test phase is suppressed.

FILES   /usr/lib/keymap   default key map directory

SEE ALSO   *curses* **keypad( )**, *terminfo*, **keymap( )**

use: query usage database

> use [−e] [−n] [−u database] [−v] [term...]

use displays information from a usage database produced by *mkuse* Schreiner (1987). All entries are shown, for which a *term* matches the beginning of their keyword. − as a *term* matches any keyword in the database.

If −e is specified, diagnostic output is used in place of standard output and the program will terminate with exit code 1. If −n is specified, the keywords are shown in place of the entries. The default database directory name is overwritten by the USE environment variable. The database file name is the basename by which *use* is called, in the database directory; it is overwritten by the option −u. If compiled into *use*, option −v provides a trace of all activities.

FILES   /usr/lib/use   default database directory

SEE ALSO   **finduse**( ), Schreiner (1987)

mkuse is distributed with the sources to this book.

2 Functions

copywin: copy window

```
#include <curses.h>

int copywin(a, b, ay0, ax0, by0, bx0, by1, bx1, ov)
     WINDOW * a, * b;
```

copywin( ) copies characters from window *a*, beginning with *ay0,ax0* as the top left position, to window *b*, beginning with *by0,bx0* as the top left position. The copy extends either to the bottom right in window *a* or to the position *by1,bx1* in window *b*, whichever is closer to the top left. If *ov* is not zero, blank characters are not copied. This is termed overlay mode. If the target character is the same as the source character, the target character is not touched. The cursor is left at or to the right of the bottom right of the copy.

SEE ALSO   *curses* **copywin**( )

copywin( ) is part of System V release 3. However, the exact behavior is not specified. **copywin**( ) would yield more predictable versions of **overwrite**( ) and **overlay**( ) than are available with System V release 2.

finduse, loaduse, seekuse: access usage database

```
#include <stdio.h>

int loaduse(fnm, db) char * fnm, * db;
int finduse(s) char * s;
FILE * seekuse(n)
```

loaduse( ) loads the index of a *use* database and returns the delimiting character. *fnm* is the pathname of a database file. If *fnm* is a null pointer, *db* is the database name in the directory specified by the environment variable USE or in a default directory. If the index cannot be successfully loaded, **loaduse**( ) returns EOF.

    finduse( ) returns the index of the key *s* in the database. Zero indicates failure, a positive result is an exact match, a negative result is the lowest matching key.

    seekuse( ) uses the index *n* returned by **finduse**( ) and returns a file pointer positioned to the database entry. A null pointer is returned on failure.

FILES   /usr/lib/use   default database directory

SEE ALSO   *use*, Schreiner (1987)

keymap, *loadmap*, *mvwgetkey*: obtain and map function key

```
#include <curses.h>

int keymap(from, to)
int loadmap(fnm) char * fnm;
int mvwgetkey(wp, y, x) WINDOW * wp;
```

keymap( ) arranges for **mvwgetkey**( ) to return *to* when *from* is pressed (or decoded). *from* must be an ASCII character code, i.e., a value between 0 and 127, or a *curses* keypad code, i.e., a value between 0401 and 0540. *to* can be any value; zero maps *from* to itself. **keymap**( ) returns the previous assignment, zero if there was none, and -1 if *from* is out of range.

loadmap( ) reads a key map from *fnm*. If a null pointer is passed, **loadmap**( ) uses the environment variable **TERM** to compose a standard file name. **loadmap**( ) returns zero if loading was successful and negative values for various error conditions: -1 for a syntax error, -2 if the file cannot be opened, -3 if **TERM** is not set, and -4 for an i/o error.

mvwgetkey( ) moves in the window described by *wp* to row *y* and column *x*, refreshes the window, reads a key press, and returns a value for the key. Keypad mode is enabled prior to reading and disabled afterwards.

If there is no key map, ASCII characters are returned as such, and function keys are represented as described in *curses* and defined in the header file *curses.h*. If requested using **keymap**( ) or **loadmap**( ), **mvwgetkey**( ) will map a key just prior to returning it. A key cannot be mapped to zero: zero is the indication that a key should be mapped to itself.

FILES   /usr/lib/keymap   default key map directory

SEE ALSO   *getkey*, *curses* **keypad**( )

loadmap: key map file format

```
# comment

ascii
0 ^A ^B          # up to 128 codes

keypad
f0 home          # KEY_F0 mapped to KEY_HOME
f(1) clear       # KEY_F(1) mapped to KEY_CLEAR
```

White space and text following # on a line is ignored. White space must separate words. The word **ascii** may be followed by up to 128 codes to map keys from the ASCII sequence. The word **keypad** may be followed by pairs of codes; the first one designates the keypad key to be mapped, the second code is its mapping.

Codes can be C integer constants in decimal, octal, or hexadecimal. `^x` designates an ASCII control character. `'x'` designates the character *x* itself; white space cannot be mapped in this fashion. `f(n)` designates **KEY_F**(*n*). Other codes must be key names taken from the list in *curses* and written in lower case.

SEE ALSO   *getkey*, **keymap**( )

macro: expand macro with parameters

```
char * macro(inp, name, text)
      char ** inp, * name, * text;
```

macro( ) returns a copy of *text* with occurrences of $i replaced by arguments from **inp*, where *i* is a single digit. $0 is replaced by *name*. If *x* is not a digit, $*x* is replaced by *x*.

If **inp* points to a left parenthesis, macro arguments are assumed to follow the parenthesis, to be separated by commas, and to be terminated by a right parenthesis. On return, **inp* will point past the trailing parenthesis. If **inp* does not point to a left parenthesis, there are no macro arguments and **inp* will remain unchanged. Arguments may contain commas enclosed by balanced parentheses as well as string and character constants. If missing arguments are referenced, empty strings will be substituted.

macro( ) returns a null pointer if parentheses or delimiters are unbalanced. The returned value is in **static** storage and can at most hold **BUFSIZ** bytes.

mvwprinta: align formatted output in curses window

```
#include <curses.h>

int mvwprinta(wp, y, x, wid, fmt, ...)
      WINDOW * wp; char * fmt;
```

mvwprinta( ) formats and aligns output in window *wp* on line *y* beginning in column *x* and extending over *wid* columns. *fmt* and the remaining arguments follow the rules of **printf**( ).

The first two characters of *fmt* control alignment and do not contribute to formatting. If the first character is **C**, the output is centered; if the character is **R**, the output is right aligned; otherwise it is left aligned. If the output has more than *wid* characters and if the second character in *fmt* is **C**, the center part of the output is shown; if the character is **R**, the rightmost part of the output is shown; otherwise the leftmost part of the output is shown.

mvwprinta( ) returns **ERR** if output cannot be produced, and **OK** otherwise.

SEE ALSO   **printf**( ), *curses* **printw**( )

A *tab* is replaced by a single blank, other control characters are not compensated.

wframe, wframe2: fancy boxes for curses

```
#include <curses.h>

int wframe(wp, nrows, ncols, y, x)
int wframe2(wp, nrows, ncols, y, x)
        WINDOW * wp;
```

wframe( ) draws a single frame, **wframe2( )** draws a double frame, with the top left corner in the window *wp* at row *y* and column *x*. The frame covers *nrows* and *ncols*; if one of these values is zero, the frame extends to the corresponding border of the window. Hopefully, the frame will be drawn using a suitable alternate character set.

The cursor is not changed. Normally the functions return **OK**. If the required frame does not fit, the functions will return **ERR**.

SEE ALSO   *curses* **box( )**

The alternate character set on the XENIX console has problems unless **msgr** is removed from *terminfo*.

winput: collect string through curses window

```
int winput(wp, buf, col, p, lim, timeout)
        WINDOW * wp;
        char buf[], ** p;
        unsigned char col[];
        int lim;
        unsigned timeout;
```

winput( ) reads characters, displays them in *wp*, and stores them in *buf*. **winput( )** implements the equivalent of **fgets( )**, can impose a time limit on input, and can be interrupted and resumed later.

For each character its column position relative to *wp* is recorded in *col*. This information is primarily used to handle control characters when editing the input line.

The next character is deposited at **p* which is then incremented. **p* must point to *buf* when **winput( )** is first called. *p* is used to continue input of a single line over several calls of **winput( )**.

lim is the dimension of the vectors *buf* and *col*; since *buf* is always terminated with a null byte, *lim* must at least be two.

winput( ) assumes that the cursor is positioned in *wp* and that **noecho( )** and **cbreak( )** are set. Normally, **scrollok**(*wp*, **TRUE**) will also be set.

If *timeout* is not zero, one call of **winput( )** will read a single character, and it will use an **alarm( )** interval of *timeout* seconds. **SIGALRM** must be intercepted while **winput( )** is called.

winput( ) interprets *backspace* and the *erase* and *kill* characters. *tab* is interpreted relative to *wp* and stored as \t. If *timeout* is zero, *return*, *newline*, and *control*-D terminate input. *control*-D is not stored in *buf*. With the exception of these control characters, only visible characters are considered.

   winput( ) normally returns zero. If *control*-D is input at the beginning of *buf*, the result is EOF. If *return*, *newline*, or *control*-D are entered, or if *lim* is reached, the result is the number of characters stored, i.e., it is positive.

SEE ALSO   *curses* **getstr( )**, **alarm( )**, **signal( )**

Once the beginning of a long input line has left *wp*, line editing can only position to the first line in *wp*.

3 Capsules

This section contains one-line descriptions of all functions and macros built into *cdc* and *wish*. Most of these functions have been used in the implementation, too. The one-liners are part of the manual pages *calc*(1) and *cdc*(1) distributed with the sources to this book.

System Calls

`int access(path, mode)`	check if file is accessible
`int chdir(path)`	change working directory
`int chmod(path, mode)`	change mode of file
`int chown(path, owner, group)`	change owner and group of file
`exit(code)`	close file connections, terminate
`_exit(code)`	terminate quickly
`int getegid()`	return effective group number
`int geteuid()`	return effective user number
`int getgid()`	return real group number
`int getpgrp()`	return process group number
`int getpid()`	return process number
`int getppid()`	return parent process number
`int getuid()`	return real user number
`int kill(pid, signo)`	send signal to process(es)
`int link(oldpath, newpath)`	make another link to a file
`int mknod(path, mode, addr0)`	make inode
`int mount(special, dir, ronly)`	mount file system
`int nice(n)`	decrease priority
`int pause()`	wait for signal
`int setgid(gid)`	set real and effective group number
`int setpgrp()`	start new process group
`int setuid(uid)`	set real and effective user number
`int sync()`	update super block
`int umask(mask)`	return and set file creation mask
`int umount(special)`	unmount file system
`int unlink(path)`	remove link to file

Successful system calls usually return zero, -1 indicates an error. **exit( )** disposes properly of open files and terminates *cdc* and *wish* gracefully, **_exit( )** does not reset the terminal.

Macros from *ctype.h*

`int isalnum(ch)`	true if letter or digit
`int isalpha(ch)`	true if letter
`int isascii(ch)`	true if in ASCII range
`int iscntrl(ch)`	true if control: \0 to \37, *delete*
`int isdigit(ch)`	true if digit
`int isgraph(ch)`	true if visible: not space, control
`int islower(ch)`	true if lower-case letter
`int isprint(ch)`	true if printing: space to tilde
`int ispunct(ch)`	true unless letter, digit, control, space
`int isspace(ch)`	true if space, *tab, return, newline, vtab, formfeed*
`int isupper(ch)`	true if upper-case letter
`int isxdigit(ch)`	true if base 16 digit: 0-9, a-f, A-F
`int toascii(ch)`	return ASCII value
`int _tolower(ch)`	return lower-case only for upper-case
`int _toupper(ch)`	return upper-case only for lower-case

Library Functions

	`abort()`	terminate with core dump
`int`	`abs(i)`	absolute value
`int`	`atoi(s)`	convert string to integer
`char *`	`getenv(name)`	value of environment variable
`char *`	`getlogin()`	login name
`int`	`isatty(fd)`	true if terminal
`char *`	`itoa(i)`	convert integer to string
`int`	`KEY_F(no)`	return *curses* function key number
`int`	`keymap(old, new)`	return and set key mapping
`int`	`putenv(asg)`	set environment value
`int`	`rand()`	pseudo random value
`unsigned`	`sleep(secs)`	suspend execution for interval
	`srand(seed)`	start pseudo random sequence
`char *`	`strcat(to, from)`	concatenate strings
`char *`	`strchr(s, ch)`	search character in string
`int`	`strcmp(a, b)`	compare strings
`char *`	`strcpy(to, from)`	copy string
`int`	`strcspn(s, class)`	length of string not in character class
`int`	`strlen(s)`	number of characters in string
`char *`	`strpbrk(s, class)`	search character from class in string
`char *`	`strrchr(s, ch)`	search character in string, from right
`int`	`strspn(s, class)`	length of string in character class
`int`	`system(cmd)`	let shell execute command
`int`	`toupper(ch)`	return upper-case for lower-case
`int`	`tolower(ch)`	return lower-case for upper-case
`char *`	`ttyname(fd)`	terminal name

Three functions are not part of the C library: **itoa()** converts an integer value into a string. **KEY_F()** returns the key value for a numbered function key. **keymap()** changes key mapping.

Values from *curses.h*

chtype	A_ATTRIBUTES	mask, extracts attribute
chtype	A_BLINK	attribute, blinking character
chtype	A_BOLD	attribute, bold character
chtype	A_CHARTEXT	mask, extracts character
chtype	A_DIM	attribute, dimmed character
chtype	A_REVERSE	attribute, reverse video character
chtype	A_STANDOUT	attribute, best emphasized character
chtype	A_UNDERLINE	attribute, underlined character
int	COLS	constant, columns on terminal screen
WINDOW *	curscr	constant, current screen
int	ERR	constant, error result
int	FALSE	constant, false condition/flag
int	LINES	constant, rows on terminal screen
int	OK	constant, success result
WINDOW *	stdscr	constant, default screen window
int	TRUE	constant, true condition/flag

These values are only built into *cdc*, not into *wish*.

Window Components from *curses.h*

chtype	wp -> _attrs	current attributes
short	wp -> _begx	left edge, physical column
short	wp -> _begy	top edge, physical row
short	wp -> _bmarg	bottom, scrolling region
bool	wp -> _clear	ok to send clear screen
short	wp -> _curx	current column
short	wp -> _cury	current row
short	wp -> _flags	misc.
bool	wp -> _leave	ok to leave cursor
short	wp -> _maxx	number of columns
short	wp -> _maxy	number of rows
bool	wp -> _nodelay	read with O_NDELAY
bool	wp -> _scroll	ok to scroll
short	wp -> _tmarg	top, scrolling region
bool	wp -> _use_idl	ok to insert/delete line
bool	wp -> _use_keypad	decode function keys
bool	wp -> _use_meta	ok to input 0x80 bit

These components are only built into *cdc*, not into *wish*.

Window Components from *view.h*

`short begx(wp)`	constant, left edge, physical column
`short begy(wp)`	constant, top edge, physical row
`short curx(wp)`	constant, current column
`short cury(wp)`	constant, current row
`short maxx(wp)`	constant, number of columns
`short maxy(wp)`	constant, number of rows

These functions are only built into *cdc*, not into *wish*.

curses Macros and Functions

Functions in the *curses* library are supposed to return **OK** on success and **ERR** on failure. Not all of them do. The lists below only indicate return types for functions and macros if they are documented.

Functions usually apply to **stdscr** unless a window pointer is supplied. Functions usually apply to and influence the current position in **stdscr** or in a window unless explicit coordinates are supplied.

`addch(ch)`	*curses.h*	add character
`addstr(s)`	*curses.h*	add string
`attroff(atr)`	*curses.h*	named attributes off
`attron(atr)`	*curses.h*	named attributes on
`attrset(atr)`	*curses.h*	set exact attributes
`int baudrate()`	`-lcurses`	terminal speed
`beep()`	`-lcurses`	ring bell / flash
`box(wp, vert, hor)`	`-lcurses`	box around edge
`cbreak()`	`-lcurses`	read single characters*
`clear()`	*curses.h*	set clear flag, erase
`clearok(wp, flag)`	`-lcurses`	set clear flag
`clrtobot()`	*curses.h*	erase to end of screen
`clrtoeol()`	*curses.h*	erase to end of line
`delch()`	*curses.h*	delete current character
`deleteln()`	*curses.h*	delete current line
`delwin(wp)`	`-lcurses`	free window
`doupdate()`	`-lcurses`	update terminal screen*
`echo()`	`-lcurses`	echo input characters*
`endwin()`	`-lcurses`	terminate screen processing*
`erase()`	*curses.h*	fill with blanks
`char erasechar()`	`-lcurses`	terminal's erase character
`flash()`	`-lcurses`	flash / ring bell
`flushinp()`	`-lcurses`	discard characters typed ahead
`getbegyx(wp, y, x)`	*view.h*	physical top and left edge*
`int getch()`	*curses.h*	input character*
`getmaxyx(wp, y, x)`	*view.h*	number of rows and columns*
`getstr(s)`	*curses.h*	input string*

`getyx(wp, y, x)`	*curses.h*	current row and column*
`int has_ic()`	-lcurses	terminal can insert/delete characters
`int has_il()`	-lcurses	terminal can insert/delete lines
`idlok(wp, flag)`	-lcurses	permit to use insert/delete line
`chtype inch()`	*curses.h*	return current character
`initscr()`	-lcurses	begin screen processing*
`insch(ch)`	*curses.h*	insert character
`insertln()`	*curses.h*	insert blank line
`intrflush(wp, flag)`	-lcurses	permit to discard output on interrupt*
`keypad(wp, flag)`	-lcurses	decode special function keys
`char killchar()`	-lcurses	terminal's kill character
`leaveok(wp, flag)`	-lcurses	permit to leave cursor at last output
`char * longname()`	-lcurses	terminal's name in *terminfo*
`move(y, x)`	*curses.h*	move current position
`mvaddch(y, x, ch)`	*curses.h*	move and add character
`mvaddstr(y, x, s)`	*curses.h*	move and add string
`mvdelch(y, x)`	*curses.h*	move and delete character
`int mvgetch(y, x)`	*curses.h*	move and input character*
`mvgetstr(y, x, s)`	*curses.h*	move and input string*
`chtype mvinch(y, x)`	*curses.h*	move and return character
`mvinsch(y, x, ch)`	*curses.h*	move and insert character
`mvwaddch(wp, y, x, ch)`	*curses.h*	move and add character
`mvwaddstr(wp, y, x, s)`	*curses.h*	move and add string
`mvwdelch(wp, y, x)`	*curses.h*	move and delete character
`int mvwgetch(wp, y, x)`	*curses.h*	move and input character*
`mvwgetstr(wp, y, x, s)`	*curses.h*	move and input string*
`mvwin(wp, y, x)`	-lcurses	move window
`chtype mvwinch(wp, y, x)`	*curses.h*	move and return character
`mvwinsch(wp, y, x, ch)`	*curses.h*	move and insert character
`WINDOW * newpad(rows, cols)`	-lcurses	create pad
`WINDOW * newwin(rows, cols, y, x)`	-lcurses	create window
`nl()`	*curses.h*	translate return and newline*
`nocbreak()`	-lcurses	read by lines*
`nodelay(wp, flag)`	-lcurses	make read non-blocking*
`noecho()`	-lcurses	do not echo input characters*
`nonl()`	-lcurses	leave newline and return alone*
`noraw()`	-lcurses	read by lines*
`overlay(src_wp, dest_wp)`	-lcurses	copy non-blanks
`overwrite(src_wp, dest_wp)`	-lcurses	copy all characters
`pnoutrefresh(wp,py,px,sy0,sx0,sy1,sx1)`	-lcurses	refresh pad*
`prefresh(wp,py,px,sy0,sx0,sy1,sx1)`	-lcurses	refresh pad, update*
`raw()`	-lcurses	read single characters, no signals*
`refresh()`	*curses.h*	refresh and update*
`scroll(wp)`	-lcurses	scroll if permitted
`scrollok(wp, flag)`	-lcurses	permit to scroll
`setscrreg(top, bot)`	*curses.h*	set scroll range
`standend()`	*curses.h*	turn all attributes off
`standout()`	*curses.h*	turn best emphasis on

`WINDOW * subwin(wp, rows, cols, y, x)`	`-lcurses`	create subwindow
`touchwin(wp)`	`-lcurses`	mark entire window changed
`typeahead(fd)`	`-lcurses`	set file descriptor for typeahead check*
`char * unctrl(ch)`	*unctrl.h*	decode character code
`waddch(wp, ch)`	`-lcurses`	move and add character
`waddstr(wp, s)`	`-lcurses`	move and add string
`wattroff(wp, atr)`	`-lcurses`	named attributes off
`wattron(wp, atr)`	`-lcurses`	named attributes on
`wattrset(wp, atr)`	`-lcurses`	set exact attributes
`wclear(wp)`	`-lcurses`	set clear flag, erase
`wclrtobot(wp)`	`-lcurses`	erase to end of window
`wclrtoeol(wp)`	`-lcurses`	erase to edge of window
`wdelch(wp)`	`-lcurses`	move and delete character
`wdeleteln(wp)`	`-lcurses`	delete current line
`werase(wp)`	`-lcurses`	fill with blanks
`int wgetch(wp)`	`-lcurses`	input character*
`wgetstr(wp, s)`	`-lcurses`	input string*
`chtype winch(wp)`	*curses.h*	move and return character
`winsch(wp, ch)`	`-lcurses`	move and insert character
`winsertln(wp)`	`-lcurses`	insert blank line
`wmove(wp, y, x)`	`-lcurses`	move current position
`wnoutrefresh(wp)`	`-lcurses`	refresh window*
`wrefresh(wp)`	`-lcurses`	refresh window, update*
`wsetscrreg(wp, top, bot)`	*curses.h*	set scroll range
`wstandend(wp)`	`-lcurses`	turn all attributes off
`wstandout(wp)`	`-lcurses`	turn best emphasis on

These functions are only built into *cdc*, not into *wish*. Functions and macros marked with * are intercepted by *cdc* and the terminal state is monitored if there is a command echo.

References

Aho, A. V., Kernighan, B. W., and Weinberger, P. J. (1988) *The AWK Programming Language*, Addison-Wesley.

Aho, A. V., Sethi, R., and Ullman, J. D. (1986) *Compilers: Principles, Techniques, and Tools*, Addison-Wesley.

Jackson, M. A. (1975) *Principles of Program Design*, Academic Press.

Kernighan, B. W. and Pike, R. (1984) *The UNIX Programming Environment*, Prentice Hall.

Kernighan, B. W. and Ritchie, D. M. (1988) *The C Programming Language*, second edition, Prentice Hall.

Knuth, D. E. (1968) *The Art of Computer Programming*, Volume 1, Addison-Wesley.

Rochkind, M. J. (1985) *Advanced UNIX Programming*, Prentice Hall.

Rochkind, M. J. (1988) *Advanced C Programming for Displays*, Prentice Hall.

Schreiner, A.-T. and Friedman, H. G. Jr. (1985) *Introduction to Compiler Construction with UNIX*, Prentice Hall.

Schreiner, A.-T. (1986) *System-Programmierung in UNIX*, Volume 2, Teubner.

Schreiner, A.-T. (1987) *UNIX Sprechstunde*, Hanser.

System V Interface Definition (1986) Issue 2, Volumes 1 and 2 describe System V release 2, Volume 3 describes extensions in release 3, AT&T.

Index